ACCOUNTABILITY AND SOCIAL ACCOUNTING FOR SOCIAL AND NON-PROFIT ORGANIZATIONS

ADVANCES IN PUBLIC INTEREST ACCOUNTING

Series Editor: Cheryl R. Lehman

Recent Volumes:

Volume 1:	1986
Volume 2:	1987
Volume 3:	1990
Volume 4:	1991
Volume 5:	1993
Volume 6:	1995
Volume 7:	1998
Volume 8:	Advances in Accountability: Regulation, Research, Gender and Justice, 2001
Volume 9:	Mirrors and Prisms: Interrogating Accounting, 2002
Volume 10:	Re-inventing Realities, 2005
Volume 11:	Corporate Governance: Does Any Size Fit? 2005
Volume 12:	Independent Accounts, 2006
Volume 13:	Envisioning a New Accountability, 2008
Volume 14:	Extending Schumacher's Concept of Total Accounting and Accountability into the 21st Century, 2009
Volume 15:	Ethics, Equity, and Regulation, 2010
Volume 16:	Managing Reality: Accountability and the Miasma of Private and Public Domains, 2013

ADVANCES IN PUBLIC INTEREST ACCOUNTING
VOLUME 17

ACCOUNTABILITY AND SOCIAL ACCOUNTING FOR SOCIAL AND NON-PROFIT ORGANIZATIONS

EDITED BY

ERICKA COSTA
Department of Economics and Management, Trento University, Trento, Italy

LEE D. PARKER
School of Accounting, RMIT University, Melbourne, Australia; School of Management, Royal Holloway College, University of London, UK

MICHELE ANDREAUS
Department of Economics and Management, Trento University, Trento, Italy

Emerald

United Kingdom – North America – Japan
India – Malaysia – China

Emerald Group Publishing Limited
Howard House, Wagon Lane, Bingley BD16 1WA, UK

First edition 2014

Reprints and permission service
Contact: permissions@emeraldinsight.com

British Library Cataloguing in Publication Data
A catalogue record for this book is available from the British Library

ISBN: 978-1-78441-005-6
ISSN: 1041-7060 (Series)

Printed and bound by CPI Group (UK) Ltd, Croydon, CR0 4YY

ISOQAR REGISTERED
Certificate Number 1985
ISO 14001

ISOQAR certified Management System, awarded to Emerald for adherence to Environmental standard ISO 14001:2004.

INVESTOR IN PEOPLE

CONTENTS

LIST OF CONTRIBUTORS

Michele Andreaus	Department of Economics and Management, Trento University, Trento, Italy
Louis Beaubien	Rowe School of Business, Dalhousie University, Halifax, Nova Scotia, Canada
Carlo Borzaga	Department of Economics and Management, Trento University, Trento, Italy; European Research Institute of Co-operative and Social Enterprises (Euricse), Trento, Italy
Giovanni Bronzetti	Department of Business Administration and Law, University of Calabria, Calabria, Italy
Anna Ciepielewska-Kowalik	Institute of Political Studies, Polish Academy of Sciences, Warsaw, Poland
Massimo Contrafatto	Department of Management, Economics and Quantitative Methods, University of Bergamo, Bergamo, Italy
Ericka Costa	Department of Economics and Management, Trento University, Trento, Italy; European Research Institute on Cooperative and Social Enterprises (Euricse), Trento, Italy
Jacques Defourny	Centre for Social Economy, HEC Management School, University of Liege, Sart Tilman, Liège, Belgium
Bernard Enjolras	Center for Research on Civil Society and Voluntary Sector, Institute for Social Research, Oslo, Sweden

Adalbert Evers	Justus-Liebig Universität, Giessen, Germany
Laurent Fraisse	CRIDA, Paris, France
Giulia Galera	European Research Institute of Co-operative and Social Enterprises (Euricse), Trento, Italy
Jean-Louis Laville	CNAM-CNRS, Paris, France
Ewa Leś	Institute of Social Policy, Warsaw University, Warsaw, Poland
Vincent Lhuillier	Université de Lorraine, Nancy, France
Laurie Mook	School of Community Resources and Development, Arizona State University, Phoenix, AZ, USA
Lee D. Parker	School of Accounting, RMIT University, Melbourne, Australia; School of Management, Royal Holloway College, University of London, UK
Pekka Pättiniemi	KSL Civic Association for Adult Learning, Helsinki, Finland
Victor Pestoff	Institute for Civil Society Studies, Ersta Skondal University College, Stockholm, Sweden; Graduate School of Human Sciences, Osaka University
Fernando Polo-Garrido	Centro de Investigación en Gestión de Empresas/Centre for Research in Business Management (CEGEA), Universitat Politècnica de València, Valencia, Spain
Daphne Rixon	Center of Excellence in Accounting and Reporting for Co-operatives, Sobey School of Business, Saint Mary's University, Halifax, Nova Scotia, Canada
Karl Henrik Sivesind	Institute for Social Research, Oslo, Norway

Roger Spear	Department of Engineering and Innovation, The Open University, Milton Keynes, UK
Yohanan Stryjan	School of Social Sciences, Södertörns Högskola, Huddinge, Sweden
Johan Vamstad	Institute for Civil Society Studies, Ersta Skondal University College, Stockholm, Sweden
Stefania Veltri	Department of Business Administration and Law, University of Calabria, Calabria, Italy
Flaviano Zandonai	Euricse, Trento, Italy

FOREWORD

Broadly speaking we know that all types of organizations are under pressure to perform better and to increase their organizational efficiency and effectiveness.

Admittedly, private organizations must deliver increasing shareholder value if they want to survive. Public organizations must deliver what is called public value in returns to taxes. Relatedly, nonprofit organizations (NPOs) too must be effective and deliver value.

But what kind of value? Like public organizations, NPOs operate under the absence of profit and shareholders as steering mechanisms. Their absence however does not mean that they must not meet and follow the universal principles of good management or that they have no obligations to deliver something called value.

In order to be clear about the kind of value we are talking, let me give a brief example. Recently I was interested in accounting for natural disasters and humanitarian interventions because I was directly touched by a tremendous earthquake in Abruzzo, and I was surprised by the fundamental efforts of volunteers and national and international NPO organizations (Sargiacomo, Ianni, & Everett, 2014). Yes, public organizations were important, but NPOs were decisive in aiding the population, and sustaining the overcoming of the very first emergency stage.

Surprisingly, I learnt that in Japan – the land of earthquakes – the term "NPO" first appeared only in 1995 – that is the year of the Great Earthquake – when approximately one and a half million volunteers were mobilized and coordinated to aid the victims of such a tremendous natural disaster. Such an impressive spontaneous wave of Japanese people tried to counterbalance the serious issues – and failures – that government organizations and public bureaucracies faced, to cope with such an awful event. This situation revealed a dramatic need to promote and incentivize altruism and social values and the organizations that were entitled to deliver it. So in 1998, the Japanese Government recognized the importance of such values and passed a new law giving them a stronger support.

Thus, generally speaking, NPOs, before being the results of contractual failures (e.g., Hansmann, 1980), are the consequences of a civil society failure in recognizing and in supporting this kind of value. Their social importance is parallel with the need to be assured that their behavior is transparent and compliant with accounting and legal rules. In fact, the 2009 L'Aquila Earthquake was not only the occasion to reaffirm the importance of altruism and the social values, but also to strengthen controls and sanctions to punish fraudulent behaviors.

This book edited by Ericka Costa, Lee D. Parker, and Michele Andreaus is very welcome as it discusses such problems and gives new perspectives on how to conceive, assess, and show the performance of the complex world of NPO organizations in parallel to the information needs of a multiplicity of internal and external stakeholders.

What is important to observe is that while many books focus almost exclusively on financial accounting, this volume gives substantial weight to social accounting because it is through the social report that we can appreciate the social and civic value of NPO organizations, and at the same time such organizations become accountable to their audience.

The articles of this book are clustered around three main general topics: the non-profit sector (articles 2, 3), accounting and accountabilities for the non-profit sector (articles 4, 5) and social accounting for the non-profit sector (articles 6–10).

The first article co-authored by Ericka Costa, Lee D. Parker, and Michele Andreaus is an introductory article. It examines the foundation of the accounting practices – measurement and reporting – of NPO's, that is, accountability.

In the article "Towards a European Conceptualization of the Third Sector," Jacques Defourny and Victor Pestoff show an interesting attempt to conceptualize third sector organizations based on subjective perceptions of the Emes Network members. This "stakeholder perspective" to NPO conceptualization is useful to elucidate the complex but often ignored process to find an agreement on what a NPO is in positive terms and not only in normative ones (what a NPO should be).

In the article "New Trends in the Nonprofit Sector in Europe: The Emergence of Social Enterprises," Carlo Borzaga and Giulia Galera in their article highlight a relation among the notion of social entrepreneurship and terms like growth, social justice, and equity. Social enterprises are seen as the response to the declining old European welfare system. These three articles shed new and interesting light on what the nonprofit sector actually is.

In the article "Intentions, Observations, and Decisions: Metrics in Insurance Co-Operatives," Louis Beaubien and Daphne Rixon investigate the metrics used in decision making activities by insurance cooperative.

The findings are very interesting because the metrics used are the same of the for-profit insurance company. So the question is: does the cooperative difference exist in the insurance sector and how (and what) performance analysis tools are used to assess their performance?

In the article "The Effects of the Accounting Reclassification of Members' Shares in Cooperatives: An approach," Fernando Polo-Garrido studies the effects of the accounting reclassification of members' shares in Spanish cooperatives as a consequence of the introduction of new accounting standards. The accounting change from equity to liability of members' shares proved to be successful, and this investigation calls for further research into the use of accounting information by capital providers which seek to finance cooperatives.

In the article "Toward an Integrated Accountability Model for Nonprofit Organizations," Michele Andreaus and Ericka Costa deeply analyze the complex question of what an integrated social report should contain with regard to NPO. This article makes a clear distinction between the institutional purpose, the adherence to the social commitment and the adherence to financial constraints, thus emphasizing the need to differentiate among the aforementioned three dimensions that underpin reporting in any firms' typology.

In the article "Stewardship Theory: Approaches and Perspectives," Massimo Contrafatto critically reflects on the notion of stewardship as a possible driver of a more sustainable way of organizing our society. In particular, he analyzes the management, organization, and accounting literature on stewardship, thus proposing a map of current theorizing on stewardship, and portraying alternative variants and approaches in stewardship framework.

In the article "An Integrated Social Accounting Model for Nonprofit Organizations," Laurie Mook presents a conceptual framework and develops a model of integrated social accounting for NPOs. Like the Balanced Scorecard the suggested model adopts four perspectives: 1. Economic and human resources; 2. Economic, social, and environmental value creation; 3. Internal systems and processes; 4. Organizational learning, growth, and innovation.

In the article "Voluntary Disclosure in a Regulated Context: the Case of Italian Social Enterprises," Ericka Costa examines the interrelations between regulation and social and environmental reporting in the Northern Italian Social Enterprises. By so doing, she emphasizes – through a longitudinal analysis – that voluntary disclosure is a real phenomenon that characterizes also nonaccredited social enterprises.

In the article "Intellectual Capital Reporting in the Italian Nonprofit Sector. An Image-Building or an Accountability Tool?," Stefania Veltri and Giovanni Bronzetti analyze Intellectual Capital (IC) measurement, management, and reporting practices at organizational level. They portray – through a case study – that voluntary disclosure – under the heading of a IC report – is used to pursue managerial ends and not only as an accountability tool.

At the end this book offers food for thought to reflect on such complex questions and on the ways to find a balance between accounting and accountability for NPOs.

Massimo Sargiacomo
Professor of Accounting
Department of Management and Business Administration
University G.d'Annunzio of Chieti-Pescara, Italy

REFERENCES

Hansmann, H. B. (1980). The role of nonprofit enterprise. *The Yale Law Journal*, *89*(5), 835–901.

Sargiacomo, M., Ianni, L., & Everett, J. (2014). Accounting for suffering: Calculative practices in the field of disaster relief. *Critical Perspectives on Accounting*, *25*(7–8). doi:10.1016/j.cpa.2014.03.011

PART I
INTRODUCTION

THE RISE OF SOCIAL AND NON-PROFIT ORGANIZATIONS AND THEIR RELEVANCE FOR SOCIAL ACCOUNTING STUDIES

Ericka Costa, Lee D. Parker and Michele Andreaus

ABSTRACT

Within the accounting discipline and its literature, attention to the role of social and non-profit organizations has been growing, particularly with respect to issues of accountability and social accounting. In response, the aim of this introductory article is to present the background for the book by highlighting (i) the relevance and rise of the non-profit sector worldwide, (ii) the limitations of the conventional accounting framework when applied/transposed to NPOs and (iii) the 'social accounting project' for NPOs. The article presents analysis and critique based on a literature review of the accountability framework for NPOs. After presenting key worldwide statistics regarding the growing non-profit sector, the article points out the skepticism regarding the adoption of traditional accounting principles and frameworks for NPOs. The article offers both an examination of how to improve the accounting system for NPOs and a discussion of the benefits emerging from the social and

Accountability and Social Accounting for Social and Non-profit Organizations
Advances in Public Interest Accounting, Volume 17, 3–21

ISSN: 1041-7060/doi:10.1108/S1041-706020140000017003

environmental accounting and reporting models. 'The social accounting project' for NPOs is presented as a pathway towards these innovative practices increasing organizational transparency. This article and the book overall provide new contributions to the research literature, fostering synergies among financial accounting and social accounting scholars engaging with the NPO subject area. Moreover it brings together studies from a range of disciplines, such as financial accounting, social accounting, economics, management, and third-sector studies. This cross-disciplinary approach offers a major contribution to our developing knowledge in this field.

Keywords: Non-profit organizations; global role; accountability; skepticism conventional accounting; social accounting

Non-profit organizations (NPOs) have expanded in number, variety, scope and societal importance and impact in many countries over past 30 years or more (Anheier, Hass, & Beller, 2013). They form not only the significant core of the third sector, but increasingly occupy centre stage in national, regional and local socio-economic development. In 2003 the United Nations, by developing the *Handbook on Non-Profit Institutions in the System of National Accounts* (United Nations Statistics Division, 2003), implicitly recommend for the regular development of statistical data in NPOs. In answering to this call in 2013, the Johns Hopkins Center for Civil Society Studies has provided 'The State of Global Civil Society and Volunteering' report which makes a step forward in this direction and provides a comprehensive picture of statistics in 16 countries around the world (Salamon, Wojciech Sokolowski, Haddock, & Tice, 2013). The report clearly shows that NPOs:

- are major employers (7.4% of the total workforce),
- play a significant economic role (4.5% of gross domestic product (GDP)),
- are major deliverers of services: that is, housing, social services, education, health care (73% of non-profit gross value added – GVA – is generated through service activities),
- exhibit a growing significance as economic drivers in national economies around the world (the non-profit sector's contribution to GDP grew at 5.8% per year over the period from the late 1990s to the mid-2000 compared to 5.2% for the economies as a whole in these countries).

Yet, only in more recent times have organizational and accounting researchers begun to seriously address the identities, roles, processes and impacts of this growing sector. Within the accounting discipline and its literature attention to and role of social and NPOs has been growing, particularly with respect to issues of accountability and social accounting. The social accounting practices of NPOs have been investigated as mechanisms of accountability, a process through which an organization evaluates, reports and enhances its social and environmental practices, especially by means of stakeholder dialogue. This book intends to shed new light on this subject area, both theoretically and empirically.

THE EMERGENT SOCIAL AND NPOS

In the past 30 years, the non-profit sector has become a key player in providing public and social services in most European and North American countries (Defourny & Nyssens, 2010; Economist, 2009). The non-profit sector brings together cooperatives, associations, mutual societies, foundations and other forms of organizations primarily aiming at something other than profit maximization. Despite considerable diversity in the kinds of organizations belonging to the non-profit sector, non-profit studies form a coherent and valuable line of academic research, one warranting further investigation and new perspectives (Steinberg & Powell, 2006).

Generally speaking NPOs could be defined as: 'private, formally-organized enterprises, with autonomy of decision and freedom of membership, created to meet their members' needs through the market by producing goods and providing services, insurance and finance, where decision-making and any distribution of profits or surpluses among the members are not directly linked to the capital or fees contributed by each member, each of whom has one vote, or at all events take place through democratic and participative decision-making processes' (Monzón-Campos & Chaves Ávila, 2012, p. 22). This sector also includes private, formally organized organizations that do not produce for the market, but on the contrary provide services for households, that is, the associations.

The definition suggested by Monzón-Campos and Chaves Ávila (2012) for the European Economic and Social Committee considers different types of organizations belonging to the non-profit sector: cooperatives, mutual societies, social enterprises, associations, foundations and other forms of organizations.

Cooperatives are private self-help organizations which operate in the market in order to satisfy the members' needs (mutualistic principle). They are organized democratically (one person one vote) and their profits are not distributed in proportion to the share capital contributed by their members. Cooperatives operate both on financial and non-financial sectors such as: labour (worker cooperatives), agriculture (agriculture cooperatives), consumer (consumer cooperatives), finance (cooperative banks).

Mutual societies are autonomous associations of persons, united voluntarily for the primary purpose of satisfying their common needs in the insurance (life and non-life), providence, health and banking sectors. There are two main sectors in which mutual societies operate: the first is the social security sector, that is, the health and social welfare risks of individuals; the second is the insurance sector both for non-life and life insurance. Similarly to cooperatives, mutual societies are grounded on the principles of solidarity among members, democracy and independence.

Social enterprises have been defined as private NPOs set up by groups of citizens oriented to creating social value and thus with an explicit aim of benefiting the community. Social enterprises are engaged in producing goods and/or services for the market with a degree of autonomy and a significant level of financial risk. They have dividend constraints and have an open and participatory governance model in which people who are affected by the activity are directly involved in the decision-making process (Borzaga & Defourny, 2001). The European Commission's Social Business Initiative (2014) considers social enterprises as a form of social businesses which operate in the market in order to provide goods and services in an entrepreneurial and innovative way, with the foremost purpose of achieving a social impact rather than generating profits for owners or members.

Associations and Foundations are private organizations which are not oriented to market production and instead produce services for families and households. They have autonomy of decision-making and freedom of membership. Any economic surplus they create cannot be appropriated by the founders/promoters of the organization.

Despite differences among these various types of NPOs, it is possible to list three main characteristics common to all these NPOs (Monzón-Campos & Chaves Ávila, 2012):

- 'They are created to meet their members' needs through applying the principle of selfhelp, that is, they are companies in which the members and the users of the activity in question are usually one and the same;

- [they] are market producers, which means that their output is mainly intended for sale on the market at economically significant prices;
- while they may distribute profits or surpluses among their user members, this is not proportional to the capital or to the fees contributed by the members but in accordance with the member's transactions with the organization' (pp. 24–25).

The emergence of NPOs in both the United States and Europe has been mainly evident in the late 1970s and 1980s, when structural societal problems, that could not be easily solved by the government (the State), came to light. This was accompanied by a global trend towards economic rationalist political philosophies that produced a preoccupation with low taxation, small government, downsizing, commercialization and corporatization of public sector organizations and the transfer of direct delivery of many former government services to outside providers (English, Guthrie, & Parker, 2003; Parker, 2012). These issues gave rise to NPOs responding to conditions in the market and to budget cuts to public funds (Kerlin, 2006). NPOs filled in as central and local governments began contracting out (Angroff & McGuire, 2003), actively rethinking social services and frequently taking over the public authority functions of directly assisting citizens (Manetti, 2014).

A DEVELOPING GLOBAL ROLE

Since this stimulus to and emergence of NPOs, the debate about their role has expanded into various types of institutions. Leading universities have designed research and training programs. International research networks have been set up. Consulting firms have been active in the market, and some European countries have considered regulations for NPOs, similar to social enterprises (Defourny & Nyssen, 2010).

Despite the growing importance of the non-profit sector at the worldwide level, we currently lack reliable estimates regarding the number and dimension of these organizations because they vary tremendously – from large organizations (such as cooperative groups) to small social enterprises (sometimes even small associations). Nonetheless, some estimates, though fragmentary, are available.

The national accounts systems play an important function in providing periodic, accurate and broad information on economic activity of NPOs and also in order to support international comparisons properly. The two most important national accounts systems currently in force are the *United Nations' System of National Accounts* – which in 2003 has for the first time developed the Handbook on Non-Profit Institutions in the System of National Accounts – and the *European System of National and Regional Accounts*. Moreover, with specific regard to US economy, the most prominent source for statistical official data is provided by the Urban Institute (Hofmann & McSwain, 2013) which periodically gather, evaluate and report information concerning non-profits that report to the Internal Revenue Service (IRS) (Blackwood, Roeger, & Pettijohn, 2012).

In 2012 the Urban Institute Report (see Blackwood et al., 2012) shows the vastness and diversity of non-profit sector, which includes more than 2.3 million organizations Approximately 1.6 million non-profits were registered with the IRS in 2010,[1] an increase of 24% from 2000. The non-profit sector contributed $804.8 billion to the US economy in 2010, making up 5.5% of the country's GDP. In 2011, 26.8% of adults in the United States volunteered with an organization, contributing 15.2 billion hours valued at an estimated $296.2 billion.

In Europe the most recent official data has been made available by Monzón-Campos and Chaves-Ávila (2012) that for the European Economic and Social Committee have delivered the 'Social Economy in the European Union' report where emerges the importance of the NPOs in both human and economic terms. NPOs in Europe provide more than 14.5 million[2] of paid employment (circa 6.5% of the working population of the EU-27 Member States) with a higher level of employment rate in some countries such as Sweden, Belgium, Italy, France and the Netherlands, where it ranges from 9% to 11.5% of the working population.

Other statistical sources are currently building up in Europe in order to make a snapshot about the overall dimension of the non-profit sector. Most European countries are indeed developing national statistics in order to estimate the overall number of NPOs. These estimates have been collected by the 'Giving in Europe' website (http://www.givingineurope.org), which counts 2 million organizations belonging to the non-profit sector in Europe. However, this is a conservative estimate because some European countries are still collecting information.

THE RISE OF THE COOPERATIVE SECTOR

Amongst the various type of organizations within the non-profit sector, cooperatives have gained increasing attention in recent years and the United

Nations recognized the importance of the cooperative sector by declaring 2012 the International Year of Cooperatives or IYC. The IYC aimed to highlight the strengths of the cooperative business model as an alternative means of doing business while furthering socio-economic development.

The cooperatives sector represents an important share of the global economy, both in terms of numbers of employees and economic performance. In 2009, the International Labor Organization (ILO) highlighted the resilience of cooperatives in turbulent economic and financial times. Broadly speaking, the financial economic crisis has had negative impacts on the majority of enterprises; however, cooperative enterprises around the world have shown resilience to the crisis: 'Financial cooperatives remain financially sound; consumer cooperatives are reporting increased turnover; worker cooperatives are seeing growth as people choose the cooperative form of enterprise to respond to new economic realities' (Birchall & Ketilson, 2009, p. 2).

Recently, the Euricse report (Borzaga & Galera, 2012) also emphasized the increasingly important role of cooperatives. The report made particular reference to the robustness of the cooperative model during the current economic crisis: 'In most countries, cooperatives have responded more effectively to the crisis than investor-owned firms. The resilience of cooperatives has increasingly been acknowledged, and policy and opinion makers are eager to understand how cooperatives can play a role in tackling the dramatic consequences of the global crisis and reforming the system that has contributed to generating it' (p. 2).

The prominence of the cooperative movement has necessitated estimates of its dimension and role in world economies; thus, the International Cooperative Alliance (ICA) recently launched the World Cooperative Monitor (WCM) Project (started in 2012). The ICA World Cooperative Monitor [WCM] (2013) has analyzed 2,032 cooperatives in 56 countries around the world and estimates that the 300 biggest cooperatives in the world account for a total turnover of $940.1 billion (excluding the banking and insurance sectors) plus $134.1 billion total net banking income and $1,023.1 billion premium income in mutual and insurance cooperatives.

ACCOUNTABILITY FOR SOCIAL AND NPOS

Despite the growing importance of the non-profit sector in providing public services in many developed countries (Dees, Emerson, & Economy, 2001), there is much that remains to be understood in terms of their institutional mechanisms, governance rules and accounting and accountability functioning (Benjamin, 2013). For the past century, conventional economic and accounting theories have dominated global economic and social activity. The vision promoted by these theories suggests that the best way to trigger human progress is through self-regulated markets populated by rational agents. Consequently, history has considered the ideal organization to be the investor-owned enterprise, which pursues the production of goods and services in order to maximize the economic value for shareholders (Palmer & Vinten, 1998).

However, research has shown that these approaches have limitations compared to NPOs (Hofmann & McSwain, 2013). Meanwhile, accounting theories encounter limitations when dealing with these organizations for two primary reasons. First, the bottom line for NPOs is not based on the maximization of economic value for shareholders, but to create 'social value' for the broader community. Second, NPOs are characterized by a multi-stakeholder profile. For instance, their governance structure includes multiple stakeholders, and their activities benefit a large range of stakeholders.

In 1993, the need to rethink the role of accounting for NPOs induced the Financial Accounting Standards Board (FASB) to revise its standards for non-profits in an effort to enhance the usefulness of disclosures and to provide greater uniformity in financial reporting. Recently, both the International Accounting Standards Board (IASB) and the FASB began a project to again revise the existing IASB Conceptual Framework by highlighting differences between NPOs and Investor-Owned Firms (IOFs) (Gordon, 2013; Sinclair & Bolt, 2013). The IASB has agreed that measuring the performance of NPOs requires information about how resources are used to provide different services as well as information about the amount and nature of net resources. Moreover, the IASB has called for more research on the broader accounting sphere in order to develop measurements for service efforts as well as different accounting and reporting systems for NPOs in general.

When dealing with NPOs' accounting and accountabilities, the IASB recognized the high level of complexity in measuring and reporting on their performance because of their multi-stakeholder nature. Indeed, NPOs must consider their economic and financial equilibrium as a requirement for long-term survival. An orientation towards creating social value does not indicate that NPOs should ignore strategies to generate earnings and cash flow; on the contrary, they must constantly create economic value in order to survive over time and to ensure that they are able to continue with their mission. In other words, while business organizations consider wealth creation to be a way of measuring value creation, NPOs consider wealth creation as a means to an end, enabling survival over time (Dees, 1998).

THE DUAL ACCOUNTABILITY CHALLENGE

As such, NPOs can be considered 'double bottom line' organizations (Dart, Clow, & Armstrong, 2010) that grapple with the dual challenge of producing both social and economic value: they have to maintain sustainability from a financial perspective while simultaneously serving a socially oriented mission. Therefore, NPOs face a daily tension between mission and margin (Chetkovich & Frumkin, 2003). A large body of literature deals with this tension with some scholars focusing on social implications and policy concerns (Simpson & Shin, 1998; Weisbrod, 1998). Other scholars analyze the role of NPOs from a strategic perspective by considering their role in the business world (Porter, 1996; Williamson, 1994). Still others investigate the role of accounting and accountabilities when dealing with NPOs (Austin, Stevenson, & Skillern, 2006; Gray, Dillard, & Spence, 2011; Tucker & Parker, 2013; Unerman & O'Dwyer, 2006; Williams & Taylor, 2013).

Most of the skepticism regarding the adoption of traditional accounting principles and frameworks for NPOs derives from the fact that there have been some attempts to adapt business concepts for the non-profit context in the past. These approaches have been glaringly misleading because of the peculiarities of NPOs. Since they are social-value oriented, they cannot simply be measured by traditional financial indicators or by market share. Therefore, economic and financial indicators fail to offer a comprehensive evaluation of organizational performance (Austin et al., 2006). For-profit organizations summarize their economic and financial performances in financial statements because shareholders consider profit to be the company's mission; in contrast, in an NPO, there is no automatic relationship between increments of achievement in the organization's mission and financial performance (Moore, 2000).

To reflect the dual nature of NPOs – with both financial and social value – these organizations began to experiment with certain accounting practices that measured not only economic performance, but also social results (Bagnoli & Megali, 2011; Manetti, 2014; Nicholls, 2009). Difficulties aligning these measurement systems arise because these two types of value creation are intrinsically connected rather than being in opposition in a zero sum equation (Emerson, 2003). This difference created a need for a more complex, multi-directional and multi-stakeholder accountability system (Christensen & Ebrahim, 2006; Ebrahim, 2005; Najam, 1996; Williams & Taylor, 2013). This 'multi-directional' approach does not simply focus on the economic bottom line, rather it deals with different cognitive needs for a great number of stakeholders in order to satisfy competing claims while simultaneously considering complexity in managing these relationships (Kanter & Summers, 1987; Unerman & O'Dwyer, 2006).

According to this view, accountability is not an absolute concept, but a relational one: 'Accountability is better viewed as a system of multi-directional and contingent relations than as a collection of independent binary links. This means that improving accountability is not only about accounting for donor funds but also about making progress toward a mission that reflects accountability to communities or clients' (Ebrahim, 2005, p. 82). Therefore, accountability cannot be considered 'as an abstract, fixed, moral ideal but instead as a strategic idea to be formulated and acted on by ... [NPOs] ... with the goal of better understanding and achieving their strategic purposes' (Brown & Moore, 2001, p. 570). As accountability involves ensuring that the various expectations of stakeholders are met, developing an NPO's mission and strategy must include a decision about structuring its accountability relationships (Williams & Taylor, 2013).

Several accounting scholars have identified the use of a multi-stakeholder approach for NPOs (Diochon & Anderson, 2009; Ebrahim, 2005; Gibbon & Affleck, 2008; Gray, Bebbington, & Collison, 2006; Nicholls, 2009, 2010; Pearce, 2003). These studies also have considered and analyzed the relevance of adopting social and environmental accounting and reporting practices for these organizations. As Gray et al. (2011) suggest that in NPOs, social accounting might be developed 'to justify their pursuit of social and environmental goals in economic terms' (p. 13). The development of social accounting practices for NPOs also might be attributed to the search for 'closeness' (Rawls, 1972) in the relationship among stakeholders: the degree of closeness might vary considerably among organizations and thus influence the search for a more formal-oriented accountability, that is, in those organizations where closeness is fairly absent – or a more informal accountability – that is, in those organizations, such as NPOs, where the relationship is based on simplicity: 'friends or family members typically do not require formal accounts' (Gray et al., 2006, p. 336). Moreover, if the accounting becomes also dynamic, that is, by addressing the expectations of critical stakeholders over time, the organization becomes dynamically transparent fully addressing the first principle of justice by Rawls (Vaccaro & Madsen, 2009).

DEVELOPING THE NPO SOCIAL ACCOUNTING PROJECT

These studies have pointed out the advantages and disadvantages of implementing the so-called 'Social Accounting Project' in NPOs. As an advantage, the authors have concluded that these innovative practices can increase organizational transparency (Unerman & O'Dwyer, 2006). However, as Gray et al. (2011) highlight, within the community of accountants and accounting scholars, there is a great deal of work that needs to be carried out in order to increase knowledge regarding accountability and social accounting for social and NPOs.

This book is an attempt to move in this direction by contributing to the debate about the role of different accountabilities in the NPO sector. The book focuses on the limitations of the traditional financial accounting system for NPOs as well as the potentialities associated with social and environmental accounting and reporting practices. It contains both an examination of how to improve the accounting system for NPOs and a discussion of the benefits emerging from the social and environmental accounting and reporting models. In this sense, the book provides new contributions to our research literature, fostering synergies among financial accounting and social accounting scholars engaging with the NPO subject area.

OVERVIEW OF THE BOOK

In order to foster accountability and social accounting studies in NPOs both theoretically and empirically, this book for the first time brings together studies from a range of disciplines, such as financial accounting, social accounting, economics, management and third-sector studies.[3] This cross-disciplinary approach offers a major contribution to our developing knowledge in this field. The book focuses on the limitations of the traditional financial accounting system for NPOs along with the possibilities associated with social and environmental accounting and reporting practices. It contains both an examination of how to improve the accounting system for NPOs and a discussion of the benefits emerging from the social and environmental accounting and reporting models. In this sense, the book provides new contributions to the accounting literature because it fosters synergies among financial accounting and social accounting scholars with regards to the NPO topic.

The book's content is summarized as follows.

Part I: The Non-Profit Sector

The first part of the book provides a broad discussion and analysis of the non-profit sector. It focuses on articles that address differences in types of organization: their characteristics, style of operation, focus and organizational cultures as well as their social, economic and political environments. In dealing with these issues, Article 2 introduces the broad European context of the third sector. Jacques Defourny and Victor Pestoff describe the colourful context of the third sector in Europe, which includes all types of NGOs, non-profit organizations (NPOs), mutuals, cooperatives, social enterprises, and foundations. The article provides brief overviews of third-sector images and concepts in 13 European countries. This article highlights the growing professionalization of third-sector organizations in most countries as well as their growing dependence on public funds for service provision.

In Article 3, Carlo Borzaga and Giulia Galera focus on the emerging concept of social enterprises in Europe by distinguishing it from the North American version of social entrepreneurship. The authors highlight the role of social enterprises and their impacts on the welfare systems of European countries. They describe social entrepreneurship as a trend across all forms of enterprises and social enterprise emerging as the institutionalization of a new typology distinguishable by specific features from inception.

Part II: Accounting and Accountabilities for the Non-Profit Sector

The second part of the book deals primarily with the limitations associated with traditional financial accounting instruments and measurement when applied to NPOs. Indeed, the conventional accounting framework has historically been designed in order to identify, gather, measure and report economic and financial data in order to reflect the stockholders' expectations. This approach effectively excludes many stakeholder groups that NPOs seek to address and assist. They include employees, clients, marginalized groups, local communities, national governments, special interest lobby groups and more. The second part of the book also discusses the recent call posed by the IASB and FASB in terms of differences between co-ops and IOFs.

In Article 4, Louis Beaubien and Daphne Rixon present a document-based review and semi-structured interviews of three large insurance co-operatives based in North America and the United Kingdom. This article examines whether or not the financial crisis of 2008 caused cooperatives to emphasize their cooperative difference from investor-owned insurance companies (IOCs) when analyzing metrics for performance measurement. The findings show that insurance cooperatives metrics are consistent with investor-owned companies; therefore, the measures do not recognize the cooperative principles and values which form the basis of these insurance cooperatives. This article thus reinforces the skepticism regarding the current practices of performance measurement in cooperatives and also theorizes how they should be developed reflecting the cooperative principles and being consistent with them.

Article 5 addresses the effects of accounting reclassification of members' shares in Spanish cooperatives. Fernando Polo-Garrido evaluates the effects of equity-liability accounting reclassification after the introduction of a change in Spain's accounting standard. The findings indicate that accounting reclassification from member shares equity to liability has effects even if there is no actual material change in terms of the members' shares. Thus, cooperatives are incentivized to modify their statutes in order to retain their equity accounting classification even when this modification is not desired. This article contributes to the literature on accounting standards for cooperatives and highlights the political impact of inappropriate equity-liability reclassification on the credit access of cooperatives. The article argues that accounting standards may have an impact on the perceptions that stakeholders – like funders – have on the cooperatives, even if no changes in the managerial activities have occurred.

Part III: Social Accounting for the Non-Profit Sector

The final part of the book deals with social and environmental accounting studies for NPOs. Michele Andreaus opens the third section by presenting his integrated accountability model for NPOs. In this sixth article, the author expands on the concept of the 'double bottom line' organization and presents his model of integrated accountability based on three dimensions: the economic, the social and the mission. This model is offered as a vehicle to better address accountability responsibilities with respect to all stakeholders. This article contributes to the debate regarding 'for what' NPOs should be accountable and makes explicit reference to the mission-related dimension which – even if it represents the very heart of the NPOs accountability – has to date been under-considered by many scholars.

In Article 7, Massimo Contrafatto introduces the concept of stewardship and stewardship-ism. In order to advance knowledge on this topic, the author has analyzed the management, organization and accounting literature on stewardship in order to propose four theoretical 'vignettes' illustrating the variants and approaches of the stewardship framework. The richness of perspectives, focus and analysis proposed in the article contribute to exploring new waves of accountability theory for NPOs. In detail, the normative and theological approach to stewardship could provide an alternative view for extending the way of conceptualize accountability in NPOs.

Article 8 presents a conceptual framework and develops a model of integrated social accounting for NPOs, namely NISA. Laurie Mook develops a framework that takes into account the specific purposes of NPOs, which are, by definition, different from for-profit organizations in terms of their peculiarities and their economic, social and environmental impacts. The integrated social accounting model proposed in this article is composed of four elements: (1) economic and human resources; (2) economic, social and environmental value creation; (3) internal systems and processes; and (4) organizational learning, growth and innovation. The article contributes to the non-profit performance management by employing a social accounting perspective and therefore by highlighting the role of stakeholders to whom accountability is owed. The NISA model presented in this work has the potential to be applied in several different contexts of NPOs since it could be adapted to different countries, regions and sectors of activities and therefore to the changing stakeholders' claims.

In Article 9, Ericka Costa analyzes the interplay between regulation and social and environmental reporting in Italian social enterprises by analyzing how 'non-accredited' social enterprises discharge voluntary accountability before and after the introduction of regulation. The findings suggest that the introduction of regulation of social and environmental reporting has increased voluntary disclosure on social and environmental matters for Italian 'non-regulated' social enterprises, thus affirming the prevalent literature arguing in favour of a mandatory approach to social reporting. The article has significant policy implications since it highlights the potential of the introduction of a new regulation regarding NPOs accountability to (indirectly) impact the voluntary disclosure. In other words, when legislators are designing any new legislative framework, they should be aware that the impact of the new accounting regulation is not only directed to those organizations affected by the law, but also other (similar) organizations could potentially be damaged (or advantaged).

Article 10 presents intellectual capital (IC) measurement along with management and reporting practices at the organizational level, with the intent of investigating whether IC reports are used for accountability or for image-building. Stefania Veltri and Giovanni Bronzetti present a case study of an Italian NPO and describe the role of IC reports as an effective managerial tool fostering true organizational accountability. The novelty of this article lies in the introduction of the IC approach within the relational approach to NPOs accountability. Thus, IC reports could be used by NPOs in order to take into consideration stakeholders' expectations in their decision-making process.

HOW TO READ THE BOOK

The book is intended as a resource for a variety of readers.

NPOs are becoming increasingly important in many economies as governments have outsourced much of their direct education welfare and other social provisions. As previously explained, in such countries, NPOs are acquiring a growing space in the 'social economy', contributing to the national welfare of many countries. Because this is a growing space, there is an urgent need to discuss accountability mechanisms that would be useful both for the organizations and for their stakeholders. Therefore, we believe that a systematic reading of this book will provide an overview and a multidisciplinary perspective regarding the contribution of social accounting for social and NPOs. It is our intention that the book be a good starting point for scholars willing to address one or more of the research avenues opened by this dialogue.

The book also fills a large gap in the textbook marketplace on this subject area. Usually, textbooks refer separately to 'the non-profit context' or 'issues in accounting for NPOs' or 'accountability for non-profits'. We believe this to be the first attempt to converge all these streams into one unique book; scholars from different disciplines have contributed under the global umbrella of a better understanding for NPO disclosure mechanisms.

NOTES

1. 'Registered organizations exclude non-profits that are not required to register with the IRS such as organizations with less than $5,000 in annual revenue or religious congregations and their auxiliary groups (although many congregations choose to register). This 1.6 million encompasses a variety of organizations including health, education, arts, advocacy organizations, labour unions and business and professional associations' (Blackwood et al., 2012, p. 2).
2. For detail regarding each EU countries, please see Tables 6.1 and 6.2 of the Social Economy in the European Union' report (Monzón-Campos & Chaves Ávila, 2012, pp. 47–48).
3. The genesis of this book occurred at the 4th Italian Conference on Social and Environmental Accounting Research. Together with Euricse, the European Research Institute on Cooperatives and Social Enterprises, we have developed a special track in order to further contribute to the broader sphere of accountability and social accounting for non-profit organizations. Several articles have been received from the scientific committee, contributing to a greater understanding of accountability and social accounting for these types of organizations while promoting future developments in these reporting issues. The articles have been evaluated with a double blind review process, and one of these manuscripts is included.

ACKNOWLEDGEMENTS

We truly appreciate the Emerald editorial team for their assistance in the development of this book. The support of Cheryl Lehman, Andrew Smith and Louise Lister is particularly acknowledged.

Special acknowledgement goes to the authors of the articles for their commitment to this editorial project and for their effort in developing high-quality work to share with the academic community.

We are also grateful to the reviewers for their meticulous work in providing comments for the enhancement of every single article.

REFERENCES

Angroff, R., & McGuire, M. (2003). *Collaborative public management: New strategies for local governments*. Washington, DC: Georgetown University Press.

Anheier, H. K., Hass, R., & Beller, A. (2013). Accountability and transparency in the German nonprofit sector: A paradox. *International Review of Public Administration, 18*(3), 69–84.

Austin, J., Stevenson, H., & Skillern, J. W. (2006). Social and commercial entrepreneurship: Same, different, or both? *Entrepreneurship Theory and Practice*, (January), *30*(1), 1–22.

Bagnoli, L., & Megali, C. (2011). Measuring performance in social enterprises. *Nonprofit and Voluntary Sector Quarterly*, *40*(1), 149–165.

Benjamin, L. M. (2013). The potential of outcome measurement for strengthening nonprofits' accountability to beneficiaries. *Nonprofit and Voluntary Sector Quarterly*, *42*(6), 1224–1244.

Birchall, J., & Ketilson, L. H. (2009). *Resilience of the cooperative business model in times of crisis.* Sustainable enterprise programme. ILO – International Labour Organization.

Blackwood, A. S., Roeger, K. L., & Pettijohn, S. L. (2012). *The nonprofit sector in brief: Public charities, giving, and volunteering.* Washington, DC: National Center for Charitable Statistics, Urban Institute. Retrieved from http://www.urban.org/publications/412674.html

Borzaga, C., & Defourny, J. (2001). *The emergence of social enterprise.* London: Routledge.

Borzaga, C., & Galera, G. (2012). *Promoting the understanding of cooperatives for a better world.* Trento: Euricse – European Research Institute of Cooperatives and Social Enterprises. Retrieved from http://euricse.eu/sites/euricse.eu/files/db_uploads/documents/1348242323 _n2208_0.pdf

Brown, L. D., & Moore, M. H. (2001). Accountability, strategy, and international nongovernmental organizations. *Nonprofit and Voluntary Sector Quarterly*, *30*(3), 569–587.

Chetkovich, C., & Frumkin, P. (2003). Balancing margin and mission: Nonprofit competition in charitable versus fee-based programs. *Administration & Society*, *35*(5), 564–596.

Christensen, R. A., & Ebrahim, A. (2006). How does accountability affect mission? *Nonprofit Management and Leadership*, *17*(2), 195–209.

Dart, R., Clow, E., & Armstrong, A. (2010). Meaningful difficulties in the mapping of social enterprises. *Social Enterprise Journal*, *6*(3), 186–193.

Dees, J. G. (1998). Enterprising nonprofits. *Harvard Business Review*, *76*(1), 55–66.

Dees, J. G., Emerson, J., & Economy, P. (Eds.). (2001). *Enterprising nonprofits: A toolkit for social entrepreneurship.* Canada: Wiley.

Defourny, J., & Nyssens, M. (2010). Conceptions of social enterprise and social entrepreneurship in Europe and the United States: Convergences and divergences. *Journal of Social Entrepreneurship*, *1*(1), 32–53.

Diochon, M., & Anderson, A. R. (2009). Social enterprise and effectiveness: A process typology. *Social Enterprise Journal*, *5*(1), 7–29.

Ebrahim, A. (2005). Accountability myopia: Losing sight of organizational learning. *Nonprofit and Voluntary Sector Quarterly*, *34*(1), 56.

Economist. (2009). *Saving the world, special report on entrepreneurship. Economist*, 12, March.

Emerson, J. (2003). The blended value proposition: Integrating social and financial returns. *California Management Review*, *45*(4), 35–51.

English, L., Guthrie, J., & Parker, L. D. (2003). A review of new public financial management change in Australia. *Australian Accounting Review*, *13*(1), 3–9.

European Commission. (2014). *The social business initiative of the European Commission.* Retrieved from http://ec.europa.eu/internal_market/publications/docs/sbi-brochure/sbi-brochure-web_en.pdf

Gibbon, J., & Affleck, A. (2008). Social enterprise resisting social accounting: Reflecting on lived experiences. *Social Enterprise Journal*, *4*(1), 41–56.

Gordon, T. P. (2013). Not-for-profit accounting in a changing world of standard setting: What professors and students need to know. *Journal of Accounting Education*, *31*, 232–243.

Gray, R., Bebbington, J., & Collison, D. (2006). NGOs, civil society and accountability: Making the people accountable to capital. *Accounting, Auditing & Accountability Journal*, *19*(3), 319–348.

Gray, R., Dillard, J., & Spence, C. (2011). A brief re-evaluation of 'The Social Accounting Project'. In A. Ball & S. P. Osborne (Eds.), *Social accounting and public management. Accountability for the common good* (pp. 12–22). New York, NY: Routledge.

Hofmann, M. A., & McSwain, D. (2013). Financial disclosure management in the nonprofit sector: A framework for past and future research. *Journal of Accounting*, *L32*, 61–87.

Kanter, R. M., & Summers, D. V. (1987). Doing well while doing good: Dilemmas of performance measurement in nonprofit organizations and the need for a multiple-constituency approach. In W. W. Powell (Ed.), *The non-profit sector – a research handbook* (pp. 154–164). New Haven, CT: Yale University Press.

Kerlin, J. A. (2006). Social enterprise in the United States and Europe: Understanding and learning from the differences. *Voluntas: International Journal of Voluntary and Nonprofit Organizations*, *17*, 247–263.

Manetti, G. (2014). The role of blended value accounting in the evaluation of socio-economic impact of social enterprises. *Voluntas: International Journal of Voluntary and Nonprofit Organizations*, *25*, 443–464.

Monzón-Campos, J. L., & Chaves-Ávila, R. (2012). *The social economy in the European Union, European economic and social committee*. Bruxelles: European Union. Retrieved from http://www.eesc.europa.eu/resources/docs/qe-30-12-790-en-c.pdf

Moore, M. H. (2000). Managing for value: Organizational strategy in for-profit, nonprofit and governmental organizations. *Nonprofit and Voluntary Sector Quarterly*, *29*(1), 183–204.

Najam, A. (1996). NGO accountability: A conceptual framework. *Development Policy Review*, *46*, 339–353.

Nicholls, A. (2009). We do good things, don't we?: 'Blended value accounting' in social entrepreneurship. *Accounting, Organizations and Society*, *34*, 755–769.

Nicholls, A. (2010). Institutionalizing social entrepreneurship in regulatory space: Reporting and disclosure by community interest companies. *Accounting, Organizations and Society*, *35*, 394–415.

Palmer, P., & Vinten, G. (1998). Accounting, auditing and regulating charities – Towards a theoretical underpinning. *Managerial Auditing Journal*, *13*(6), 346–355.

Parker, L. D. (2012). From privatised to hybrid corporatised higher education: A global financial management discourse. *Financial Accountability and Management*, *28*(3), 247–268.

Pearce, J. (2003). *Social enterprise in anytown*. London: Calouste Gulbenkian Foundation.

Porter, M. (1996). What is strategy? *Harvard Business Review*, *74*, 61–78.

Rawls, J. (1972). *A theory of justice*. Oxford: Oxford University Press.

Salamon, L. M., Wojciech Sokolowski, S., Haddock, M. A., & Tice, H. S. (2013). *The state of global civil society and volunteering: Latest findings from the implementation of the UN nonprofit handbook*. Working Paper No. 49. Johns Hopkins Center for Civil Society Studies, Baltimore.

Simpson, J., & Shin, R. (1998). Do nonprofits exercise market power? *International Journal of the Economics of Business*, *5*(2), 141–157.

Sinclair, R., & Bolt, R. (2013). Third sector accounting standard setting: Do third sector stakeholders have voice? *Voluntas: International Journal of Voluntary and Nonprofit Organizations*, *24*, 760–784.

Steinberg, R., & Powell, W. W. (2006). *The nonprofit sector: A research handbook*. New Haven, CT: Yale University Press.

Tucker, B. P., & Parker, L. D. (2013). Managerial control and strategy in nonprofit organizations doing the right things for the wrong reasons? *Nonprofit Management & Leadership*, *24*(1), 80–107.

Unerman, J., & O'Dwyer, B. (2006). Theorising accountability for NGO advocacy. *Accounting, Auditing & Accountability Journal*, *19*(3), 349–376.

United Nations Statistics Division. (2003). *Handbook on nonprofit institutions in the system of national accounts*. Series F, No. 91. St/ESA/Stat/Ser.F/91. New York, NY: United Nations.

Vaccaro, A., & Madsen, P. (2009). Transparency: The new ICT-driven ethics? *Ethics and Information Technology*, *11*(2), 113–122.

Weisbrod, B. (1998). Institutional form and organizational behavior. In W. W. Powell & E. S. Clemens (Eds.), *Private action and the public good* (pp. 69–84). New Haven, CT: Yale University Press.

Williams, A. P., & Taylor, J. A. (2013). Resolving accountability ambiguity in nonprofit organizations. *Voluntas: International Journal of Voluntary and Nonprofit Organizations*, *24*, 559–580.

Williamson, O. (1994). Strategizing, economizing, and economic organization. In R. P. Rumelt, D. E. Schendel, & D. J. Teece (Eds.), *Fundamental issues in strategy* (pp. 361–401). Cambridge, MA: Harvard University Press.

World Cooperative Monitor. (2013). *Exploring the co-operative economy*. Explorative Report 2013. Retrieved from http://euricse.eu/sites/euricse.eu/files/wcm2013_web_0.pdf

PART II
THE NON-PROFIT SECTOR

TOWARDS A EUROPEAN CONCEPTUALIZATION OF THE THIRD SECTOR

Jacques Defourny and Victor Pestoff

ABSTRACT

There is still no universal definition of the third sector in Europe, but it can be seen as including all types of non-governmental not-for-profit entities such as non-profit organizations, mutuals, cooperatives, social enterprises and foundations. This article attempts to make sense of the current shifting conceptualization of the third sector in Europe. It is based on short country summaries of the images and concepts of the third sector in 13 European countries by EMES Network's members, first presented in 2008 (Defourny and Pestoff, 2008; nine of them were recently revised and are found in the appendix to this article.). The perception and development of the third sector in Europe is closely related to the other major social governance institutions/mechanisms, like the market, state and community and through the third sector's interaction with them. Moreover, many third sector organizations (TSOs) overlap with these other social institutions, resulting in varying degrees of hybridity and internal tensions experienced by them. TSOs can generate resources from their activities on the market, by providing services in partnership

Accountability and Social Accounting for Social and Non-profit Organizations
Advances in Public Interest Accounting, Volume 17, 25–87

ISSN: 1041-7060/doi:10.1108/S1041-706020140000017001

with the state and/or by promoting the interests of a given community or group. The country overviews document a growing professionalization of TSOs in most countries and a growing dependency of public funds to provide services. This has important theoretical and practical implications for orienting the articles included in this book. Thus, it can provide a key for better understanding the discussion and analysis in the remainder of this volume.

Keywords: Third sector; third-sector organization; cooperatives; welfare triangle; overlapping area; professionalization

INTRODUCTION

In European economies, the importance of a 'third sector', distinct from the private for-profit and public sectors, has increasingly been acknowledged, from various points of view. First, it clearly appears that beyond the diversity of conceptions and labels used to identify such a third sector, the latter has gained economic significance in terms of employment and production. This growth is especially apparent in service provision. Because of different definitions, there are no universally accepted measures of the sector's economic weight. But although its importance remains modest in some countries (in particular in the new EU member states), it represents, according to some figures, more than 10 per cent of total employment in countries such as Ireland, the Netherlands and Belgium.[1]

It also appears that public authorities have paid greater attention, in recent decades, to third sector organizations (TSOs); the latter have increasingly been recognized as partners for the implementation of public policies. Although such an acknowledgement may sometimes remain purely instrumental or only focus on particular fields, numerous public initiatives have been undertaken to increase the role of TSOs in areas of public interest.

In academic spheres as well, the third sector has benefited from an increasing interest in the last three or four decades (Defourny, 2013). More precisely, the broad set of non-governmental organizations that do not distribute a profit or may be qualified as 'not-for-profit' has been studied by various disciplines within the social sciences, including sociology, political science, social policy, economics, management, history, law, psychology, etc. Based on this growing body of scientific literature, a number of courses and training programs have been developed and are being offered by universities and other higher educational institutions.

However, in spite of those clear trends, the image of the third sector in public opinion and among many other socio-economic actors generally remains unclear. Even within the third sector itself, the degree of consciousness of belonging to a wide and distinct sector varies significantly across organizations and often remains low.

In such a contrasting context, the major objective of this article is to document these apparently divergent developments and to lay the foundations for a better understanding of the evolving place, profiles and roles of TSOs in European economies and societies. In order to do so, members of the EMES European Research Network from nine EU countries[2] revised their brief overview of the images and recent trends of the third sector in their respective national contexts. These country contributions represent the major part of the present study and they are included in the Appendix to this article. On the basis of those short and precise descriptions, we first try to point out the common features which may contribute to better and more integrated knowledge of the third sector, while not ignoring the strong diversity of national specificities.

Diversity of the Third Sector's Historical Roots

Although the main forms of the modern third sector in Europe took shape during the 19th Century, its history dates back to the oldest forms of human association. Indeed, it is fair to say that the genesis of the third sector parallels to a large extent the gradual emergence of freedom of association. Collective relief funds, trade guilds, guild masterships, fraternities, craft brotherhoods, convents, as well as many other forms of community life involving economic activities that could be found in most world regions throughout centuries (Defourny, Develtere, Fonteneau, & Nyssens, 2009). However, most of those initiatives in Europe could not exist outside tight control of the State, the Church or other institutional power. In the 18th Century nevertheless, friendly societies grew (especially in England), some types of charitable institutions gained more autonomy and learned societies, including secret ones (especially in France), were increasingly created. It then took almost 100 more years to see freedom of association making critical breakthrough in most Western European countries: laws were passed in the late 19th or early 20th Century to provide legal frameworks to organizational forms (non-profit organizations, associations, cooperatives, mutual societies, foundations) that made up the modern third sector.

Such a common basic trend could be found in several parts of Europe, but the emergence of TSOs took place in quite different ways as national and local contexts were marked by major cultural, social, political and economic specificities. In the midst of various factors which clearly contributed to shape the third sector, it is possible to identify a diversity of streams which proved to be particularly influential in specific countries (Evers & Laville, 2004). These streams may be summarized as follows, while such a classification clearly deserves more comments than space allows:

- the tradition of philanthropy (charities, the community sector, etc.) was and still is particularly influential in the United Kingdom and Ireland, as in the United States (through foundations) with a clear mutual influence between these two regions;
- the tradition of civic commitment to the entire community, aiming to foster equality and democracy has been prevailing in Scandinavian countries;
- the principle of 'subsidiarity' has been central, especially with respect to Church-related initiatives that tried to maintain their autonomy with respect to the State, in countries such as Germany, Belgium, Ireland and the Netherlands;
- in various countries, the cooperative movement was closely linked to the development of the voluntary sector, either through a common civic background fostering participation and democracy (as in Denmark, Sweden, etc.), or through a common religious or associationist-socialist inspiration (as in Italy, Belgium, France, etc.);
- finally, the role assigned to the family in countries such as Spain, Portugal, Greece and Italy also had a major influence on the pace of development of the third sector, especially as regards the provision of personal services (childcare, elderly care, etc.) which remained informally organized within the family much more than elsewhere.

Diversification of Organizational Forms within the Third Sector

More recently, a new generation of initiatives appeared in the final quarter of the 20th Century that were often dealing with new challenges, not usually addressed by traditional organizations. Such challenges included the fight against unemployment (e.g. worker cooperatives, worker-owned firms, work integration enterprises), the need to combat social exclusion (e.g. housing and urban revitalization initiatives, new services for the poorest and people at risk in many respects) and local development of remote areas (community development enterprises or agencies). Many other fields such as fair trade, organic food processing, micro-credit, social finance, renewable energy, waste collection and new methods for re-using second-hand materials have witnessed the emergence of initiatives inventing new business models, which combine social or societal aims with a reliance on a diversity of resources. Public authorities acknowledged the public benefit dimension of many activities undertaken by associations of all kinds and designed specific programmes and schemes to support them. As a result, various types of initiatives have become registered, labelled and identified with such public schemes. In several countries legislations created new legal forms, better suited to some types of organizations. In some cases, these new legal forms were associated with general frameworks designed for cooperatives (e.g. in Greece, France, Italy, Portugal and Spain), in others, they referred to the wider notion of social enterprise to encompass various types of enterprises pursuing a community interest or a social aim (e.g. in Belgium, Italy and the United Kingdom); while elsewhere they narrowly focused on the work integration of disadvantaged groups (e.g. Finland, Poland).[3] In any case, it is striking to see how the concept of social enterprise has been a major vehicle in recent years to revisit the role of TSOs in today's societies, although this concept sometimes goes beyond the borders of the third sector (Defourny, Hulgård, & Pestoff, 2014).

In a somewhat contrasting way, we are currently witnessing the rise of new generations of associations, marked by a stronger orientation to members' interests, for instance in leisure activities, while traditional organizations pursuing the benefit of the whole community may sometimes experience a decline. Newer local associations also tend to remain quite autonomous, avoiding affiliation to national umbrella structures – something that was previously unknown in some countries, like Norway only a few years ago. Generally speaking, there appears to be a major difference between powerful nationwide umbrella organizations, such as the German ones, and the quite vivid, diversified and autonomous associative life that can be observed today at the local level in most countries, including new EU member states like Poland.

Moreover, in some countries, the move towards greater 'corporate social responsibility' (CSR) has led big companies to establish corporate foundations or funds or to become involved in community foundations. In Italy, for example, foundations have also been created on the basis of collective reserves accumulated by public banks which were privatized, and endowments made by wealthy individuals to philanthropic organizations supporting civil society activities or social entrepreneurs. Similarly, actors like national lotteries may play an important role in the third sector. The National Organization of the Blind in Spain, the ONCE foundation, based on a lottery, is by far the largest employer in the Spanish third sector, with over 100,000 employees. In Norway, lotteries traditionally play a crucial funding role for voluntary organizations. What is new in this regard is the increasing competition among associations to attract gamblers' interest and the strengthening of this competitive market by new funds set up by large for-profit firms. As a result of all these trends, the third sector increasingly appears to include a wide spectrum of organizational forms and a wide variety of aims, although it still has many major and well identified components.

TOOLS FOR CONCEPTUALIZING A THIRD SECTOR WITH BLURRED FRONTIERS

As noted above, TSOs are increasingly involved in the provision of socially necessary services. Much of the literature on non-profit organizations and the social economy argues that the state and private for-profit companies provide certain services, but these services may not be of the desired quality for some groups (this is often true of uniform public services), or, as a result of their price, they will not be affordable to the individuals who need these services most (as is often the case with market provision). Thus, TSOs generally provide a necessary complement to both public and private for-profit provision of basic welfare services, or they deliver the bulk of some specific services. Therefore, several European third sector scholars have discussed the 'welfare mix', made of shared responsibilities among various types of providers, which has increasingly taken place in Europe, while others have proposed a 'welfare triangle', represented in Fig. 1, to better understand the relations between the various sectors (Eme, 1991; Evers, 1990, 1995; Evers & Laville, 2004; Laville, 1992, 1994; Pestoff, 1998, 2005, 2008).

From a macro perspective, the idea of the welfare mix, at an abstract level, expresses variations in the relative importance attributed to the major social institutions/mechanisms of the community, market and state as well as to associations in the governance of society. At the same time, the third

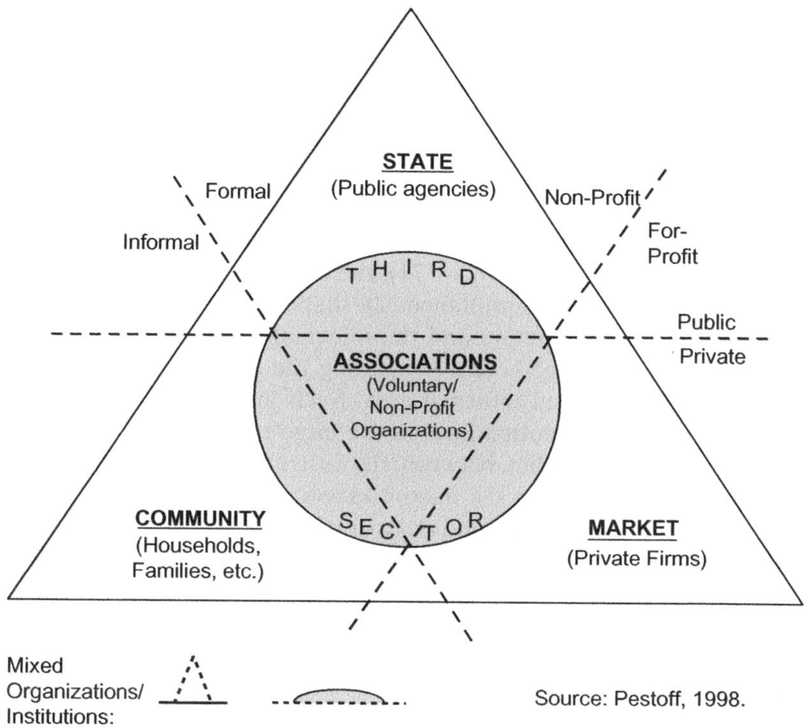

Fig. 1. The Third Sector in the Welfare Triangle.

sector is depicted as an intermediate sector, which is clearly interrelated with the state, private for-profit companies and the informal sector. Conceiving the third sector as an intermediate sector makes an important difference for research in at least four respects (Evers, 1995, p. 160):

- first, it calls attention to the importance of the social and political role of TSOs, which are otherwise usually only recognized for their economic role as alternative service providers;
- second, it underlines the intermediating role of TSOs, in relation not only with the state and the market, but also with the informal or community sphere;
- third, it emphasizes the need for a synergetic mix of resources and rationales available to organizations in the third sector, rather than pursuing a substitution or assimilation process between clear-cut sectors, and

– fourth, it leads to a recognition of the great variety of ways in which intermediary organizations act as hybrids, intermeshing different resources and connecting with different areas, and it therefore underlines the limits of attempts to map the third sector precisely and to assess its accurate size.[4]

As noted earlier, the role of organizations with social- and service-related purposes varies according to historical and political traditions. According to Evers (1995, pp. 162–171), the characteristics of the third sector are shaped by, but also simultaneously shape the respective influence of state institutions, market actors and the informal sector of families. There is a constant tension at the border separating the central triangle in Fig. 1 from the market, state and informal area. Such 'behavioural' tensions are represented by the three dotted lines in the large triangle. The first type of tension concerns the conflict between the instrumental rationality of the market, which is oriented to the maximization and distribution of profits, and the solidarity-based, social and democratic values both of the third sector and the state. The second type of tension is related to state institutions and their universalistic values, which contrast with the particularistic logic of most private actors, including TSOs. Finally, there is a third type of tension, between formal organizations and the informal worlds of the family, personal relationships, neighbourhoods, social networks, etc., thereby making it harder to draw a clear line between the latter and the third sector in areas of help and self-help.

Those behavioural tensions give a polyvalent and hybrid nature to TSOs, which must act under the multiple influence of and are dependent on the other sectors, and in extreme cases this may result in organizational transformation. TSOs often pursue multiple goals simultaneously, for example, providing services to members and others, lobbying for changes in the law or regulations, etc. Balancing various activities can be very challenging, and also require greater transparency between the managers of TSOs and their strategic stakeholders.

In relation to the tensions that have just been highlighted, let us now try to interpret and illustrate more precisely the areas in the figure where the third sector overlaps with the other spheres of society. Indeed, such overlapping areas are crucial to fully understand the current blurring of the third sector's borders, emphasized in various country notes in the appendix. Even more importantly, they allow diverse conceptions of the third sector's place and role in Europe to coexist, while stressing that such views still have a lot in common. We will therefore look closer at each of these overlapping areas one at a time.

Overlap between the Third Sector and Market

The overlapping area between *the third sector and the market* highlights that some third sector enterprises, such as cooperatives, operate entirely on the market and seek profits while adopting rules other than those of typical capitalist companies. For example, shareholders only receive a limited return on capital and the decision-making power is distributed among members, like in many other TSOs, on the basis of the 'one member, one vote' principle. These cooperative principles are rooted in a historical matrix of the 19th Century when cooperatives, friendly societies and all kinds of associations emerged as expressions of the 'civil society'.

This overlapping area includes most of the established cooperative movement, but it also illustrates the dangers inherent in such intermediary positioning: a multiplicity of goals increases the risks of goal displacement or organizational atrophy associated with the pursuit of conflicting goals, as seen in many big cooperative firms which increasingly behaved like their capitalist counterparts and do not make enough effort to maintain or reinvent their cooperative specificity (Pestoff, 2012a). The same area also provides some insights on the rapid development of so-called 'social enterprises'. Indeed, many social enterprises are clearly market-oriented while pursuing primarily a social aim, so they may be found in this area as well.

During most of the 20th Century, cooperatives developed their activities to meet their members' needs to gain better access to markets (as consumers, savers, producers, etc.). Their specialization in specific fields, the pressure of market forces and their increasing size led most cooperatives to follow a more commercial path that differed from most other components of the third sector. The later were generally oriented to non-market activities, such as advocacy, material assistance or the delivery of services outside market channels. This is one of the key reasons why scholars in several countries have been and still are reluctant to develop a conception of the third sector that encompasses both cooperatives, social enterprises and community or voluntary organizations.

In recent decades, however, newer forms of cooperatives appeared, in fields such as personal services, which do not solely rely on commercial or market resources. Therefore, social cooperatives and, more broadly, social enterprises operating on the basis of public subsidies or contracts as well as market resources can help to bridge part of the gap between traditional cooperatives and associations.[5] Of course, it should be stressed that such bridging forces have also been associated with the concept of social economy as it was revitalized at the end of the 1970s in France and subsequently in various countries like Belgium, Italy, Spain and Sweden and in an increasing number of other European and non-European countries (Argentina, Canada, South Korea, etc.).

As a result of these developments, the third sector has become increasingly associated with its productive role, especially as a service provider. Such an image is being reinforced in all fields where TSOs have to compete in the market with other private or public (for instance municipal) providers. The need for and the trend towards a professionalization of the third sector's labour force also reinforces this evolution, as do business schools by offering degrees in non-profit management.

However, an emphasis on the third sector's economic dimension and business-like methods may generate tensions within this sector, similar to those that have divided cooperatives and associations for a long period. In the current context, such tensions are especially likely to appear between production-oriented organizations, on the one hand, and associations for whom advocacy and/or civic commitment represent the core of their identity, on the other hand.[6] Thus, major components of the British community sector reacted negatively to the strategy of vigorously promoting social enterprise as it was implemented by the Blair/Brown government from 2002. That is why the latter decided to set up an Office of the Third Sector, in 2006, within the Cabinet Office. It also provided a definition of the third sector that encompassed 'voluntary and community organisations, charities, social enterprises, cooperatives and mutuals, both large and small'.[7] The previous British government also took a major initiative in promoting research on the third sector by financing the Third Sector Research Centre for five years.[8]

Overlap between the Third Sector and State

Shifting emphasis, social enterprises may also appear in the upper zone of the circle. This leads us more broadly to the overlap between *the third sector and the state*, where the increasingly blurred border between the public and the private (non-profit) sectors may result in new or hybrid types of organization. An example hereof is provided by quasi-public organizations, or what Streeck and Schmitter (1985) refer to as 'private interest government'. Here the division between the public and the private sectors almost disappears: private non-profit organizations are given explicit public responsibilities in terms of defining and implementing public policy. Such quasi-public organizations often comprise the nexus of networks of public and private bodies with strong mutual interest in regulating a certain field (Kenis, 1992). TSOs get involved in the regulation of certain public matters, like when farmers' cooperatives in Sweden became heavily involved in regulating agricultural production, prices, import quotas and export subsidies prior to membership in the EU and CAP (Pestoff, 1991). This overlapping area also integrates the increasingly important partnerships between TSOs and public authorities. For instance, in the fields of education and health as in various other fields, it is quite common for the state to prefer to delegate the provision of social services and to conclude contractual arrangements with private non-profit schools, hospitals or mutuals that it heavily finances. The strict regulation and supervision that the state imposes on these organizations explain why such TSOs appear to be located closer to the public sector than at the very centre of the third sector.

In several countries, public authorities have historically supported the voluntary sector as a service provider, on the basis of the subsidiarity principle, while in other countries, such as the Scandinavian ones or, to a lesser extent, Italy, the state chose to act as the main – if not the sole – provider of social services. In all cases, transformations of the welfare state in recent decades led to drastic changes in the relations between the third sector and public authorities. New types of partnerships were set up, with the state increasingly focusing on its regulatory function and contracting out the delivery of personal services. Thus, Voluntary Compacts[9] are now found in many European countries, both at the national and local level.

The state not only recognized and supported existing or emerging civil society initiatives, it sometimes took the lead in shaping and fostering voluntary organizations according to its priorities. One extreme example is provided by the former communist regime of Poland, which left its heritage in fields like sports and leisure, where large and wealthy quasi-public organizations are now supposed to behave along more autonomous and voluntary lines. Other more subtle examples include those public schemes that transform independent organizations into instruments of personal or collective service provision by regulating them very strongly and imposing norms in terms of targets, standardized processes or public accountability.

Work integration of hard-to-place unemployed people represents one of the areas where the collaboration between the state and the third sector has particularly developed and has taken many forms.[10] It seems reasonable to assert that recent moves towards institutionalization of the third sector probably reached a peak in that area. In several countries, like Germany, Ireland, Portugal or, more recently, Sweden, as well as in some Belgian regions, the concept of 'social economy' and 'social enterprise' appear to be reduced to work integration initiatives by the public authorities. This is very notable in Poland, which benefited greatly from the EU Equal programme – a programme which fostered a rather narrow understanding of the social economy concept (Pestoff, 2012b) and in Sweden (Levander, 2011).

However, the increase in the (sometimes close) interactions between the third sector and the state has tended to blur the boundaries between both spheres, as well as between public and civic responsibilities. Third sector provision of social services based on a long-term citizen/user commitment to contributing their time and effort for a better quality outcome is a growing phenomenon in Europe and elsewhere. It is often known as co-production and examples of parent participation in childcare and preschool services can be found in several European countries (Pestoff, 2008, 2009). Of course, this makes it even more difficult to define clear-cut borders for a truly distinct third sector.

Overlap between the Third Sector and Community

Finally, when examining the overlap between *the community and the third sector*, we note numerous examples of mixed organizations. A non-profit organization may for example attract the support of numerous individuals who are not formally members of the organization, but who nevertheless contribute their time and/or money to support its activities and to help this organization achieve its goals. A variety of mutual-aid and self-help groups also belong to this category; in some cases, the 'members' have not yet created a formal association, while in other cases, the association does not restrict its activities to 'dues-paying members', but is open to all persons in the community who are supported by the mutual-aid or self-help group. Moreover, some new local non-profit initiatives not only start without any legal framework, relying exclusively on the work of volunteers, but many of them also remain informal, do not register or adopt a clear legal status, although they actually provide some services. In any case, this third overlap area also helps, as the two others, to avoid establishing a strict frontier between stages in organizations' trajectories. The varying organizational response to HIV/AIDS in different European countries clearly illustrates this (Marin & Kenis, 1997).

BROAD CHANGES IN THE POLITICAL LANDSCAPE

Broad changes in the political landscape can have far-reaching consequences for the third sector and can impact the possibility structures for TSOs and their leaders, opening new ones and constraining or closing old ones. This can be seen in a situation where TSOs that usually operate in one area of overlap in the welfare triangle, for example, with the state, must shift rapidly and substantially to another area of overlap, like with the market. However, they may be unprepared to cope with the challenges and demands of their new environment and the new 'rules of the game'. This can expose TSOs to increasing hybridity, tensions and the uncertainty it implies. Thus, with the introduction of New Public Management (NPM) across Europe, many TSOs lost their previously cosy relations with public authorities that recognized their inherent social value added and therefore financed their activities through public grants. Once governments began to privatize public services and competition and efficiency became the principal criteria for distributing funds this cosy relationship ended. They have to adapt to and operate in a new, highly competitive and insecure environment, where many of their earlier partners or collaborators are now their competitors, along with many new entries in the form of private for-profit firms, including multinational companies and venture capitalists.

Continued funding for TSOs depends on winning a tender for providing services, but in order to succeed in this competitive environment they must become more professional. Their very survival in the competitive NPM environment demands greater professionalization. This, in turn, may introduce a new stakeholder into the management of a TSO, that is, a new type of professional staff with a strong managerial orientation who can develop separate and sometimes different interests than the board and/or the clients of a TSO. Moreover, the new 'rules of the game' are often very complex and demanding, subjecting TSOs to new and sometimes contradictory logics, thus increasing their hybridity. This more political perspective would, therefore, emphasize the potential status inconsistencies of a TSO leaving its 'comfort zone' and shifting its operations to new and uncharted waters. Here a high degree of hybridity might imply more challenges and hurdles to overcome, diverting attention from the TSO's original mission and could have an impact on its ability to survive in a highly competitive environment (Pestoff, 2014).

This also reflects the growing complexity of the bidding processes adopted by most New Public Management regimes, along with the heavy emphasis on competition and efficiency. Here large actors, often international venture capitalists, appear to have a competitive advantage, particularly when strict financial criteria are applied to the bidding process and little, if any, consideration is given to social criteria and service quality. Some argue that TSOs must become more 'business-like' and make more professional bids in order to be more competitive. However, becoming more professional and business-like may come into conflict with their social goals. Thus, the increasing overlap between the third sector and market logics will result in greater hybridity, complexity and both internal and external tensions that many if not most TSOs may find difficult to cope with.

Beyond Change, Permanent Features: Volunteering and Values

In spite of a clear trend towards professionalization, volunteering is increasing or remains at high levels in several countries. In Scandinavian countries, one third to one half of the population contribute to volunteer work; this is also the case in the United Kingdom, where volunteering and philanthropy seem embedded in citizens' duties. Although in a completely different context, volunteering is also developing across the Polish nongovernmental sector. In countries like Ireland and Belgium, a national committee on volunteering was recently established to better take into account and promote the specific role of volunteers in the third sector. The previous red-green government in Germany adopted a major report on the 'Future of civic engagement' (2002), which did not focus exclusively on volunteers but nevertheless stressed strongly the importance of the latter.

Moreover, beyond all transforming forces experienced by the third sector, the latter seems to remain associated primarily with values that are promoted and diffused in the overall society. The British government even speaks about 'value-driven NGOs' to describe the entire third sector. It is also through its values that the German third sector remains a point of reference for the whole society, while some EU countries now define the social economy by a specific set of values.

Service Provision and Advocacy: Avoiding a Zero-Sum Perspective

In many of the brief country reports contained in this study, the growing tendency towards third sector provision of some kinds of social services is associated with an increasing dependency of TSOs on government funds, and these are increasingly allocated under strict contractual arrangements and in competitive contexts. However, in spite of the risks of isomorphism already mentioned, a growing dependency on state funding and a trend towards professionalization are not by definition a threat to the independence or influence of the third sector.

By providing services, a TSO may obtain more resources and recognition than otherwise to pursue its key social mission and promote its core social values. This is not a zero-sum situation, in which more service provision would mean that less effort is devoted to advocacy and opinion formation. Both continued professionalization and increasing government funds may give an organization more – rather than less – political impact. The TSO can evolve from being a 'powerless outsider', competing for the attention of 'political insiders', to assuming the role of an influential, if somewhat more moderate, insider, and still remain dedicated to promoting its key mission and core social values. In other words, clear-cut situations of either advocacy or service provision are becoming less frequent in most of the European countries included here.

While the brief country overviews found in the Appendix merely scratch the surface, they do nevertheless underline the growing complexity of the changing role of the third sector in Europe. This is why various EMES scholars have long tried to contribute to a conceptualization of the third sector allowing a more dynamic and variegated picture of change and growth (Defourny et al., 2014).

Need for Greater Accountability by TSOs, NPOs, NGOs, Co-ops and Social Enterprises

Several factors discussed above underline the growing importance of accountability and social accounting for all types of TSOs, be they non-profit organizations, non-governmental organizations, cooperatives or social enterprises. All these changes increase the need for greater transparency and accountability, particularly in order to avoid mission drift, goal displacement and isomorphic tendencies. Until recently social accounting was a marginal and underdeveloped area of academic endeavour. However, thanks to the pioneering efforts of Gray, Owen, and Adams (1996) at CSEAR and Zadek and Evans (1993) at the New Economic Foundation, social accounting and audit are no longer *terra incognita*.

Previously, this lack of interest reflected, in part, the fact that the third sector itself was found at the crossroads of many different academic disciplines, economics, politics, sociology, etc., and no single one could cover all important aspects of the field. Moreover, accounting was closely tied to business administration with a clear focus on private for-profit firms. Therefore, it was necessary to ask to whom should TSOs be accountable? Unerman and O'Dwyer (2006, 2010) argue that it is possible to distinguish three main types of third sector accountability: *upward* accountability, where the organization is accountable to those who provide funds; *downward* accountability to their beneficiaries and finally *holistic* accountability. The latter combines both upward and downward accountability and implies TSOs should be accountable to all those upon whom they impact (Simaens & Koster, 2013). Furthermore, legal requirements in most countries only stipulate that TSOs provide an annual account of their economic activities or a financial statement that is subject to audit, but not a social account.

Such considerations make the following articles in this volume all the more relevant, topical and important for the development and future of the third sector.

NOTES

1. For figures focusing on non-profit organizations only, see the various publications of the Comparative Non-profit Sector Project, led by the Johns Hopkins University since the early 1990s. For figures covering the whole social economy, understood as encompassing cooperatives, mutuals and the non-profit sector, see Boniver, Defourny, and Richelot (1991) for an early attempt as well as the recent publication by CIRIEC (2012) for the European Economic and Social Committee.
2. Thirteen countries were included in the EMES WP No. 08/02. Nine of them were recently revised and updated for this report. They are found in the Appendix.
3. For more details, see Defourny and Nyssens (2008, 2010).
4. In spite of those limits, such attempts do of course make a significant contribution to a better understanding of the third sector.
5. This was a central point of the first book of the EMES European Research Network (Borzaga & Defourny, 2001).
6. In Italy, some non-productive associations go so far as to promote the idea of a 'fourth sector', different from the third sector.
7. Economic and Social Research Council and Office of the Third Sector (2007).

8. Such a policy promoting the third sector concept was not endorsed by the subsequent Cameron government which preferred to emphasize the notion of civil society and the 'Big Society'.

9. Voluntary Compacts embody Public Private Partnerships and take various forms in different countries. They first appeared in the United Kingdom during the Major Government and are now found in many European countries.

10. For results of a large EMES research programme on work integration social enterprises across Europe, see Nyssens (2006).

REFERENCES

Boniver, V., Defourny, J., & Richelot, C. (1991). Cooperative, mutual and nonprofit organizations in the European community. In *Panorama of EC industry 1991–1992*. Luxembourg: Publications Office of the European Community.

Borzaga, C., & Defourny, J. (Eds.). (2001). *The emergence of social enterprise*. London: Routledge.

CIRIEC. (2012). *The social economy in the European union*. Brussels: European Economic and Social Committee.

Defourny, J. (2013). Third sector. In L. Bruni & S. Zamagni (Eds.), *Handbook on the economics of reciprocity and social enterprise*. Cheltenham: Edward Elgar.

Defourny, J., & Nyssens, M. (Eds.). (2008). *Social enterprises in Europe: Recent trends and developments*. Working Papers Series 08/01. EMES European Research Network, Liege.

Defourny, J., Develtere, P., Fonteneau, B., & Nyssens, M. (Eds.). (2009). *The worldwide making of the social economy*. Leuven: Acco.

Defourny, J., Hulgård, L., & Pestoff, V. (Eds.). (2014). *Social enterprise and the third sector, changing European landscapes in a comparative perspective*. London: Routledge.

Defourny, J., & Nyssens, M. (2010). Conceptions of social enterprise and social entrepreneurship in Europe and the United States: Convergences and divergences. *Journal of Social Entrepreneurship*, *1*(1), 32–53.

Defourny, J., & Pestoff, V. (2008). *Images and concepts of the third sector in Europe*. Working Paper No. 08/02. EMES, Liege.

Economic and Social Research Council & Office of the Third Sector. (2007). Call specification for a centre for third sector research, London.

Eme, B. (1991). Les services de proximité. *Informations Sociales*, *13*(August–September), 34–42.

Evers, A. (1990). Im intermediären Bereich. Soziale Träger und Projekte swischen Hanshalt, Staat und Markt. *Journal für Sozialforschung*, *2*(30), 189–210.

Evers, A. (1995). Part of the welfare mix: The third sector as an intermediate area. *Voluntas*, *6*/*2*, 119–139.

Evers, A., & Laville, J.-L. (2004). Defining the third sector in Europe. In A. Evers & J.-L. Laville (Eds.), *The third sector in Europe*. Cheltenham: Edward Elgar.

Gray, R., Owen, D., & Adams, C. (1996). *Accounting & accountability. Changes and challenges in social and environmental reporting*. London: Prentice Hall.

Kenis, P. (1992). *The social construction of an industry*. Boulder, CO: Campus Verlag & Westview Press.

Laville, J.-L. (1992). *Les services de proximité en Europe*. Paris: Desclée de Brower.

Laville, J.-L. (Ed.). (1994). *L'économie solidaire*. Paris: Desclée de Brower.

Levander, U. (2011). *Utanförskap på entreprenad. Diskurser om sociala företag i Sverige*. Göteborg: Daidalos Förlag.

Marin, B., & Kenis, P. (Eds.). (1997). *Managing AIDS. Organizational responses in six European countries*. Aldershot: Ashgate.

Nyssens, M. (Ed.). (2006). *Social enterprise – At the crossroads of market, public policy and civil society*. London: Routledge.

Pestoff, V. (1991). *Between the market & politics: Cooperatives in Sweden*. Boulder, CO: Campus Verlag & Westview Press.

Pestoff, V. (1998). *Beyond the market and state. Civil democracy and social enterprises in a welfare society*. Aldershot: Ashgate.

Pestoff, V. (2005). *Reforming social services in Central and East Europe – A Eleven Nation overview*. Cracow: Cracow Academy of Economics.

Pestoff, V. (2008). *A democratic architecture for the welfare state*. London: Routledge.

Pestoff, V. (2009). Towards a paradigm of democratic participation: Citizen participation and co-production of personal social services in Sweden. *Annals of Public and Cooperative Economics*, *80/2*, 197–224.

Pestoff, V. (2012a). Hybrid tendencies in consumers cooperatives: The case of Sweden. In D. McDonnell & E. Macknight (Eds.), *The co-operative model in practice. International perspectives*. Aberdeen: University of Aberdeen & Co-operative Educational Trust Scotland.

Pestoff, V. (2012b). *Lost in translation: Social enterprises in Poland*. Siena: ISTR Conference.

Pestoff, V. (2014). Hybridity, co-production and third sector social services in Europe. *American Behavioral Scientist*, *58*(11), 1412–1424.

Simaens, A., & Koster, M. (2013). Reporting on sustainable operations by third sector organizations. A signaling approach. *Public Management Review*, *15/7*, 1040–1062.

Streeck, W., & Schmitter, P. (1985). *Private interest government – Beyond market and state*. Beverly Hills, CA: Sage.

Unerman, B., & O'Dwyer (2006). Theorizing accountability for NGO advocacy. *Accounting, Auditing & Accountability Journal*, *19/3*, 349–376.

Unerman, B., & O'Dwyer (2010). NGO accountability and sustainability issues in the changing global environment. *Public Management Review*, *12/4*, 475–486.

Zadek, S., & Evans, R. (1993). *Auditing the market. A practical approach to social auditing*. London: New Economic Foundation.

APPENDIX: COUNTRY OVERVIEWS

Belgium

Jacques Defourny

Concepts

The 'third sector' concept is almost unknown in Belgium, but other terms are frequently used to point out some of its main components: the 'associative sector' or the 'non-market sector' in the French-speaking part of the country and the 'midfield' (*middenveld*) or the 'social-profit sector' in the Flemish region.

However, when considering Belgium as a whole, the term which corresponds more closely to the notion of third sector is that of 'social economy'. Since 1990, this notion has been increasingly recognized, on the basis of a first official 'Report on the social economy in Wallonia'. The latter states that *the social economy is made up of economic activities* (in a broad sense) *carried out by cooperatives and related enterprises, by mutual societies and by associations whose ethical stance is represented by the following principles: a purpose of serving members or the community rather than seeking profit, an independent management, a democratic decision-making process, and the primacy of people and labour over capital in the distribution of income* (Conseil Wallon de l'Economie Sociale, 1990). This definition was confirmed and institutionalized in a decree of the Walloon parliament in 2008. In Flanders, although the concept of social economy has not yet achieved the same legitimacy (among field actors and public authorities) as in the southern part of the country, a related definition has been proposed later by a group of field organizations.

Positive Effects of Public Recognition and Promotion

From an institutional point of view, the recognition and the promotion of the social economy in Belgium may seem impressive. All regional governments now have a minister in charge of the social economy (often with other spheres of competencies) and the federal (national) government includes a State secretary only devoted to the 'social and sustainable economy'. Moreover, various tools have been set up in the last 10 years to provide social economy initiatives with credit facilities, securities and seed capital as well as technical support through dedicated consultancy agencies.

In this context, various parts of the social economy have experienced a significant growth – in the recycling industry and environmental activities, in quite diverse activities carried out by work integration initiatives, as well as in the wide spectrum of personal services. In the last four years, a subsidized 'voucher system' for house cleaning and related home services has extracted 100,000 unskilled workers (mainly women) from the black market by offering them a normal labour contact; about one fourth of these jobs (one third in terms of worked hours) have been created within social economy organizations.

In the last decade, the importance of the associative sector has been heavily underlined by the pioneering work carried out jointly by the National Bank of Belgium and the Centre for Social Economy (University of Liege) to set up a first 'satellite account of the non-profit sector'. According to the latter which is now built every year, non-profit associations represent around 15 per cent of all wage-earning employees in Belgium when including private non-profit (catholic) schools and hospitals, and still about 8 per cent without these two major industries. When taken globally, the associative sector accounts for more than 90 per cent of the whole social economy. Moreover, official figures reveal that 36 per cent of net jobs creation took place in associations from 2000 through 2010 and that the growth rate in employment was 4 times higher in associations than in the rest of the economy. The cooperative movement, for its part, has experienced major transformations and a strong decline in job numbers over the last decades and this was particularly true with cooperative banks in the 15 years. Cooperatives still play a significant role in services provided to agricultural producers as well as in pharmaceutical distribution and the insurance industry. The case of the Cera cooperative also deserves to be noted: while merging its banking activities with a traditional bank, it remains a major shareholder of that new group, and the 500,000 members agree that part of the cooperative's dividends are allocated to social projects as a kind of 'cooperative foundation' where members are involved in the selection of projects. As already mentioned, new cooperatives also appear as work integration social enterprises in various emerging fields. As to mutual societies, although they manage various types of home care services under the legal form of association, they are mainly seen as delegates of the public authorities, serving as an interface between the central health insurance public fund and their members (practically all Belgian adults belong to a mutual). Mutuals have also launched various types of insurance services on a solidarity basis, for instance to cover hospital costs not covered by the compulsory health insurance scheme.

In spite of several major failures in traditional industries, it seems the cooperative idea has gained a new attraction power in reaction to the global financial crisis and several embryonic, but emblematic cooperatives have been set up with hundreds or even thousands of members.

The Rise of Social Entrepreneurship

In the last two or three years, the notions of social entrepreneurship and social entrepreneurs have spread in various spheres in a surprizing way. Some perceive these new concepts as a threat to existing social economy organizations. On the overall however, one can also see them as new vehicles to give more visibility to and to convincingly revisit the social economy as well as hybrid organizations at its borders. In any case, many initiatives are being taken to promote social entrepreneurship and social enterprises, bringing new actors in the third sector such as business schools, major companies and foundations as well as umbrella organizations.

Challenges Ahead: Tensions and Traps

In spite of all these steps towards its recognition and promotion, the social economy still has to face major challenges as several tensions and traps tend to create confusion in the perception of the sector.

The first of these traps could be named the 'Flemish trap': as many initiatives aiming to reintegrate very disadvantaged people into society and the labour market have long been referred to as 'social', various public policies (first in Flanders and now in Brussels) tend to see the social economy as reduced to its part focussing on that mission.

Secondly, there is also a 'Walloon trap': as the Southern part of Belgium needs more SMEs and market-oriented entrepreneurial initiatives, its government tends to put the emphasis on the 'market social economy', that is, cooperatives and associations selling goods or services to customers; this leads to a vision of the social economy leaving aside a very significant part of the sector – namely the part relying on public subsidies, private contributions and volunteering. Although most umbrella organizations have constantly opposed such a temptation to see the market social economy as the only true and credible social economy, various public policies measures are designed for this sole kind of initiatives.

Finally, it is possible to identify a 'borders' trap': several components of the social economy cannot be located within neat borders. For instance, mutual societies are clearly on the bridge linking the public and the third sector. Among the latest developments, a growing number of work integration social enterprises are being set up by public bodies, especially to benefit from the attractive 'voucher system' in house cleaning services; these initiatives too are obviously 'borderline cases'. Therefore, any attempt to draw clear-cut frontiers may lead to more confusion as it underlines the difficulty of getting a neat picture.

But beyond these traps on the road towards the recognition and promotion of the social economy as a third sector, what is most striking is the growing interest for it, not only on the political scene, but also for a growing audience, as a matter whose understanding has to be deepened: for instance, most Belgian universities now have courses and/or research programs explicitly devoted to the social economy, now often associated to social entrepreneurship.

REFERENCES

Center for Social Economy and National Bank of Belgium. (2004). Satellite account of nonprofit institutions 2000–2001. Brussels: National Accounts Institute.

Conseil Wallon de l'Economie Sociale. (1990). *Rapport à l'Exécutif Régional Wallon sur le secteur de l'économie sociale*. Namur: CWES.

Defourny, J., Adam, S., & Simon, M. (2002). *The cooperative movement in Belgium: Perspectives and prospects*. Brussels: Ed. Luc Pire.

Defourny, J., Henry, A., Nassaut, S., & Nyssens, M. (2010). Does the mission of providers matter on a quasi-market? The case of the Belgian 'service voucher' scheme. *Annals of Public and Cooperative Economics*, *81*(4), 583–610.

Marée, M., Gijselinckx, C., Loose, M., Rijpens, J., & Franchois, E. (2008). *Les associations en Belgique. Une analyse quantitative et qualitative du secteur*. Brussels: Fondation Roi Baudouin.

Mertens, S., Adam, S., Defourny, J., Marée, M., Pacolet, J., & Vande Putte, I. (1999). The nonprofit sector in Belgium. In L. M. Salamon et al. (Eds.), *Global civil society. Dimensions of the nonprofit sector*. Baltimore, MD: Johns Hopkins University Press.

Mertens, S., & Marée, M. (2007). *Les contours de l'économie sociale: clarification conceptuelle*. Liege: Centre d'Economie Sociale, Université de Liège.

Finland

Pekka Pättiniemi

Various labels have been used in the Finnish context to refer to the third sector: unofficial sector, voluntary sector, non-profit sector, non-governmental sector, organizations of general interest, social economy, civil society and intermediate sector. The most suitable term nowadays to refer to the Finnish third sector may be that of 'civic organizations' (Julkunen, 2006, p. 118), but the latter only corresponds to the associative part of the sector. Defining which types of organizations belong to the third sector has often been problematic in Finland, as elsewhere, but there is agreement in the general public about the terms best describing the sector (general interest, ethical, social, voluntary and non-profit) and the activities of its organizations (which are often referred to using the words of solidarity, individual, freedom of choice and flexibility) (Harju, 2000, pp. 11–14).

Boundaries and Importance of the Finnish Third Sector
During the past 20 years the Finnish third sector has grown considerably. The economic crisis of the 1990s and the problems in employment and financing of the welfare state highlighted the potential of voluntary and civic associations, especially in solving the mass-unemployment which rose in early 1990. But also in large, the third sector became more visible as an actor in social policy. Also co-operative development has been notable and since 1995 nearly 200 cooperatives have been established yearly.

Taking into account cooperatives, mutual societies, foundations and associations, we obtain total figures for the third sector of some 144,000 organizations, 10,000,000 members and 208,000 employees (about 8.5 per cent of the total employment). Associations represent by far the largest group in terms of number of organizations: in 2012, there were 136,000 registered associations in the country that represented about 15,000,000 memberships, with 77,000 (full-time-equivalent) employees and about 500,000 volunteers. Despite their comparatively small number, only 4,600 organizations, cooperatives constitute the main employer in the third sector, with some 105,000 employees in 2012 (Ot-lehti 4/13:28; Ruuskanen, Selander, & Anttila, 2013, p. 10; Pättiniemi, 2007, p. 99; Karjalainen, 2014). The third sector, mainly associations, produces part of the social and health services in Finland. In 2008 municipalities (which are the most important providers of social services) purchased about 16.3 per cent of social services and 4 per cent of health services from third sector organizations.

Public procurement acts and competition in the sector has affected the position of social and health care associations in the market. Up till 2004 they were the major private providers of social and health care providers, but today the private enterprises have taken the leading role. However, in certain sectors associations are still major service providers: for example sheltered housing, housing for alcoholics and drug addicts (Peltosalmi, 2012, pp. 26–27). Quite a few of the major welfare association or foundations have incorporated their service production as companies that they own totally. This is due to changes in the base for income taxation as well as to efficiency and competition reasons. This has resulted in more private sector-type of organizing services.

Contrary to many other countries the results of a recent study shows that the rapid extension of employment and new methods of organizing service production has led to serious challenges. According to one report 'Third sector work offers more autonomy in terms of schedule control. At the same time, however, skill discretion is lower and high work intensity more common, so employees find their work less secure in third sector both in terms of employment security and qualitative security. Furthermore, employees experience more work-family conflicts than their counterpart in public and private sectors. They also report significantly more turnover intentions than employees in other sectors. This suggests that greater third sector co-production of public services may lead to a loss of job quality in terms of deskilling and insecurity' (Ruuskanen, Selander, & Anttila, 2013, p. 106).

In 2004 the major source of income for third sector organizations was private donations (57.9 per cent of the total income), followed by public sector funding (36.2 per cent), while for organizations providing health care and social services they derive 51 per cent and 27 per cent respectively of their income from public sector funding, whereas members' fees and sales represent 46 per cent of the income of health care organizations and 38 per cent of the income of social services organizations (Kari & Markwort, 2004, p. 59).

The boundaries between the Finnish third sector and the public sector or the private for-profit sector are not clear-cut. The cooperation between the public sector and welfare associations is often centred on established activities of large-scale associations. Some of these associations have no special democratic organizational characteristics; they are providing services with public sector funding and are closely monitored by the state. Many traditional associations for disabled persons, for example, perform as extensions of the state and their way of working closely resembles that of public sector organizations. On the other hand, many of the associations providing welfare services are hard to distinguish from private sector providers.

The Role of the Third Sector

With the development of welfare pluralism, the third sector nowadays finds itself in a situation of competition with the other actors (private companies, public entities and unofficial providers – that is – families that provide welfare services). In such a context, values and ways of working are adapted from each other and are being reorganized in all the sectors. The overall intention is not necessarily to abandon the characteristics of the Nordic welfare state, but rather to test the adaptability of the model's universality. In this changing context, new questions emerge; for example, are third sector organizations supplementing the existing public sector services, or do they embody a wholly new way of providing services? As a service provider, the third sector is regarded as quite heterogeneous: it may include organizations as diverse as self-help groups, cooperative service provider organizations and working and housing communities. The third sector has more and more turned from lobbying for its members interest to service provision. This is illustrated in Table 1.

The economic perspective emphasizes the economic importance of well-established associations. Through its economic modernization, the third

Table 1. Finnish Third Sector Can Be Divided into Traditional and New Third Sectors.

Key Features	Traditional Third Sector	New Third Sector
Purpose of the activity	Lobbying interests of certain group and organizing activities for the group	Producing and selling certain services and/or goods, employing
Relation with the public sector	Depending on the case	Part of the service structure of public sector
Basic principle of economic activity	Non-profit, possible surplus invested to the activities of the organization	Pursuit for profit
Legal form	Registered association	Registered association, foundation and social enterprise
Majority of employees	Volunteers	Paid professionals

Source: Huotari, Pyykkönen, and Pättiniemi (2008, p. 7).

sector is incorporated closely into markets and into the structures of the welfare state (Matthies, 1999, pp. 40–45). But this modernization of the third sector should not be realized only by adopting market economy principles; the ethical aspect should not be forgotten in the process.

Present Expectations for the Third Sector

The change from a lobby organization to service provider and simultaneous changes in the environment and organization has increased the need to rethink the role of third sector. There is urgent need for new strategies, the development of managerial attitudes and skills, upgrading the methods of managing volunteers and attract new members. Moreover, the third sector is still regarded as societal experiment and development area which could help in the pursuit for solving societal problems.

REFERENCES

Huotari, T., Pyykkönen, M., & Pättiniemi, P. (2008). Johdanto; Suomalaisen sosiaalisen yrityksen muodostuminen. In T. Huotari, M. Pyykkönen, & P. Pättiniemi (Eds.), *Sosiaalisen ja taloudellisen välimaastossa. Tutkimusnäkökulmia suomalaiseen sosiaaliseen yritykseen*. Helsinki: Sosiaali- ja terveysturvan keskusliitto ry.

Harju, A. (2000). Uusi työ – projekti työllistämisen tutkimus- ja kehittämishankkeena. In A. Harju, & K. Backberg-Edvards (Eds.), *Kohti uutta työtä. Uusi työ – kansalaisjärjestöjen yhteinen työllisyysprojekti*. Helsinki: Suomen Nuorisoyhteistyö Allianssi, Suomen Liikunta ja Urheilu, Sosiaali- ja terveysturvan keskusliitto.

Julkunen, R. (2006). *Kuka vastaa? Hyvinvointivaltion rajat ja julkinen vastuu*. Helsinki: STAKES.

Kari, M., & Markwort, J. (2004). *Kolmas sektori EU:ssa ja eräissä Euroopan maissa*. Helsinki: RAY.

Karjalainen, J. (2014). *Palveluja tuottavat yhdistykset, yritystoiminta ja kasvu*. [Service providing associations, enterprising and growth.] Helsinki: FinSERN2.

Matthies, A.-L. (1999). Ekonomisen ja eettisen vuoropuhelu. In L. Hokkanen, P. Kinnunen, & M. Siisiäinen (Eds.), *Haastava kolmas sektori*. Helsinki: Sosiaali- ja terveysturvan keskusliitto ry.

Pättiniemi, P. (2007). Yhteisötalous Suomessa (Social Economy in Finland). In J. Laurinkari (Ed.), *Yhteisötalous* [Social Economy]. Helsinki: Helsinki University Press, Palmenia.

Peltosalmi, J., Hakkarainen, T., Särkelä, R., & Eränen, A. (2012). *Järjestöbarometri 2012*. Helsinki: SOSTE Suomen sosiaali- ja terveys ry.

Ruuskanen, P., Selander, K., & Anttila, T. (2013). *Paid work in the third sector*. Helsinki: MEE Publications, Ministry of Employment and the Economy.

France

Jean-Louis Laville, Laurent Fraisse and Vincent Lhuillier

Third Sector Images and Concepts

In France, the term 'third sector' has so far been little used by public authorities and representatives of civil society. Its use remains, for the moment, limited to an academic and predictive field of debate. At this level, behind a common rejection of a philanthropic conception of the third sector founded principally on charity and voluntary participation, lies, on a larger scale, a certain French reticence to conceive the third sector as an exclusively not-for-profit sector (Evers & Laville, 2004). Indeed, such a conception is perceived as an acceptance of the dichotomy between the economic and the social – a dichotomy which is rejected by the French 'social and solidarity economy' (SSE).

The concept which comes closest to the North-American approach adopted by the Johns Hopkins Project (Salamon & Anheier, 1997) – which is dominant at the international level and defines the third sector as the sector grouping together all non-profit organizations – is maybe that of 'the associative life' (*la vie associative*).[11] But this concept not only excludes mutual societies and cooperatives from the third sector, it also fails to take into account the social entrepreneurship dimension of associations. This latter aspect has become particularly important in France with the development of economic activities carried out by associations and the creation of numerous jobs by the latter in the past 20 years. Contrary to what is the case in some other European countries, leaders and promoters of the associative life consider themselves – for historical and institutional reasons – to belong to the same world as cooperatives and mutual societies, as they are all part of a different way of 'being actors in the economy'.

The concept of social economy combines a legal approach based on legal forms (cooperatives, associations and mutual societies) with the definition of common ethical and organizational principles, among which a limitation (rather than an absolute ban, as in the non-profit approach) on the distribution of profits. The social economy, considered as a whole, represents 11.7 per cent of French GNP and 1.8 million full-time-equivalent jobs.

As for the solidarity economy approach,[12] it emphasizes the development model, citizen participation in the production of goods and services and the economic mix of resources; it also insists on the plurality of economic principles (market resources, public redistribution and voluntary commitment) to understand the political dimension of some new economic initiatives in the resistance to the extension of the market and in the new interactions between economy and democracy.

The border between the social economy and the solidarity economy could appear as thin from an external point of view; however, the existence, before the French elections of 2007, of two different manifestos (one of which, the 'Manifesto for the solidarity economy', was published in *Le Monde*) to promote these two sets of organizations underlines the ambiguous relationship between these two dominant French approaches. To summarize, one can say that beyond strong analogies between the two concepts, marked differences appear when considering the empirical and concrete initiatives they refer to, but also regarding the level of radicalism of their respective political proposals.

Recent Trends

Public Policies Supporting the SSE. Whereas the 1980s corresponded, to a certain extent, to the first phase of institutionalization of the social economy at the national level, with the recognition of some national umbrella organizations (such as the CNLAMCA), a national committee of liaison between activities of mutual, cooperative and associative types and the creation of a National delegation to the social economy, the 2000 witnessed the first signs of integration of the solidarity economy in the public action.

Since the short existence of a State secretary to the solidarity economy (2000–2002), a significant change has been the emergence of local public policies dedicated to the SSE,[13] with the election of hundreds of solidarity economy delegates in local authorities. In many cities (Nantes, Lille, Grenoble, etc.) and regions (Nord-Pas de Calais, Provence-Alpes-Côte d'Azur, etc.), local policies mobilizing SSE organizations and local networks have gradually been implemented. The most important initiative is the setting up of the 'Réseau des territoires pour l'économie solidaire' (http://rtes.fr); this network gathers several hundred public servants and elected representatives in charge of SSE for regular meetings and exchanges. Almost all French regions have dedicated schemes for the SSE that are integrated in their economic policies. In 2012, a minister of the SSE, mainly dedicated to preparing a law for 2014, was created in the national government.

The SSE Act: Towards a Legal Basis for the SSE. Although the SSE Act is still under discussion at the French Parliament, the main aspects are advanced enough in the political process to be mentioned. The primary scope of this law is symbolic, in that it gives enterprises of the SSE a legal basis that is mainly inspired from the statutory approach gathering cooperatives, associations, foundations and mutual societies. However, Article 2 enlarges the borders of the statutory approach by defining the conditions under which a company with another legal form but with an explicit social utility goal could be considered as falling under the scope of the act. Others articles particularly discussed in the medias have been the right of priority information, which is intended to facilitate the takeover of companies by their workers, and a new definition of public grants to associations, which underlies the bottom-up process, the activities subsidized as well as their contribution to the general interest.

The main representatives of the field consider the act as an important step towards the recognition of the SSE in the French society; however, some limits could be underlined. The act defines the SSE mainly from the supply-side point of view, as an economy of production based on a particular population of enterprises – a definition that reduces the economy to an entrepreneurial perspective. The citizens and their potential commitments as ethic consumers, volunteers or activists in the everyday act of economic life are not taken into consideration by the law. Indeed, the connection of the SSE Act with the Consumption Act, elaborated by the same Ministry, has not been done. Finally, the financial impacts of the law, in a context of budget restrictions for SSE initiatives and organizations, are highly uncertain.

New Academic Networks. In recent years, politicians have often been at the forefront of demands for improved quantitative and qualitative understanding of the sector, as well as for evaluations of the programmes implemented. This resulted in an increase, over the past few years, in the number of reports, studies and publications focusing on the social economy, the solidarity economy and associations.[14] Besides, the existence of platforms for academic dialogue (such as the *Réseau Inter-Universitaire de l'économie sociale et solidaire*[15]) has contributed to strengthen the ties between professors and doctoral students, and collaborations among research centres and universities. This new kind of academic networking has been the consequence of the development of numerous Masters programmes[16] dealing with the SSE.

The New Legal Status of 'Collective Interest Cooperative Society'. Following Lipietz's report on the need for the creation of a new legal status for economic initiatives producing positive and collective externalities, the legal framework for cooperatives, which had been defined in 1947, has been adapted to current needs, after collective debates on the matter,[17] leading to the creation of a new legal form, namely that of 'collective interest cooperative society' (*société coopérative d'intérêt collectif*, or SCIC). If the number of SCICs still remains quite low (306 in 2013), their development seems to accelerate. Above all, the qualitative changes they imply are meaningful, both regarding the French debate and the place of the solidarity economy, in particular in relation with traditional initiatives from the social economy. Fields of activities are broader than before and original; they include social housing, cultural broadcast initiatives, work integration, microfinance and micro-insurance, and support to environmental development.[18] Democratic principles and support to alternative economic rationality are also underlined through the multi-stakeholder principle and the ways in which decisions are to be made, particularly regarding the use of financial surplus. Since 2010, the former 'production workers cooperative society' (*Société coopérative ouvrière de production*, SCOP) has been renamed and integrated, by his main representative network, into a general category of 'participatory and cooperative society' (*Société coopérative et participative*, SCOP), in which former SCOPs coexist with new SCICs. If we add the new focus on 'employment and activities cooperative' (*Coopérative d'activités et d'emploi*, CAE) to this cooperative landscape, we understand that, following the creation of the SCIC legal form, new attention has been paid to governance matters and innovative way of organizing cooperation.

The Controversial Emergence of the Social Entrepreneurship Movement. Whereas the concept of 'social enterprise' was practically not used by entrepreneurs and researchers 10 years ago, a progressive appropriation of this notion in the public sphere has led to an emerging coalition. The founding act has been the creation of the 'movement of social entrepreneurs' (*Mouvement des entrepreneurs sociaux*, Mouves)[19] in 2010. Gathering former leaders of historical work integration social enterprises as well as newcomers from international networks or business schools, this coalition emphasizes the individual role of the entrepreneur and the social goals of economic activities, whatever the legal forms and statutes of the enterprises. The quantitative assessment of the social innovations, the partnership with the business world and the acceptance of competition rules (even for delivering social services) are also strong themes among Mouves promoters who try to find a new space between the traditional social economy, solidarity-based initiatives and new kinds of economics projects with strong social innovations. However, within SSE spheres, the relevance of this platform has been questioned, both from a political and from a conceptual point of view. Mouves has been analyzed by some authors less as an organization offering a perspective complementary to the SSE approach than as an importation from the Anglo-Saxon approach, not compatible either with the continental conceptualization of the third sector nor with the SSE ambitions of transforming the dominant economic system. Despite some interest by the medias, the institutional recognition of this coalition of social entrepreneurs remains limited in a context where the new Ministry institutionally enshrines the concept of the SSE. However, the extension of the perimeter of the SSE to for-profit companies with social utility goals could also be interpreted as an implicit recognition of social enterprises.

SSE: Solutions to the Crisis or Victims of Austerity. In the first phase of the financial crisis of 2008, SSE initiatives and enterprises appeared as more resilient than other companies, much more exposed to the globalization process. Moreover, part of the SSE circles adopted an pro-active position, through the organization of the 'Etats généraux de l'ESS', in 2011, with proposals for a new economic development[20] based on SSE experiences and values. However, the present period, dominated by austerity and strong budget constraints, weakens many small and medium not-for-profit organizations. In 2012, for the first time in 30 years at least, the number of organizations and jobs in the associative field decreased. This silent restructuration of the non-profit sector has been sped up by the growing diffusion of public procurements for the delivery of social services of general interest, on the one hand, and by the governmental promotion of for-profit companies in fields such as personal home services or childcare facilities, on the other hand. In this context, local authorities are crucial for maintaining places, programmes and funding in favour of the SSE.

NOTES

11. In the academic field, Edith Archambault, economist, who participated in the John Hopkins project for France, or, in a political science perspective, Martine Barthélémy may be considered as the main promoters of this concept of 'associative life'.

12. The solidarity economy is not a sector properly, but rather a theoretical and practical perspective, which overlaps with the social economy. For instance, it is possible to analyze social economy organizations through a solidarity economy framework.

13. For a first analysis, some studies and an international comparison of local public action in the field of the solidarity economy, see Laville, Filho, Magnen, and Medeiros (2005).

14. All regional studies undertaken as part of the research programme of the *Secrétariat d'Etat à l'économie solidaire* can be consulted on the DIES website: http://www.association.gouv.fr/rubrique.php3?id_rubrique=18

15. For more details, see www.riuess.org/

16. Over 20 at least if we only consider RIUESS members, and far more if we take into account all the Masters Degrees delivered in France with an SSE mention.

17. Note that these debates often involved academic representatives of the networks mentioned above, thus establishing clear relationships between theoretical reflexions on the matter and concrete developments in the field.

18. For more details, see www.scic.coop

19. For more details, see http://mouves.org/

20. *Pour une Autre Economie*, Labo ESS, Alternatives Economiques.

REFERENCES

Archambault, E. (1996). Le secteur sans but lucratif. Associations et fondations en France. Paris: Economica.

Barthélémy, M. (2000). *Associations: un nouvel âge de la participation?* Paris: Presse universitaire de sciences politiques.

Evers, A., & Laville, J.-L. (2004). *The third sector in Europe*. Cheltenham: Edward Elgar.

Laville, J.-L., Filho, G. C., Magnen, J.-P., & Medeiros, A. (2005). *Action publique et économie solidaire, une perspective internationale*. Ramonville: Eres.

Laville, J.-L. (Ed.). (2006). *Dictionnaire de l'Autre économie*. Paris: Seuil.

Salamon, L. M., & Anheier, H. K. (Eds.). (1997). *Defining the non-profit sector – A cross national analysis*. Manchester: Manchester University Press.

Germany

Adalbert Evers

Historical Developments

If one wants to understand the ways 'third sector issues' are taken up in Germany, one has to look back onto both long-time and more recent historical developments.

'Long-time development' goes back as far as the turn from the 19th to 20th Centuries, when the Churches in Germany engaged in creating local responses to various social problems and needs, especially in the field of social policies. The various associations created in the process national umbrella organizations ('*Wohlfahrtsverbände*'). In the framework of the subsidiarity concept, they became (and have remained until today) important partners of municipalities, state institutions and social insurance in providing health and social services. In the 1920s, the social democratic movement also created its own national umbrella organization. Today, about 50 per cent of all social services and a large part of hospital services remain provided by such organizations – which could, in abstract terms, be referred to as third sector organizations, even though more than 80 per cent of their resources come from public funding. However, cooperatives did not fare as well; the broad and powerful cooperative movements, particularly those linked with the labour movement and the Left were destroyed by the fascist regime. It was reconstructed in parts after the war, but did not regain the same impact with its large organizational units as in decades before. In the early days of the new German welfare state that took shape in the 1950s, with a social democracy focussing on state-based welfare and the dissolution of the old milieus that had supported the cooperatives, they died off or lost most of their earlier far-reaching reformist goals. Those parts of the broad inter-class cooperative movements that survived best belonged to the less ambitious formerly bourgeois and peasant-oriented strands. They preserved their role as effective umbrella bodies for small craftsmen and peasants on larger markets (on this subject, see Bode & Evers, 2004).

Winds of change date from more recent historical developments, namely the 68 movements and their social and cultural follow-ups: the blossoming of a vast plurality of small-scale initiatives, projects and self-help groups, loosely networked alongside policy fields (culture, health) and receiving, in most cases, public support in the form of unstable municipal support. Later on, these developments, together with concerns about social integration and the evolution of the welfare state, led to the emergence of topics which are still the most important points of reference of this new generation of initiatives: the idea that they have to strengthen the civil society and citizens' common sense and to revive or find new forms of individual commitments, such as volunteering. At the same time, the former generation of organizations and their '*Wohlfahrtsverbände*' have further expanded in their socio-economic key role, but they have also taken a more commercial and managerial route; throughout their evolution, their credibility has been (and remains) fairly good, but they do not have a sharp reform profile nor an approach that gives or revives, in future-oriented forms, a civic and popular image.

The Presence: Blurred Sectorial Borders

In the course of the red-green government period (1998–2006), concepts such as 'the activating state' complemented the overarching themes of civil society, public commitment, volunteering and citizens' participation. An important landmark was the official report of the Parliamentary Commission on the Future of Civic Engagement (Enquete-Kommission, 2002). These issues have won significance among public and third sector actors in fields like culture, local urban renewal, childcare services, labour market integration and all kinds of initiatives fighting against social exclusion and discrimination. Latest developments include debates on the increasingly important role of foundations, corporate citizenship and CSR, on the one hand, and – given the increasingly central role of consumption and private provision of public goods – issues of consumers' movements and rights.

It is sometimes difficult to assess the extent to which participation, activation and volunteering represent new faces of civil society, and the extent to which they are parts of new forms of policies implemented by the state and administrations in the social field. Many projects, initiatives and participatory approaches depend on public money, programs and action. The civil society discourse, even though it is strong on the more general level of cultural aspirations and discourses, has very little impact on the conception and implementation of social reforms in such central areas as health, social security and labour market integration.

Third Sector Concepts in the General Public and the Academic World

All in all, in Germany, the issues and points of reference of the general public regarding the third sector have less to do with notions of a sector than with values, forms of commitment and new forms of joint governance crosscutting sectorial lines.

In academic research different streams coexist. There are first basic theoretical studies on the various notions of civil society. Much can be found here about the size and economic power of the third sector according to the Johns Hopkins approach (Zimmer et al., 2013). There are studies about the managerial shift in the big voluntary agencies. Much research takes the form of evaluation studies accompanying government programs that deal with associations and participation in various policy fields. Research on CSR (partly funded by private corporations and their organizations and foundations themselves) and on foundations is increasing. Finally there is a beginning of basic research on consumers' movements and the emergence of 'citizen-consumers'. Every second year starting in 2013 an expert commission on civic engagement collects facts and findings, features, trends and discusses a special key problem-area each time. Its first report in 2013 focused on the existing and potential role of CSR. The next report for the federal government (2015) will focus on the repercussions of demographic changes for civic commitment and voluntary action, especially with respect to its challenges for public policies on local levels.

Major Recent Trends in Germany

The most recent trends, challenges and chances concerning the third sector and specific parts of it such as social enterprises can be summed up in seven points.

1. After abolishing conscripted military service, its counterpart became abolished as well – a civil service to be taken up by those, who refused to serve in the army. The government has installed then as a follow up a new federal voluntary civil service, addressing foremost young people but as well elderly citizens. Now it competes with existing similar activities run by the voluntary associations and the federal states, strengthening the impact of the federal government. In the meantime it has grown as large as the older volunteering efforts, with both comprising more than about 30,000 citizens volunteering each. How to develop this considerable resource as a means for staffing public services has become a major concern of the government. It appears to take this possibility more seriously than the other much more relaxed, but less governable forms of civic commitment and volunteering.
2. Since 2013 there is a new report that complements the regular surveys on individual membership and volunteering (see Gensicke & Geiss,

2009), portraying the third sector as a landscape of different organizations (the ZIVIZ survey, Krimmer Priemer, 2013). It has measured and counted the main organizational forms and their profiles, that is, associations, foundations, cooperatives and companies with limited liability and the official status of being for the common good (gGmbH, a status often taken by social enterprises). Among many other interesting facts and findings two issues deserve special attention. From the about 616,000 organizations that populated the third sector in 2012, 95 per cent were made up by usually small local associations with little public support and few paid staff, if any. They are an important sociocultural given, yet not so important factor in terms of occupation and 'service output' issues that are so dear for many politicians. In addition, there are more than 18,000 foundations, about 10,000 gGmbhs and 7,600 cooperatives. Thus, in this very divided and polarized sector most government funding goes to few relatively big organizations.

3. A second interesting and new outcome of the ZIVIZ report is the fact that a special type of association shows the biggest growth rate: associations that see their main role in supporting an established public service or institution such as a school, a swimming hall, a public garden, museum or similar goods that operate in arm-length to the citizens and users as a kind of commons. Nowadays about a quarter of all organizations addressed by the ZIVIZ survey said that they consider themselves 'fully' as support organizations for such services. This is a strong hint to the crisis and austerity of the public households and the municipal and state welfare agencies. It points to the incremental development of new forms of cooperation and partnership between citizens and public institutions when it comes to preserving public goods in changing times and circumstances.
4. An important point of reference for developments in the third sector is the ecological movement and the declared goal of the present government to get through with a change in policies dealing with issues of energy and sustainability ('Energiewende'). While there is a strong tendency to do this with big infrastructure projects, such as wind-parks and new power supply lines for electricity, there are as well many small-scale organizations such as energy-cooperatives and local action groups working out with municipalities and authorities concepts towards sustainable ways of dealing with energy. Here, social, community-based and cooperative dimensions intertwine with orientations and knowledge from the field of technology, economics and financing and management.

5. Given the fact that there has been a steep increase in rents and prices for housing within many of the metropolitan regions, a combination of the classical problems of a housing shortage and lacking access for poorer groups combined with the search for new ways and rooms for urban living and housing among the better off has politicized housing, urban and community development. Local protest movements about limited access to housing and quests for a more social and community oriented style of living and housing has led to a renaissance of cooperatives especially in this field. The older and well-established ones now have to rethink their policies and the number of new small-scale cooperative endeavours in housing is rising remarkably. Presently more than one quarter of all cooperatives in Germany are housing cooperatives, ranging from very small projects of a few families over to long-time established organizations, administering 10,000 of flats, being redetected as a major force and instrument in local public housing policies.
6. The last years have seen economic issues questioning in various ways notions of the third sector as a purely social, cultural and beneficial subject. This has not only come about by a managerial modernization of existing third sector organizations but as well by debates about the potential of and innovative nudges that come from social and policy entrepreneurs, be it as 'intra-preneurs' in existing organizations, or as founders of new undertakings. The latter has as well renewed and increased a concern with cooperatives, gGmbhs (social enterprises) and enterprises run by the municipalities. Overall, these developments and debates do not support a special notion of organizational form of 'social enterprise' as proposed, for example, by the EMES-group (Defourny et al., 2014). Work integration social enterprises, for example, exist in large numbers but they have difficulties to be perceived and recognized as a specific type of organization. What is absent is the overall strict separation of economic and social concerns and issues, by looking for pragmatic ways of tying both together. This happens in discussions on issues of local economy, ethics and economies, etc., that take place in the context of policies of urban renewal and local concepts for integrating cultural and ethnic minorities. The approaches and styles of debate range from those that are oriented towards civic entrepreneurialism, US style and community-based endeavours, over to those that want to revitalize their own cooperative traditions. Remarkable is the fact that the new organizations are usually small less formalized and bureaucratized, much more in touch with peoples' and participants' lifestyles and concerns than the older generation of social enterprises, cooperatives and

municipal providers (see, Hackenberg/Empter, 2011; Jansen a.o., 2013). All in all the blurring of the long established frontiers between (market) economic and social (policy) thinking by the developments and debates sketched above is ambivalent – from attempts to think the economical more in social terms over to attempts to plug the rhetoric of the market economy and managerialism into the third 'social' sector.

7. While all the points mentioned before have touched on issues of civic engagement with a strong service and self-help dimension, the overall context should not lose sight of concerns about democracy and engagement in politics. In recent decades the self-esteem of many citizens has increased and likewise the willingness to follow simply top-down decisions from institutions, public or private, has decreased. Big public projects not only around atomic energy but as well about mega building projects like airports, train stations or traffic lines have in a densely populated country led to a new upswing of debates on more participatory ways of public planning and policy making, more public deliberation as part of decision-making (Geissel, 2009). In many areas of concern, such as about the future design and daily administration of schools, local concepts for mobility, energy-consumption, socio-economic projects of associations, initiatives and cooperatives intertwine, collide with or complement public planning, governance systems and routines of public authorities. Democracy is then a question both of giving space and support for the broad variety of such third-sector projects and for finding more participatory ways of making them part of politics. The future of activities and organizations in the third sector can hardly be understood and debated properly without linking it with questions about new forms of democratic governance, both big and small.

REFERENCES

Bode, I., & Evers, A. (2004). From institutional fixation to entrepreneurial mobility? The German third sector and its contemporary challenges. In A. Evers & J.-L. Laville (Eds.), *The Third Sector in Europe*. Cheltenham, UK: Edward Elgar.

Defourny, J., Hulgård, L., & Pestoff, V. (Eds.). *Social enterprise & the third sector. Changing European landscapes in a comparative perspective*. London: Routledge.

Enquete-Kommission. (2002). *Bericht – Bürgerschaftliches Engagement: auf dem Weg in eine zukunftsfähige Bürgergesellschaft*. Opladen: Leske und Budrich.

Geissel, B. (2009). Participatory governance: Hope or danger for democracy? A case study of local agenda 21. *Local Government Studies*, *35*(4) S401–S414.

Gensicke, T., & Geiss, S. (2009). Hauptbericht des Freiwilligensurvey 2009 Zivilgesellschaft, Soziales Kapital und freiwilliges Engagement in Deutschland 1999–2004–2009, S. 5–46. Retrieved form http://www.bmfsfj.de/RedaktionBMFSFJ/Broschuerenstelle/Pdf-Anlagen/3._20Freiwilligensurvey-Hauptbericht,property=pdf,bereich=bmfsfj,sprache=de,rwb=true.pdf

Hackenberg, H., & Empter, S. (Hg.). (2011). *Social entrepreneurship – Social business: Für die Gesellschaft unternehmen*. Wiesbaden: VS-Verlag.

Jansen, S. A., Heinze, R. G., & Beckmann, M. (Hg.). (2013). Sozialunternehmen in Deutschland. Analysen, Trends und Handlungsempfehlungen. New York, NY: Springer.

Krimmer, H., & Priemer, J. (2013). ZIVIZ Survey (2012) Zivilgesellschaft verstehen S. 8–33; 50–67. Retrieved form http://www.ziviz.info/fileadmin/download/ziviz_survey2012.pdf

Priller, E. u.a. (Hg.). (2011). *Zivilengagement. Herausforderungen für Gesellschaft, Politik und Wissenschaft*. Berlin/Münster: LIT Verlag.

Zimmer, A., Priller, E., & Anheier, H. K. (2013). Der Nonprofit-Sektor in Deutschland. In R. Simsa, M. Meyer, C. Badelt (Hg.), *Handbuch der Nonprofit-Organisation. Strukturen und Management*. Stuttgart: Schäffer-Poeschel Verlag. 5. überarbeitete Auflage, S. 15–36.

Italy

Carlo Borzaga, Giulia Galera and Flaviano Zandonai

Growth of the Italian Third Sector

Similarly to other EU countries, in the 1990s Italy registered a considerable quantitative growth of the third sector as a whole,[21] which was distributed rather homogeneously across the entire national territory. This quantitative evolution has been accompanied by an increasing trend, among public administrations, to contract out the supply of social services. The development and increase in number of TSOs has been strongly related to the production of traditional welfare services, but it can also be accounted for by the fact that the supply of services increased as well in fields other than welfare, including culture and art, education and environment.

Organizational Forms and Fields of Activity

At the theoretical level, the main concepts used to refer to entities other than public agencies and for-profit organizations are the ones found by the literature at the international level, that is, the non-profit sector, the third sector and social enterprise. At a more practical level, the definition of the third sector used by both practitioners and policy-makers refers to the sum of the organizational forms that have been legally recognized in the last two decades. This was done in a progressive way through a number of specific laws, including those regulating traditional non-profit organizations such as voluntary organizations, social promotion associations and non-governmental organizations, as well as new types of organizations, such as social cooperatives and social enterprises. A general policy law addressed to the third sector as a whole has not been issued yet, and a cross-fiscal legislation has added further to the confusion of the sector.

According to this approach, the basic legal forms usually included in the third sector in 2001[22] were associations (202,059), social cooperatives (4,651) and foundations (3,008).[23] By 2011, the number of associations increased to 269,353 (including *de facto* associations), social cooperatives reached 12,647, while there were 6,220 foundations. In 2001 most of these organizations (63 per cent) were active in the field of culture, sport and entertainment. The second most important field of activity in terms of number of organizations was that of social care (8.7 per cent of organizations); followed by trade unions and interest groups (7.1 per cent), education and research (5.2 per cent) and health (4.4 per cent) (Euricse, 2013; ISTAT, 2013). A similar pattern can be noted one decade later. In 2011 most of these organizations (195,841) are still active in the field of culture, sport and entertainment. The second most important field of activity in terms of number of organizations is that of social care (25,044 entities), followed by trade unions and interest groups (16,526), education and research (15,519) and health (10,969) (ISTAT, 2013).

Heterogeneity and Diversification of the Third Sector

A hallmark of the Italian third sector has always been its heterogeneity – hence the attention paid by this brief document to aspects of diversity. In recent years, the various organizational types that compose the third sector have not grown at the same rate: whereas voluntary organizations and traditional associations have registered a slight growth, both entrepreneurial (social cooperatives and associations) and grant-making organizations (such as banking foundations) have increased more markedly.

Over the decade 2001–2011, the third sector has emerged as the only dynamic sector in Italy and within the third sector the most dynamic component is social enterprise. Over the past decade social cooperatives, the most developed typology of social enterprise in Italy, have registered a dramatic increase in number and have demonstrated the ability to create new employment even in times of crisis, more so than the economy as a whole and more so than other types of cooperatives (Euricse, 2013). Indeed, contrary to the general trend of the Italian labour market, which has registered a decrease in the total number of workers occupied (–1.2 per cent) between 2007 and 2011, the number of workers employed by social cooperatives increased over the same period by 17.3 per cent.

In 2011 there were 12,647 social cooperatives, employing 322,875 workers, out which 30,534 disadvantaged workers. Social cooperatives are the most significant component of the entire sector both in light of their economic impact and the social relevance of the services supplied. In 2011, as a sector, social cooperatives had a turnover of 10.1 billion and had an invested capital of 8.3 billions of euros (Euricse, 2013).

Moreover, the quantitative growth of the third sector has been coupled with a diversification trend at various levels, which was the result of various forces at play:

- the multiplication of legal forms and the increasing differentiation of the organizational types that compose the third sector (entrepreneurial organizations vs. voluntary organizations), as well as the acknowledgement of the relevance of local contexts by legislation;

- the engagement in sectors other than the welfare sector, including culture, education, environment;
- an increasing territorial differentiation, generated by the various welfare models (centralized vs. liberal) implemented at the regional level and by the more or less favourable attitude of local administrations towards certain organizational types (social cooperatives vs. associations);
- the increase in competition among various organizational types engaged in the supply of social services induced by competitive tenders;
- the growth of isomorphic tendencies generated by the strong public demand for services.

Overall, the third sector is divided into several components, which have not yet found a synergy; the various groupings and families that compose the sector find it difficult to ensure unitary representation and speak with one voice at the national and local levels. By contrast, we are witnessing the multiplication of umbrella organizations tailored to specific legal forms, sectors of activity, territorial areas, etc.

Research

The process of growth of the third sector has been accompanied by new research devoted to the study of the third sector phenomenon and the creation of new research groups by an increasing number of universities, including the establishment of a national network of research centres: IRIS Network.[24] IRIS Network brings together a growing number of research institutes with a view to supporting empirical and theoretical research aimed at promoting a better understanding of the role and potential of social enterprises in Italy.

This confirms the increasing relevance of the topics related to the development of the third sector and the existence of a growing demand for new managerial and organizational tools apt to improve the performance of TSOs.

NOTES

21. According to the first census on non?-profit? institutions and enterprises, which was conducted in 1999, 55.2 per cent of the existing organizations were founded in the 1990s (ISTAT, 2001).

22. Including *de facto* associations.

23. According to ISTAT (2001). To these add 7,861 entities with other legal forms.

24. http://www.irisnetwork.it/

REFERENCES

Barbetta, G. P., Cima, S., & Zamaro, N. (2003). *Le istituzioni nonprofit in Italia*. Bologna: Il Mulino.

Borzaga, C. (2004). From suffocation to re-emergence: The evolution of the Italian third sector. In A. Evers & J.-L. Laville (Eds), *The third sector in Europe*. Cheltenham: Edward Elgar.

Euricse. (2013). *La Cooperazione Italiana negli Anni della Crisi*. Trento: 2° Rapporto Euricse.

ISTAT. (2001). *Istituzioni nonprofit in Italia*. Retrieved form http://www.istat.it; http://www.irisnetwork.it/

Istat. (2013). Rapporto Annuale 2013. La situazione del paese, Istituto nazionale di statistica, Roma.

Norway

Karl Henrik Sivesind and Bernard Enjolras

Images and Concepts
In Norway, the dominant term in the field of the third sector is that of 'voluntary organizations' (frivillige organisasjoner), which are primarily associated with membership, participation, volunteering and democratic structures. The term 'non-profit sector' is seldom used or understood outside a narrow group of researchers and experts.

Many civil associations in Norway were formed as national voluntary organizations. Those with their roots in the first half of the 19th century reflect the processes of nation building and political mobilization; this first wave of national civil associations was based on a broad mobilization of people around religious, social and cultural issues. During the latter part of the 19th century, concepts such as association and spirit of association (associationsaand) were commonly used. The common denominator of the 19th century's national movements was the broad mobilization of members, with engagement based on morals and the desire to contribute to necessary changes as the prime motivations for membership.

In the course of the 1980s, this picture changed in several ways. The centre of gravity in the voluntary sector clearly shifted in the period 1960–2000. Membership in religious organizations has declined strongly since 1960. Social and humanitarian organizations peaked in the 1960s due to the strength of the broad social welfare organizations at that time. Local community, leisure and international organizations reached their maximum in the 1980s. However, in sports associations, membership has increased until present and 'culture, nature and environment' organizations have shown the strongest growth rate in the 1990s. The paid employment is small from a European perspective; it represents only 3.9 per cent of the non-agricultural employment (compared to 7 per cent for the EU7[25]), but the Norwegian voluntary sector nevertheless has considerable resources at its disposal in terms of voluntary inputs (6.8 per cent of the total non-agricultural employment compared to 4.2 per cent for the EU7). Indeed, as much as half the Norwegian population reports contributing their time to voluntary organizations during any given year.

Recent Trends
Decline of the Social Movement Tradition. The traditional organizational structure characteristic of the social movements, with its roots in rural

communities and affiliations with national movements, was not truly challenged before the 1980s, when new types of organizations appeared, leading to the emergence of the *two-part organizational society*. On the one hand, several national organizations loosened their ties to the local level. Some (although not many) national organizations even appeared which were not membership-based. The weight given active membership diminished, even within traditional associations. On the other hand, the local level became increasingly anchored in areas of local development or local neighbourhood. These new local activities grew independently of any national association: thus, the majority of local associations formed since the 1980s are not affiliated with a national organization – a structure which was almost inconceivable 20 years ago.

Recent Changes at the Local Level. The total number of associations is approximately the same today as 10 years ago; by comparison, an increase of 25 per cent was registered between 1980 and 1990. But underneath this apparent stability, both the types of activities and the organizational structure of the associations have been changing in the last decade. Measured in per cent of the entities existing in 1990, educational associations have been most severely hit. In terms of absolute numbers of associations, however, the religious associations have experienced the strongest reduction. Another historically important group gradually losing appeal consists of the traditional humanitarian organizations. However, new types of association are developing. Interest associations for the handicapped have proliferated at an impressive rate over the past decade, and so too have leisure, sports and culture associations. The main development trend in local associations is a growth in activities with an individual focus. Organizations directing their activities towards their own members' interests (leisure or others) are expanding, while activities directed towards the community at large are in decline.

Increasing Marketization. In Norway local and national lotteries have for a long time been an important income source for voluntary activities. As the Norwegians' personal incomes and enthusiasm for gambling gradually increased, lotteries became increasingly perceived as a marketplace where associations compete for the stakes of the gamblers. Gaming automats generated rapidly growing revenues for a few years before the ban in 2007. Although voluntary associations may operate lotteries under an exemption from the general ban on gaming in Norway, competition from the state-owned games company Norsk Tipping has made such lotteries a less profitable source of income than they used to be. To compensate for this, money raised by regular donations and personal sponsorships has strongly increased, accounting for 15 per cent of the income of major Norwegian fundraising organizations in 2011. The lottery and fundraising market have been supplied by a 'sponsor market' – mostly for-profit firms that want to support certain purposes or improve their public image. These types of marketization have enlarged the income potential of voluntary associations, and have opened up for new, business-like ways of thinking among the professional staff.

Relations with the Public Sector. Most voluntary organizations in Norway have established close contact and cooperation with public authorities, while at the same time remaining largely autonomous. Thus, changes in government policies significantly affect the voluntary sector and the voluntary sector–government relationship. In several fields, the borderlines between public and civil responsibilities become diffuse. Voluntary associations and non-profit activities have been integrated in the public sphere in ways that at times make it difficult to categorize an activity as either 'public' or 'private'.

Recent Changes in Third Sector Images and Concepts

As noted earlier, the dominant term in the field of the third sector is that of 'voluntary organizations' (frivillige organisasjoner), which are primarily associated with membership, participation, volunteering and democratic structures, but it is losing significance. However, in recent years the term 'ideal organizations' (ideelle organisasjoner) has in policy-making contexts become synonymous with welfare service providing TSOs.

There has been increased focus on the welfare service provision of the third sector, as a result of a broader use of quasi-markets and open tenders by the state, municipalities and by semi-autonomous public agencies (regional health authorities, child and family protection, etc.). Advocacy organizations (Frivillighet Norge, Virke) feared that the number of third sector's welfare service institutions would be decreasing as a result of this. However, employment data show that non-profit organizations have been able to retain a share of about 7–8 per cent of the rapidly growing welfare employment in the period 1997–2010 (Sivesind, 2013). This is low compared to 13 per cent in Denmark and 20–25 per cent in corporatist countries as France, Austria and Germany (Sivesind & Selle, 2010). Therefore, several political parties saw a need for addressing the frame conditions of the third sector welfare provision. In October 2012 the red-green coalition-government's (2005–2013) response was to sign a compact with the 'ideal' organizations providing health and social services, inspired by similar agreements in the United Kingdom, Denmark and Sweden. The goal was to establish shared principles and guidelines for effective and high quality services and dialogue, while securing predictability, autonomy and distinctiveness for the 'ideal' organizations.[26] This has resulted in negotiations exclusively with 'ideal' organizations and more long-term contracts in certain areas.

The red-green coalition-government also saw a need for a more unified policy for voluntary organizations, and for clarifying the characteristics of voluntary activity as a sector in society, different from market and state. The Labour Party and the Socialist Left Party have previously been less concerned with the voluntary sector in general terms (Selle & Strømsnes, 2012). In June 2007, Parliament passed a law of a Register for Voluntary Organizations proposed by the red-green Government (Ot.prp. nr. 55, 2006–2007). The register is intended to simplify the interaction between voluntary associations and public authorities, and should result in systematic statistics, research and policy-relevant information, and thereby strengthen the legitimacy of voluntary activity. The Register for Voluntary Organizations is not obligatory, but is a pre-requisite for getting compensation for sales tax or VAT, access to the so-called grass root share (the gamers/gamblers may decide which local voluntary association should get 5 per cent of their stakes), and an increasing number of types of public support. In 2013 the number of registered organizations passed 30,000.

In Norway, there is a multitude of third/voluntary sector definitions implemented in various registers, laws, tax-laws and exemptions, and support arrangements that outline different partly overlapping target groups. This means that, whereas a foundation is defined by law, a 'nonprofit' or 'voluntary organization' is still not a distinct legal category in Norway.

NOTES

25. Austria, Finland, France, Germany, Ireland, the Netherland and the United Kingdom.
26. http://www.regjeringen.no/upload/FAD/Vedlegg/Konkurransepolitikk/Anskaffelser/Samarbeidsavtale.pdf

REFERENCES

Ot.prp. nr. 55. (2006–2007). *Om lov om register for frivillig virksomhet*. Oslo: Kultur- og kirkedepartementet.

Selle, P., & Strømsnes, K. (2012). Organisasjonene og det offentlige. *Har vi fått en ny frivillighetspolitikk?* Oslo: Senter for forskning på sivilsamfunn og frivillig sektor.

Sivesind, K. H., Lorentzen, H., Selle, P., & Wollebæk, D. (2002). *The voluntary sector in Norway*. Oslo: Institute for Social Research.

Sivesind, K. H. (2013). Ideella välfärdstjänster: en lösning på den skandinaviska modellens framtida utmaningar? In L. Trägårdh, P. Selle, L. S. Henriksen, & H. Hallin (Eds.), *Civilsamhället klämt mellan stat och kapital. Välfärd, mångfold, framtid* (pp. 75–88). Stockholm: SNS Förlag.

Sivesind, K. H., & Selle, P. (2010). Civil society in the Nordic countries: Between displacement and vitality. In R. Alapuro & H. Stenius (Eds.), *Nordic associations in a European perspective* (pp. 89–120). Baden-Baden: Nomos Verlagsgesellschaft.

Wollebæk, D., & Selle, P. (2002). *Det nye organisasjonssamfunnet*. Bergen: Fagbokforlaget.

Wollebæk, D., Lorentzen, H., & Selle, P. (2000). *Frivillig innsats*. Bergen: Fagbokforlaget.

Poland

Ewa Leś in collaboration with Anna Ciepielewska-Kowalik

Key Figures

Number of Organizations. The last 25 years of the Polish transition from totalitarian system to democracy have seen the renaissance of TSOs such as foundations and associations (although it has to be noted that most TSOs still do not identify themselves as being part of a 'third sector'). There are also terms used to differentiate voluntary organizations from public and for-profit private institutions, such as 'the non-profit sector', 'non-governmental organizations' (NGOs), 'civil society organizations', 'social economy' and 'social enterprises'. Social economy and social enterprise are new terms in Poland. They have emerged after the 1989 from the concepts of third sector and cooperatives. In Poland the concept of social enterprise has received initial recognition among government officials, professionals, academics and the third sector due to EU programs on social inclusion and economic reintegration, such as EQUAL and Human Capital. In the years 1990–1999, the number of foundations multiplied by 20 and that of associations, by 14.5 – an increase only comparable to the increase registered in the immediate post-WWII period. According to estimates made by the Polish research team of the Johns Hopkins Comparative Non-profit Sector Project, in 1997 there were in Poland approximately 36,000 active associations and other social organizations (including Voluntary Fire Brigades); 8,100 labour unions; 3,100 foundations; 2,100 professionals, business and employers' organizations; and 900 church-based social institutions. The growth of the sector continued after 1997; in 2010 there were some 75,000 active associations and foundations in the country. As to cooperatives, they are not perceived as being part of the third sector. In public statistics, they are part of the private sector, together with private commercial firms. Unlike non-profit organizations, which proliferated in Poland after 1989, cooperative enterprises underwent a decline in this period. In 2012, however, the number of cooperatives exceeded 8,000 with 8 million members.

Employment. Among non-profit organizations (foundations, associations and other voluntary organizations), the employment generating function is not their explicit role. Instead, they are producers of goods and services for their members and broader communities, relying predominantly on temporary jobs as a less expensive form of employment. The worse financial situation of many small non-profit organizations forces them to use less expensive hiring options than permanent jobs. The 'convenience' of this type of hiring in the non-profit sector is reflected in the dynamic between temporary and permanent positions. In 2010, only 15 per cent of the non-profits employed permanent workers. Yet, non-profits generated a significant portion of temporary positions, 23 per cent of all paid employment in the Polish non-profit subsector, while 62 per cent of the associations and foundations did not have any paid staff (Gos-Wogcicka, Nalecz, 2013).

This phenomenon is related to the still weak role of the Polish third sector as a long-term, full-fledged partner of the public sector in social service delivery. Most TSOs have short-term contracts with public authorities and work on a project basis, which does not allow for full and stable employment. In the case of associations and foundations, their potential in fulfilling a role in public policies continues to be largely untapped. On the other hand, cooperatives remain a significant employer in Poland despite their weakening role (Leś, 2004). In the period 1995–2012 we observed a decreasing employment dynamic in most branches of the co-operative sector and a drop in employment by more than half, from 642,000 in 1995 to 290,000 in 2012. However, cooperatives still provide about 2.9 per cent of all hired employment in Poland and 2.1 per cent of all paid employment in the national economy (Nalecz, 2008).

Financial Base. Another feature of the third sector in Poland is its extremely high economic polarization. A majority of resources belong to a relatively small group of organizations, a phenomenon which might be termed 'oligarchization' of the Polish third sector's financial base. Ten per cent of Polish non-profit organizations represent 88 per cent of the sector's resources. The paid workforce and good financial position usually concentrate in big cities, while local organizations often lack paid personnel and public support. In terms of its revenue structure, the biggest part of the non-profit sector's revenues (45 per cent) is generated from public subsidies. The second important funding base (31 per cent) for the non-profit subsector is revenue from market sources (selling goods and services), and private donations (33 per cent).

Socio-Political Considerations

Roles of TSOs. Political and legal re-institutionalization of the third sector as an advocacy agent has been much more advanced than the evolution of the sector's role in the rapidly transforming public welfare system, where third sector is still perceived rather as a 'dumping grounds' for acute social problems than as a full-fledged partner in public services delivery.

Although, the third sector has become a part of the private sector since 1989, whereas, before the transition, the so-called 'social organizations' existed as quasi-state agencies and were part of the public – or 'socialized ownership' – sector. Thus, in general the structure of the Polish third sector's paid workforce still reflects both the legacy of the socialist welfare state, where these organizations did not play a role of structurally independent service providers, as well as their still weak institutional recognition as possible public delivery agents. To some extent, however, TSOs have been recognized as often cheaper and more flexible in terms of modes of service delivery than public or private sector entities (Golinowska, 2003, p. 23), but this has not yet been translated into a delegation of public tasks on a permanent basis, except for a few subfields. Nevertheless, the Polish third sector's social and economic roles have evolved in the national economy and society during the transition.

Taking early childhood education and care services as an illustration of recent developments, we note that since 1989 the third sector, along with public and market institutions, have formed a new social infrastructure based on institutional pluralism of providers of these services. In 2008 less than 1 per cent (0.79 per cent) of TSOs declared that they were providing preschool services. However, this represents a slow increase in this field. In 2005 TSOs ran 5.6 per cent of preschool institutions providing services to 3.7 per cent children, while in 2013 they comprised 8 per cent preschool institutions and were attended by 4.9 per cent of children. Thus, we note a slow change in the direction of childcare and preschool educational policy between 2007 and 2013, representing a move towards a culture of cooperation and partnership between public administration (especially the local governments) and TSOs (Ciepielewska-Kowalik, 2013a). So we can discuss about new models of cross-sector relations, including experimental public–private forms of partnership (e.g. common local governing bodies in education and modular public-owned preschool buildings for TSOs) as well as new ways of providing services by the third sector in terms of pedagogic and management aspects based on different stakeholders participation. In 2008 the main sources of financing the activity of TSOs providing childcare and preschool services were from public sources (2/3), while, 1/5 of their budget came from the market sources (Ciepielewska-Kowalik, 2013b).

From Coerced Membership to Voluntary Participation. The high upsurge in the formation of citizens' organizations (which, as we have already mentioned, was particularly marked during the years 1990–1999) was accompanied by a shift from mechanical and mass participation in officially sanctioned organizations of the 'ancient regime', often with coerced membership, to multidimensional, locally oriented participation, not limited to membership in formalized citizens' organizations and combined with a phenomenon of growing volunteering without membership. According to the most recent estimates (2011), some 30 per cent of Poles volunteer, both in formal organizations and informal groups, which is the highest level since the breakthrough of 1989.

Networks, Legitimacy and Corruption. The Polish third sector has developed several links and networks on both the local and national levels, namely branch federations representing fields such as social services and education, centres and different platforms grouping local voluntary organizations. However, the interactive patterns of the third sector are still not strong enough to promote the sector's mission among the general public, to strengthen its legitimacy, or to discourage the dishonest practices and misconduct of some of the sector's organizations.

The Third Sector in Academic Fields and Public Statistics
With the growth of the non-profit and social economy, training programmes developed at the higher education level for voluntary organizations' leaders and staff as well as staff of public institutions in several academic centres of Poland. Since 2006 The Polish National Statistical Office (GUS) has undertaken systematic research aimed at measuring socio-economic potential and impact of the TSOs. At present, it is possible to reliably monitor the economic importance of non-profit organizations and partially their contribution to Poland's economy and public policies.

REFERENCES

Ciepielewska-Kowalik, A. (2013a). Final results of the research project. The role of non-profit organizations in early childhood education and care policy in Poland in transition period. A new model of social investments and activation. *Paper for National Science Centre*. Warsaw: Institute of Political Studies Polish Academy of Science.

Ciepielewska-Kowalik, A. (2013b). Institutionalization of social enterprises and co-production in Poland (1989–2013). A case of early childhood education and care. Paper presented at 4th EMES International Research Conference on Social Enterprise 'If Not For Profit, For What? And How?', University of Liege.

Golinowska, S. (2012). System of social assistance. Main challenges of changes and reforms. In E. Leś (Ed.), *Social assistance: From clientelism to participation*. Warsaw: The Publishing House ELIPSA.

Goś-Wójcicka, K., & Nalecz, S. (2013). *The third sector in Poland. Associations, foundations, faith-based charities, professional and business associations, employers' organizations in 2010* (in Polish). Warsaw: Central Statistical Office.

Juros, A., Leś, E., Nalecz, S., Rybka, I., & Rymsza, M. (2004). From solidarity to subsidiarity: The nonprofit sector in Poland. In A. Zimmer & E. Priller (Eds.), *Future of civil society. Making central European nonprofit-organizations work.* VS Verlag Fur Sozialwissenschaften with Robert Bosch Stiftung.

Leś, E. (2004). Cooperatives in Poland: From state-controlled institutions to new trends in cooperative development. In C. Borzaga & R. Spear (Eds.), *Trends and challenges for cooperatives and social enterprises in developed and transition countries.* Trento: Edizioni31.

Leś, E., Nalecz, S., Toepler, S., Sokolowski, W., & Salamon, L. (2004). *Poland: In global civil society. Dimensions of the non-profit sector* (Vol. 2). Bloomfield: Kumarian Press with The Johns Hopkins Comparative Sector Project.

Nalecz, S., & Goś-Wójcicka, K. (2012). *Volunteering through organizations and other types of unpaid work outside own households in 2011.* Warsaw: Central Statistical Office.

Nalecz, S. (2008). *Social economy in Poland.* Warsaw: Institute of Political Studies. Polish Academy of Science.

Sweden

Victor Pestoff, Yohanan Stryjan and Johan Vamstad

The Third Sector's Changing Roles and Labels

The images of the third sector in Sweden and the terminology used to label it have shifted over time, in tune with changing Swedish political and welfare policy discourses. The *role* played by organizations has evolved (Lundström & Wijkström, 1997; Olsson, Nordfeldt, Larsson, & Kendall, 2005; Pestoff, 2004; Stryjan & Wijkström, 1996) – from a role of independent actors in a laissez-faire state, through a vanguard-role in a nascent welfare state and a role of complement of the mature welfare state – back again, from the late 1980s onwards, to a service provider with an ambiguous position of a potential ally and an implicit challenger of the state.

Labels have changed too; organizations that are active in the field tend to adopt labels in order to enhance their legitimacy and facilitate access to resources, thus, they shift labels when the political climate so requires. So, the 'charity' label was largely abandoned in the first decades of the 20th Century, while the 'popular movement' (*folkrörelse*) label gained followers across the political spectrum and became the dominant term for several decades among organizations in the field. However, it came under sharp attack, from left and right alike, in the 1970s (Berggren & Trägårdh, 2006); and it was also challenged by the emergence, in the mid-1980s, of the term 'civil society'. This concept, which entered Swedish political discourse under impact of developments in Central and Eastern Europe (Reuter, 2007), emphasized independence from the state. In parallel, the transformation of welfare services created demand for a more adequate term to address service-producing organizations: as a result, the 'third sector' concept was adopted, primarily by researchers. As to the term 'voluntary sector' (two Swedish correspondents, namely '*frivillig*' and '*ideel*', are in circulation), it was introduced in the wake of the public sector's reforms of the early 1990s, in an attempt to bridge the popular movement tradition, the more service-production-minded 'third sector' approach, and residues of yet older charitable traditions.

Rhetorics of Change versus Legitimacy after EU Accession

The social economy concept was introduced in the mid-1990s, in the context of Sweden's accession to the EU and of the Union's increasing involvement in the field of social (cohesion) policy. Indeed, the developments of this period created the need for bridges between Swedish institutional vocabulary and that of the emerging social policy instruments of the Union. The introduction in Sweden of the social economy concept, hitherto unknown in the country, was initiated expressly for this purpose by the Swedish Government. A report by an inter-departmental team, delivered in July 1998 and aptly subtitled 'Tradition and Renewal', enlists EU terminology as a new source of legitimacy for the *folkrörelse* tradition. Democratic governance and social goals are singled out as the defining properties of the social economy, while the importance of voluntarism and mutuality is toned down. While stressing continuity, the report also provides an opening towards voluntary organizations, by pointing out that the social economy is a *sector of the economy*, not bound by any particular incorporation form.

The social economy concept also spread to the local government level. It was adopted by public authorities and provided focus, in the 2002–2005 period, for several EQUAL projects, which called for the formal inclusion of social partners in development partnerships. The central government's interest waned gradually, even though social economy was taken up in practically all national budgets for 1997–2006. The government's way of envisaging the concept also evolved over time: from a conception of the social economy as a general approach, the government gradually narrowed its definition of the term to labour market integration issues (Levander, 2011). On other fronts, the pressures by non-socialist municipalities and counties for privatization of housing, health and welfare services led to a retrenchment of service-providing organizations in more traditional positions. By June 2002, the government signalled a renewed interest in popular movements, as a subject for policy and research (Vetenskapsrådet, 2003). In a sense, the end of the decade was nearly as ambiguous, from a conceptual point of view, as its beginning: no consensus had been reached, though the concept of social economy gained some ground with grassroots' groups and at the highly heterogeneous local government level.

Recent Trends

In 2008 the Swedish government finalized an agreement with the national civil society organizations in the public sphere and the Swedish Association of Local Authorities and Regions, following the example of the British compact and several similar agreements in a number of other countries. The agreement was, as in the British case, an effort to establish a long-term understanding of the different roles of the state and civil society in the Swedish welfare state. Several evaluations have been conducted and their results lead to the conclusion that the agreement has been well received at the national level but the implementation at the local level, where most welfare services are governed and produced, has been a disappointment (Johansson, Kassman, & Scaramuzzino, 2011). The Swedish agreement might, in other words, have been important as a matter of principle, but the actual policy implications have so far been limited by both suspicion among civil society organizations and lack of interest from municipalities (Gavelin, 2010). Moreover, the chairmen and women from seven TSOs recently published an appeal to public authorities and municipalities for greater respect for the TSOs' value base and demanded that they stop being treated as private firms (DN, 16.11.13).

There are, however, some interesting examples of Swedish civil society organizations moving from a traditional Scandinavian role of 'voice' representation to a new role of delivering services in a manner more similar to the continental European tradition. Perhaps most notable among them is the former state church of Sweden, which since its separation from the state in the year 2000 has been seeking to find a role as provider of social services for the elderly, different minority groups and others (Edgardh, 2012; Pettersson & Edgardh, 2012). This is rather typical for civil society involvement in welfare services today. The Church of Sweden is a very large organization, with 6.4 million members in a country of just 9.5 million and a lot of capital to invest. The marketization of many central welfare areas in Sweden in recent years has favoured large, for-profit corporations at the expense of small-scale social enterprises. Large civil society actors, like the Church of Sweden and a handful of old foundations with their historical roots in pre-welfare state Sweden, seem to be the ones best equipped to compete under present conditions.

Another significant development in the area in recent years was when Sweden, as the last country in Europe, introduced tax deductions for charitable gifts, on January 1, 2012. Those opposing the reform, mainly from the left of the political spectrum, argued that taxes should be spent on causes selected in a political process, not by encouraging individual citizens to give money to civil society causes they choose themselves (Trägårdh & Vamstad, 2009).

The issue of who should provide the welfare services of tomorrow has become one of the most discussed topics among political representatives as they enter the race for the General Elections of 2014. There seems to be a growing weariness of the market-oriented welfare policies of recent years, but it is too soon to know if this will result in a turn from for-profit to non-profit and public providers, as has been suggested by party leaders on the left, union leaders and others (DN 4.07.13). However, the development of the third sector since 2006, when the ruling Center-Right coalition came to power, paints a bleak picture. In spite of signing a Compact with major third sector providers of social services, TSOs often lose out to private for-profit actors that have more resources to promote their interests and understand the rules of the competitive game better. Two trends are notable in the past decade: first the dramatic growth of private for-profit providers of welfare services, often international venture capitalists, and second the marginalization of the third sector as a welfare provider (Statistiska Meddelanden, 2012). This, in part, reflects the growing complexity of the bidding processes adopted by the Swedish New Public Management regime, with its heavy emphasis on competition and efficiency. Here large actors, often international venture capitalists, appear to have a competitive advantage, particularly when strict financial criteria are applied to the bidding process.

REFERENCES

Berggren, H., & Trägårdh, L. (2006). *Är svensken människa? Gemenskap och oberoende i det moderna Sverige*. Stockholm: Norstedts.

Dagens Nyheter. (2012). *Så skapar vi en välfärd fri från kommersiella intressen. [Creating welfare without commericial interest.] Dagens Nyheter*, DN Debatt, 4 July.

Dagens Nyheter. (2013). *Sluta behandla ideela föreningar som företag. [Stop treating third sector organizations like private firms.] Dagens Nyheter*, DN Debatt, 16 November.

Edgardh, N. (2012). Overview of the National Situation. In A. Bäckström (Ed.), *Welfare and values in Europe – Transition related to religion, minorities and gender*. Uppsala: Uppsala University.

Gavelin, K. (2010). *Uppföljning av Överenskommelsen mellan regeringen, idéburna organisationer inom det sociala området och Sveriges Kommuner och Landsting*. Stockholm: Överenskommelsen.

Johansson, H., Kassman, A., & Scaramuzzino, R. (2011). *Staten och det civila samhällets organisationer i ett föränderligt välfärdssamhälle – Perspektiv på en överenskommelse*. Stockholm: Överenskommelsen.

Levander, U. (2011). *Utanförskap på entreprenad. Diskurser om sociala företag i Sverige*. Göteborg: Daidalos Förlag.

Lundström, T., & Wijkström, F. (1997). *The nonprofit sector in Sweden*. Manchester: Manchester University Press.

Olsson, L.-E., Nordfeldt, M., Larsson, O., & Kendall, J. (2005). The third sector and policy processes in Sweden: A centralised horizontal third sector policy community under strain. Third Sector European Policy (TSEP) Working Paper 3. LSE Dept. of Social Policy, London.

Pettersson, P., & Edgardh, N. (2012). Gävle case study report. In A. Bäckström (Ed.), *Welfare and values in Europe – transition related to religion, minorities and gender*. Uppsala: Uppsala University.

Pestoff, V. A. (2004). The development and future of the social economy in Sweden. In A. Evers & J.-L. Laville (Eds.), *The third sector in Europe*. Cheltenham: Edward Elgar.

Reuter, M. (2007). *Networking a region into existence? Dynamics of civil society regionalization in the Baltic Sea area*. Berlin: Berliner Wissenschafts-Verlag.

Statistiska Meddelanden. (2012). *Finansiärer och utförare inom vård och omsorg 2010*. Stockholm: SCB, Sveriges Offentligt Statistik, OE 29 SM 1201.

Stryjan, Y., & Wijkström, F. (1996). Cooperatives and nonprofits in Swedish social welfare. *Annals of Public and Cooperative Economy*, *67*(1), 5–27.

Trägårdh, L., & Vamstad, J. (2009). *Att ge eller att beskattas: Avdragsrätt för gåvor till ideell verksamhet i Sverige och andra länder*. Stockholm: Sektor 3.

Vetenskapsrådet. (2003). *Svensk forskning om demokrati, offentlig förvaltning och folkrörelser. En kartläggning av forskning 1990–2003.* utförd av vetenskapsrådet på regeringens uppdrag, Rapport 2003, rapport 15, Vetenskapsrådet, Stockholm.

The United Kingdom

Roger Spear

Conceptions, Images and Quantitative Importance of the Third Sector

In the United Kingdom, the term third sector is used differently by different groups: voluntary and community sector (VCS) people tend to call their sector the third sector, while co-ops people tend to use the term to refer to co-ops, mutuals and voluntary organizations, rather than using the term social economy, which is not widely used.

The New Labour Government (mid-1990s to 2010), through the Office of the Third Sector (OTS) defined the third sector as non-governmental organizations which are value-driven and which principally reinvest their surpluses to further social, environmental or cultural objectives. The sector includes voluntary and community organizations, charities, social enterprises, cooperatives and mutuals. The third sector, in this conception, is equivalent to the social economy.

In 2009/2010, the social economy employment (Monzón Campos and Chaves, 2012) in the United Kingdom was 236,000 FTEs in cooperatives, 50,000 FTEs in mutuals and 1,347,000 FTEs in the voluntary sector, that is, a total of 1,633,000 FTEs. This represents 5.64 per cent of the total employment in the country, but is a decline of 4.57 per cent from 10 years previously.

Social enterprise has been a major plank in policy for more than 15 years, the definition used in surveys has varied, with very large variations in estimates (Lyon, Teasdale, & Baldock, 2010). The most recent survey (BMG Research, 2013) specifies five criteria: mainly social or environmental aims; not pay more than 50 per cent of profit or surplus to owners or shareholders; not generate more than 75 per cent of income from grants and donations; not generate less than 25 per cent of income from trading; and agree that it is 'a business with primarily social/environmental objectives, whose surpluses are principally reinvested for that purpose in the business or community rather than mainly being paid to shareholders and owners' (self-identification criterion). This small business survey reports numbers of social enterprise with both a 'good fit' and a 'very good fit' to the above criteria, and thus it allows different headline figures: a Cabinet Office fact sheet (Cabinet Office, 2013) declared: 'there are 180,000 social enterprise SME employers, representing 15 per cent of SME employers', while the representative body Social Enterprise UK (based on the very good fit data) states 'there are approximately 70,000 social enterprises in the UK' (representing 5.7 per cent of SME employers). Both sets of figures represent a slight decline from previous years.

In early surveys (2005) of social enterprise, 'third sector' and 'social enterprise' overlapped almost totally. The only area of difference was advocacy and small self-help organizations (i.e., the non-trading part of the third sector which is not considered as social enterprise). However recent survey approaches and definitions emphasize the business aspect of social enterprise. These underestimate the numbers of third sector organizations which are social enterprise, although in government discourse and amongst social enterprise lead organizations, social enterprises would include voluntary and community organizations, charities (foundations), and many cooperatives. Thus, there has been a gradual policy shift towards constructing social enterprise in the UK to cover both the small business and the third sector.

Policy Developments

Several policy developments have helped shape the framework for the development of the third sector. Firstly, for many years there have been policy measures to reform the provision of public services through public procurement. This was informed by new public management approaches internally (by moving towards more enterprise-like management structures internally – cost centres, internal marketing of services, etc.), and, more importantly, by contracting out public services to the private for-profit and the third sector, alongside a declining level of state provision. Central and local government have also attempted to maintain control through managerialist systems of targets and measures, and a procurement system which strongly emphasizes payment by results contracts.

Changing systems of governance have also influenced the framework in which third sector organizations operate and develop. The changing shape of the state has led to partnership structures, and participative governance arrangements that attempt to bring together different stakeholders associated with specific areas of provision, or specific policy issues. An example illustrating these changes in the systems of governance is provided by multi-stakeholder governance structures associated with local transport where private and third sector (social enterprise) providers attempt to coordinate policy and operations for local communities and for the state as contractor.

After a long period of government investment in policy measures (such as Future-Builders[27]) to improve the professional operation and the capacity of the VCS to provide public services, post crisis budgetary cuts have eliminated much of this support. But to a certain extent this has been replaced by great emphasis on the development of social finance markets accessible to third sector organizations; this represents a major policy initiative (Spear and Paton with Mendell & Thornley, 2014), firstly towards community investment, then towards social enterprise, and more recently for social innovation and social impact.

The Coalition government (formed in 2010) initiated some policy changes from the previous government, but there was also substantial continuity. New Labour raised the profile of the third sector, with programmes for increased support and capacity building through a Compact (TS\Government partnership agreement), and there were increased levels of public procurement. In contrast the Cameron sponsored 'Big Society' policy which was intended to be seen as counter to Labour's Big State, and emphasize closer links between the community and the third sector. To achieve this, policy aimed to reduce red tape, to encourage voluntary action, to make it easier to set up voluntary and community organizations, to facilitate them getting resources (particularly by growing the social investment market, and philanthropy and volunteering), and to improve their working relationship with the state. The Coalition government also renamed the OTS as the Office for Civil Society (OCS), with the target of pursuing the 'Big Society' agenda. The Minister for Civil Society 'responsible for charities, social enterprise, voluntary organisations'[28] is supported by the OCS in the Cabinet Office; but *the OCS has had its budget cut by 75 per cent.* The Compact was renewed, but crisis driven budget cuts particularly at local levels had considerable negative impact on the third sector, thus further undermining the credibility of Big Society policy.

The relabelled OCS indicates a shift in ideology from the previous government, and 'Big Society' represents a major shift from the days when Thatcher announced 'There's no such thing as society, there are individual men and women and there are families'. One strong narrative developed by the primarily Tory agenda of Coalition policy for the sector was a continuation of a strong social enterprise role in public procurement – a major welfare to work public service was outsourced, but its implementation was through such large contracts that in most cases it relegated social enterprise to roles subcontracting to large private sector contractors. This raised the issue of alternative narratives about social enterprise as covers for privatization; and although commitment to TS was clearly apparent in policy, budget cuts led to withdrawal of much capacity building support, at a time when the contracting regime is getting tougher with payment by results contracts (Alcock, 2012).

Legislative Changes
Several important legislative measures have been adopted to facilitate the entrepreneurial functioning of the third sector in the United Kingdom.

First, a Charities Act was approved in November 2006 and gradually implemented; it aims to improve the regulation of charity operation and fundraising, and to provide a clearer definition of charity, emphasizing public benefit, thereby improving the general public's understanding of charities. And in 2013 a new legal form was established, the *charitable incorporated organization*, which gives limited liability and reduces the bureaucracy for charities to trade, since the previous alternative was to register both as a company and a charity.

Secondly, Community Interest Companies (CICs) regulations came into force in July 2005; CICs are limited companies (by guarantee or shares), created for businesses for community benefit, and not purely for private profit. This legal form involves a 'community interest test' and an 'asset lock', thereby ensuring that the CIC is established for community purposes and the assets and profits are preserved for such purposes (in the event of dissolution, the assets pass to another social enterprise). CICs are also required to produce a stakeholder report annually, in addition to normal accounting reporting. By the end of 2013, there were about 8750 CICs registered, some of which were conversions from other structures.[29]

Finally in 2013, the Public Service (Social Value) Act was passed, in order to emphasize the importance of social value in procurement; it obliged local authorities to consider how they could improve the social impact of public contracts.

NOTES

27. See http://www.futurebuilders-england.org.uk/
28. https://www.gov.uk/government/news/nick-hurd-appointed-minister-for-civil-society
29. See http://www.cicregulator.gov.uk/

REFERENCES

Alcock, P. (2012). *The big society: A new policy environment for the third sector?* TSRC WP82. Birmingham.

BMG Research. (2013). *Social enterprise: Market trends.* Based upon the BIS Small Business Survey 2012. London: Cabinet Office.

Cabinet Office. (2013). *G8 factsheet: Social investment and social enterprise*. London.

Lyon, F., Teasdale, S., & Baldock, R. (2010). Approaches to measuring the scale of the social enterprise sector in the UK. Third Sector Research Centre WP 43.

Monzón Campos, J. L., & Chaves, R. (2012). *The social economy in the European union*. Liege: Ciriec International.

Spear, R., & Paton, R., with Mendell, M., & Thornley, B. (2014). Public policy for social finance. In A. Nicholls, R. Paton, & J. Emerson (Eds.), *Social investment*. Oxford: Oxford University Press.

NEW TRENDS IN THE NONPROFIT SECTOR IN EUROPE: THE EMERGENCE OF SOCIAL ENTERPRISES

Carlo Borzaga and Giulia Galera

ABSTRACT

This article has two objectives: to clarify the organizational and managerial differences between social entrepreneurship *and* social enterprises *and to investigate the role of social enterprises and their impacts on the welfare systems of European countries. The authors describe* social entrepreneurship *as a* trend *across all forms of enterprises and* social enterprise *as the institutionalization of a new typology that is distinguished by specific features from its inception. By relying on a theoretical analysis, the article supports the interpretation of social enterprise as an innovative institutional tool that can have a role in supporting growth and welfare. The essential features of social enterprise, which justify their competitiveness vis-à-vis public and for-profit organizations in the production and delivery of general-interest services, are thoroughly investigated. The article sheds light on the contribution of social enterprises to reforming and democratizing the traditional European welfare systems,*

Accountability and Social Accounting for Social and Non-profit Organizations
Advances in Public Interest Accounting, Volume 17, 89–110

ISSN: 1041-7060/doi:10.1108/S1041-706020140000017002

which – since the 1980s – have revealed their inability to distribute welfare services inclusively and cope with the growing phenomena of poverty and inequalities.

Keywords: Social entrepreneurship; social enterprise; social value creation; contracting out; social innovation

INTRODUCTION

Since the 1980s, the management of economic systems worldwide has been characterized by a widespread trust in the ability of markets to ensure growth and welfare. This belief contributed to the undesirable environmental and social consequences that generated the 2008 financial and economic crises (Sabeti, 2011).

As a reaction to the environmental and social costs generated by market fundamentalism, the "social side" of entrepreneurship has gained momentum. This situation is confirmed by the recent dramatic increase in scientific publications and the growing attention of researchers and policymakers to emerging concepts such as *social entrepreneurship* and *social enterprise*. In addition to the conceptual boom, the interest in entrepreneurial pluralism has also grown in importance (Stiglitz, 2009).

However, one should be aware that the general sense of social responsibility that is pervading entrepreneurship has generated two different dynamics, which ought to be maintained and investigated separately to be fully understood and supported.

The first dynamic concerns all types of enterprises and is related with the idea that enterprises should pay more attention to the social impact of entrepreneurial action. Expressed differently, all enterprises should fully take charge of addressing the social problems affecting local communities and take the lead in reconciling business and society (Porter, 2011). What drives this idea is the increasing awareness that the market alone is unable to manage a changing, increasingly complex, and unstable economy. As a result, enterprises cannot limit themselves to pursuing profit maximization. The crisis has further confirmed the need to seek credible alternatives to entrepreneurial behaviors supported by the mainstream economy and has dramatically questioned the traditional concept about profit maximization that notably reigned unconditionally from the 1980s until the early 2000s. Over the last decade, a new mindset has taken hold, encouraging all enterprises to take due account of the consequences of their actions. The responsibility of enterprises for their impacts on society has driven them to modify their business models to create social and economic value. The concept of *social entrepreneurship* has been expanded to embrace a diverse set of entrepreneurial initiatives, which are aimed at generating social value. These encompass corporate social responsibility practices promoted by single entrepreneurs, conventional enterprises, nonprofit organizations, and profit-nonprofit ventures in an attempt to pursue both economic and social objectives. Such aims include the design of innovative processes that integrate social, environmental, and ethical human rights and consumer concerns into the business operations of conventional enterprises, as well as the change of strategic objectives in close collaboration with their stakeholders. An increasing number of social entrepreneurship initiatives have gone even further by applying the technique of business entrepreneurship to address specific, unresolved environmental, or social needs.

In essence, in social entrepreneurship initiatives, the desired social change benefits from an innovative, entrepreneurial, or enterprise-based solution. Social entrepreneurship activities are normally characterized by a dual bottom line, and they are voluntarily promoted by entrepreneurs and managers committed to become more responsible. However, while all such initiatives are characterized by a social mission, they may not lead to the setting up of an enterprise. There is also no guarantee that the social orientations will survive over time, simply because they are subject to the will of the entrepreneur (Helm & Andersson, 2010; Light, 2006).

The second dynamic refers to the emergence of new economic actors that have managed to institutionalize the pursuit of explicit social aims and are clearly dedicated to create value from their inception. Indeed, following the crisis of the welfare states, the development of new organizational forms (called *social enterprises*) explicitly aimed to deliver and manage personal and community services (which traditional welfare systems are no longer able to provide) has become of utmost importance in several European Union (EU) countries. What distinguishes social enterprises from traditional nonprofit organizations is their clear entrepreneurial stance, which is a function of the pursuit of explicit social aims and presupposes the supply of general-interest goods or services. In other words, in social enterprises, the production and delivery of general-interest services are organized in an entrepreneurial way by means of a dedicated enterprise. In an increasing number of countries, these new actors have been gradually integrated into the welfare system, in several cases turning into the most important providers of vital welfare services. Interesting examples of the above-mentioned institutionalization processes are provided by several European countries, including Italy and the United Kingdom (UK). In Italy, social cooperatives, which are the most widespread social enterprise model, have registered a 10–20 percent average annual growth rate since they were first created. In 2011, 12,647 social cooperatives employed 322,875 workers, out of which 30,534 were disadvantaged workers (Rapport Euricse, 2013). In the same year, social cooperatives had a turnover of 10.1 billion Euros and an invested capital of 8.3 billion Euros (Rapport Euricse, 2013). In the United Kingdom, social enterprises have been legally recognized through the introduction of the regulation on community interest companies (CICs) in 2005. Since their formal recognition, CICs have multiplied; in 2012, there were 6,391 registered CICs with an annual turnover of at least £1 billion (Regulator of Community Interest Companies, 2012).

While operating on distinguished albeit parallel tracks, the above-mentioned dynamics are often confused by both researchers and policy-makers, who sometimes consider them as a single concept. Due to this misunderstanding, the terms *social entrepreneurship* and *social enterprise* are frequently used interchangeably. More precisely, the term social enterprise is often wrongly employed to describe social entrepreneurship initiatives, ignoring the intrinsic differences between the concepts of *entrepreneurship* and *enterprise*, as far as the actors, beneficiaries, and aims are concerned.[1]

This lack of conceptual clarity explains the need to shed light on the typical characteristics distinguishing each dynamic. In brief, we believe that the first dynamic (*social entrepreneurship*) should be branded as a *trend* across all types of enterprises. The second dynamic should be regarded as the institutionalization of a new typology of enterprise (*social enterprise*) that is distinguished by specific features from its inception. These two development paths are clearly intertwined; indeed, *social enterprise* is an integral part of the first dynamic, which encompasses all types of enterprises.

This article's aim is twofold: to clarify the organizational and managerial differences between social entrepreneurship and social enterprises, and to investigate the role of social enterprises and their impacts on the welfare systems of European countries. The interest in social enterprises stems from its connections with profound changes significantly affecting public policies, on the one hand, and questioning the mainstream interpretation of economic behaviors, on the other hand. The emergence of social enterprises challenges key concepts that have so far dominated policy and economic thinking. Key changes primarily involve the common interpretation of general-interest services. The assumption that the latter should be provided directly by the government is challenged by the upsurge and consolidation of social enterprises supplying welfare and general-interest services to the entire community (Nyssens, 2006). Second, the emergence of enterprises that explicitly pursue social goals challenges the conventional profit-oriented goal, which had dominated social science thinking until recently.

After clarifying the distinctive features of each development path, this article defines social enterprise that is grounded in the European tradition and is often used to describe a "different way" of both conducting business and providing social services, which encompasses the more entrepreneurial component of the nonprofit sector and some innovative aspects of the cooperative movement (Becchetti & Borzaga, 2010; Nyssens, 2006). As such, social enterprise is a specific type that pursues social goals, performs specific functions, develops distinctive governance forms, and shows precise limitations. The article briefly investigates the essential features manifested by social enterprises, which justify their competitiveness vis-à-vis public and for-profit organizations in the production of general-interest services. Then it analyzes the key factors explaining social enterprise success from a historical perspective. Finally, the article sheds light on the contribution of social enterprises to reforming and democratizing the traditional European welfare systems, which – since the 1980s – have proven their inability to distribute welfare services inclusively and cope with the growing phenomena of poverty and inequalities.

DEFINING SOCIAL ENTREPRENEURSHIP

The relevant literature illustrates that social entrepreneurship is interpreted as the widespread trend of designing innovative solutions to address unresolved economic, social, and environmental concerns. Social entrepreneurship is thus regarded as "*an umbrella term for a considerable range of innovative and dynamic international praxis and discourse in the social and environmental sector*" (Nicholls, 2006, p. 5).

Accordingly, social entrepreneurship initiatives can be promoted alternatively by individuals, private organizations, or public agencies, and are not necessarily designed to last for a long time. Thus, social entrepreneurship does not result in a specific type of enterprise, as it encompasses social initiatives of profit-seeking businesses; institutionalized entities pursuing social goals, relations, and practices that yield social benefits; entrepreneurial trends in nonprofit organizations; and ventures developed within the public sector (Johnson, 2000; Mair & Martì, 2006; Roper & Cheney, 2005).

Social entrepreneurship also comprises a number of diversified initiatives. Among others, these include initiatives that generate innovative products to respond to the needs unfulfilled by conventional commodities, the delivery of low-cost products for recipients in need, welfare protection initiatives to the workers' advantage, and work integration schemes for disadvantaged people. Overall, social entrepreneurship initiatives are carried out voluntarily by their promoters. This explains their alleged transitory life cycle and the multiple goals that promoters may pursue at a time (Santos, 2012). Given the complexity and voluntary nature of such innovative entrepreneurial solutions, social entrepreneurship is rarely regulated by a specific piece of legislation.

To conclude, when analyzing social entrepreneurship, the focal unit of analysis becomes the entrepreneur rather than the organization involved. The entrepreneur is typically described as a heroic individual who builds innovative solutions to address social problems and improve people's lives, but who does not exclude profit as a goal to be pursued. In other words, the social entrepreneur has a double bottom line that balances the pursuit of profit with the aim of achieving social benefits.

DEFINING SOCIAL ENTERPRISE

As already highlighted, the concept of social enterprise differs from that of social entrepreneurship, because the former refers to a specific type of institution that is distinguished by precise features. Compared with social entrepreneurship, this interpretation of social enterprise has a longer history and has found greater resonance in Europe, where a gradual convergence toward a common understanding of what constitutes social enterprise is noticeable.

The process of developing a common understanding of social enterprise has been strongly supported by the EMES European Research Network through a permanent dialogue among researchers from all parts of the EU, which has been backed by concrete experiences (Borzaga & Defourny, 2001; Nyssens, 2006). Conversely, the concept of social enterprise in the United States is generally much broader and more focused on entrepreneurial initiatives set up by nonprofit organizations for the sake of revenue generation (Kerlin, 2010).

According to the European perspective, a social enterprise is an economic entity that explicitly aims to benefit the community (Defourny & Nyssens,

2008). Thus, different from most managerial studies' definition of social enterprise, such enterprises are here described as a single bottom-line organization, whose social aims are prioritized and profit generation is instrumental (Lee & Battilana, 2013; Eikenberry & Kluver, 2004; Zahra et al., 2009).

The EMES Network's conceptualization of social enterprise, initially built on a set of social and economic criteria (Borzaga & Defourny, 2001), was subsequently reclassified along three lines: the social dimension, the entrepreneurial dimension, and the inclusive ownership-governance (Defourny & Nyssens, 2014). However, these criteria are mainly meant to describe an "ideal type" that enables researchers to position the experiences they are studying within the "galaxy" of entrepreneurial initiatives pursuing social aims (Defourny & Nyssens, 2008).

The working definition of social enterprise that was elaborated on by the EMES Network has met with significant success in several European member states, which have embraced it by incorporating its core principles into their legal frameworks that have been designed to regulate this new type of enterprise (Galera & Borzaga, 2009).

Essential Characteristics of Social Enterprises

To sustain their complex economic and socially oriented mission, social enterprises have innovated governance models and have assumed peculiar characteristics, which are meant to enhance their ability to produce high social surplus and distribute it fairly to the advantage of either the community or its beneficiaries. In this regard, social enterprise-specific features come to the fore, in addition to the characteristics normally shown by all types of enterprises.

The specific characteristics that social enterprises exhibit have often been assumed spontaneously at the very beginning of their development, when such initiatives first emerged from the bottom up, in response to existing needs. However, as social enterprises have advanced from the start-up toward the consolidation phase, the need for institutionalizing their essential characteristics has become increasingly important. Drawing on the EMES definition of social enterprise, it can be useful to better analyze the three dimensions,[2] taking into account that they may be fulfilled in different ways; indeed, it is the interplay among the three dimensions that determines whether an organization may or may not qualify as social enterprise.

Entrepreneurial Dimension

Social enterprises are firstly production units that either fully belong to the universe of enterprises or are distinguished by an increasingly entrepreneurial stance. Accordingly, social enterprises represent a break with traditional nonprofit organizations, which are mainly interested in advocacy activities and typically rely on donations and public subsidies to pursue their institutional aims. They also signify a separation from the idea that general-interest services must be produced by public agencies. This means that social enterprises are expected to engage in a process, creating value that must be expressed in monetary terms (Somerville & McElwee, 2011). However, in contrast to social entrepreneurship initiatives, social enterprises have only one bottom line: the pursuit of explicit social aims. In other words, what distinguishes social enterprises from conventional ones is that their economic behavior is aimed at sustaining their socially oriented mission. For conventional business organizations, wealth creation is an end in itself; whereas for social enterprises, wealth creation is important primarily as a path to social value creation, since it enables the enterprise to be financially sustainable and to continue functioning (Dees, 1998). Profit here is channeled toward the fulfillment of social or other public-interest goals rather than private appropriation (Santos, 2012).

To sum up, the double bottom line perfectly fits for-profit enterprises that are interested in taking charge of the social consequences of their entrepreneurial activities, such as the vast array of social entrepreneurship activities. However, it has little to do with enterprises that are structured to prioritize the pursuit of social aims by using production factors that are normally purchased and only occasionally obtained for free.

Social Dimension

As opposed to conventional enterprises, the aims pursued by social enterprises imply the production of goods or services that generate direct benefits for the entire community or specific groups of disadvantaged people, thanks to the specific products or services delivered and allocation processes adopted. The explicit social aims must be clearly defined at the statutory level, and the products or services delivered by social enterprises must be distinguished by a social or meritorious nature that is recognized as such by the community. Having said this, social enterprises' engagement should not be limited to a restricted set of activities like welfare service delivery and work integration, but should encompass all types of general-interest services. Since the concept of general-interest services is context specific, depending on the judgment of a given society, the typology of services supplied can significantly vary. According to the diversity of unmet needs that may arise at the local level in different countries and contexts, the set of services delivered can comprise welfare, health, educational, and cultural services; utilities (e.g., water supply, gas, and electricity); credit services addressed to nonbankable recipients; and even private goods and services, provided that they are allocated according to a "social" rather than market rationale.

Inclusive Ownership-Governance

To succeed in identifying needs and involving the stakeholders concerned in designing adequate solutions, social enterprises have developed peculiar ownership structures and governance models that are meant to strengthen the enterprise's social orientation, on the one hand, and to support a distribution of outcomes that is consistent with the nature of goods delivered, on the other hand. These strategies are meant to identify a community's needs effectively and to help create and strengthen mutual trust among the stakeholders. Two key mechanisms ensure that the inclusive nature of the social enterprise is safeguarded over time: adoption of participatory ownership and governance structures, and compliance with a nonprofit distribution constraint.

In many instances, both strategies have been voluntarily implemented by social enterprises and have subsequently become a widespread practice, sometimes following their compulsory formalization by means of legal regulations. Whereas the voluntary decision to adopt a participatory governance structure and comply with a nonprofit distribution constraint can be sufficient to ensure inclusiveness during the start-up phase, once the social enterprise consolidates, the inclusive dimension must be safeguarded through a formal institutionalization at the statutory level.

Concretely, participatory ownership implies that ownership rights and control power are assigned to all of the most relevant stakeholders that directly benefit from the enterprise's activities. The participatory nature of social enterprise is consistent with its social foundations, which often lie in the community that hosts the social enterprise (Santos, 2012; Somerville & McElwee, 2011), and it presupposes that the social enterprise is controlled either by people living within the benefit area or by a group that shares a certain need or aim. While ensuring access to basic services, the participatory structure also increases efficiency, enabled by the reduced opportunism that is facilitated by the reciprocal relationship between the producer and consumers (e.g., *coproduction*) (Pestoff, 2008).

Depending on the type of social enterprise under consideration, ownership rights and control power can be assigned to more than one category at a time, giving grounds for a multi-stakeholder ownership asset.

The participatory ownership and governance structure implemented by social enterprises is backed by an additional mechanism, the nonprofit distribution constraint, which is meant to further lock the social and inclusive dimension of social enterprise. However, it has another function; by preventing the sale of the social enterprise, it ensures self-survival over time in its endeavor to pursue explicit social goals.

The experiences in various countries show that the nonprofit distribution constraint can be operationalized in three ways, through a series of alternative combinations. It can be applied to the profits generated, the assets accumulated, or the remunerations gained by the workers and managers employed. Moreover, the nonprofit distribution constraint can be annually based or lifelong. It can also have a total distribution constraint in terms of both dividends and assets, hence forbidding any dividend distribution and asset transfer in case of enterprise dissolution. At the same time, it can envisage capped dividends and a total asset lock, or it can allow for capped dividends and provide for a partial asset lock. Finally, it can foresee capped dividends without being accompanied by an asset lock.

The nonprofit distribution constraint can be addressed to either the social enterprise owners or to its financers, who do not exercise control over the enterprise. Finally, the nonprofit distribution constraint should also be conceived as a mechanism contributing to the firm's capitalization. Indeed, its observance implies that net earnings, if any, are devoted to financing the general-interest activities that the organization was formed to carry out (Hansmann, 1996).

Several scholars have considered the nonprofit distribution constraint as the crucial institutional tool that reduces asymmetric information and fosters relationships of trust, thus building legitimacy and public confidence and helping guarantee that resources are employed in the stakeholders' interests (Anheier, 2014). In addition to its trust-enhancing capacity, the nonprofit distribution constraint has been regarded as a utility-strengthening device that can attract stakeholders (users, workers, and managers) whose individual goals are consistent with the social aims pursued by the social enterprise (Valentinov, 2008).[3] However, further research is needed to investigate the rationale and key functions of the nonprofit distribution constraint.

To conclude, the nonprofit constraint's basic guarantee that the enterprise will remain social over time is strengthened by participation. Together, both mechanisms are meant to safeguard the fair distribution of outcomes, and they ensure that the quality of the services delivered is monitored and that the wealth generated will be used to pursue general-interest goals (Vamstad, 2012).

Social Enterprise as a New Typology: A Historical Analysis

Over the past decades, social enterprises have been increasingly recognized by social science researchers, practitioners, and policymakers as a new institutional architecture for adequately exploiting and channeling citizens' ability to solve key societal problems innovatively in several general-interest domains, including health, social services, education, culture, and the environment. Social enterprises have thus emerged as an additional actor, which complements the actions of public and for-profit organizations.

In this regard, from a historical perspective, several key factors have played roles in supporting the rise of social enterprise as a new typology. A key driver influencing the upsurge of social enterprises has been the bottom-up mobilization and self-organization of citizens' groups, who have collectively decided to take charge of key problems affecting local communities. Evidence from diverse countries, including Italy, the United Kingdom, Sweden, and Poland, shows that many social enterprise initiatives were initially established on a voluntary basis, but they have subsequently evolved into stable organizations that are now fully integrated into the welfare systems and provide continuous and often innovative services (Becchetti & Borzaga, 2010). Thanks to the mobilization of citizens' groups to address local concerns, social enterprises have been set up in various fields of activities that are of interest to the communities.

In most EU-15 countries, social enterprises have initially emerged in the welfare sector. Interesting examples of social enterprises driven by the voluntary commitment of citizens' groups include parent cooperatives providing childcare services in Sweden and community interest companies supplying diverse personal and community services that are supported heavily by volunteers in Italy and the United Kingdom (Borzaga & Defourny, 2001; Defourny & Nyssens, 2008). Nevertheless, over the last years, social enterprises have expanded into other fields as well. The new fields of activities are the provision of educational, cultural, environmental, as well as public utility services. Among the wide range of innovative areas of intervention, noteworthy are bioenergy villages in which agricultural producers are closely linked to private households, community facilities, and energy provision, and citizens' attempts to collectively take over formerly privatized energy grids or water and wastewater plants. There are also interesting examples of social enterprises that use new technologies either to improve the delivery of traditional welfare services or to provide new ones, such as the establishment of technological platforms matching the demand and supply of various social and personal services. Generally, social enterprises have been demonstrated as likely to work in any field of activity that is of interest to the entire community or specific, fragile segments of the population.

The supply of social services by social enterprises has assumed a key role, especially in certain countries, Italy for instance, where the public and private supply of social and personal services was limited. Indeed, in the 1970s, when the Italian welfare state started to face the first symptoms of a financial crisis, both the public and private supply of social and personal services was inadequate, mainly public, standardized, and poorly managed. Except for the provision of health and education services, most public spending was allocated in the form of cash benefits (mainly pensions). In Italy, the subsequent development of social enterprises was thus boosted by the increasing public support in favor of service provision. In the United Kingdom, social enterprises have grown in relevance during the phase of privatization of general-interest services, becoming in many instances the end result of privatization policies. Conversely, in countries that traditionally have been distinguished by strong and universal welfare states, such as Denmark or Sweden, social enterprises have become particularly attractive as alternative welfare providers over the last decade or so.

Among the most innovative initiatives, work integration social enterprises (WISEs) deserve particular notice. Work integration is emblematic of the dynamics of social enterprises and a major sphere of their activity that can be found in many European countries (Nyssens, 2006). The philosophy of these organizations, which first emerged in the 1980s, has been to empower and integrate excluded people. Against this background, disadvantaged workers have been encouraged to participate in social enterprises that offer them an opportunity both to reassess the role of work in their lives and to gain control over their personal projects. This concept implies assisting disadvantaged workers not only to develop an occupation, but also to acquire specific values through democratic management structures, as disadvantaged workers are often involved in the governance of WISEs (Galera, 2010).

Additional spaces of intervention of social enterprises have been generated by the 2008 financial crisis, which has worsened the public sector's ability to finance the traditional infrastructure-based services of general interest. Public budget cuts have therefore strengthened further the policy interest in social enterprises as vehicles for achieving balanced and fair economic growth. Against this background, issues such as the regulation of social enterprises and social contracting have suddenly come to the fore and are now at the center of policy discussions at national and European levels.

Institutionalization of Social Enterprises in Europe

Thanks to the availability of suitable organizational forms, a growing number of social enterprise initiatives have been spreading, developing from informal actions into institutionalized endeavors and from spontaneous undertakings into regulated activities.

The cooperative and associative forms have been the most exploited models by citizens' groups involved in initiating entrepreneurial activities aimed at tackling unsatisfied needs arising in society. Neither the cooperative nor the associative models had been originally conceived to conduct entrepreneurial activities that aimed to pursue explicit social goals. However, the intrinsic flexibility of both organizational models has allowed their adjustment to strengthen their social and entrepreneurial dimensions, respectively.

More precisely, we have witnessed the evolution of cooperatives toward the pursuit of social aims and the contextual shift of associations toward an entrepreneurial stance. New cooperative initiatives that involve enhancing collaborative, intrinsic social responsibility for the entire community have developed in an experimental way in countries where the cooperatives' social function was politically recognized, and associations were prevented from carrying out economic activities. These countries include Italy and several Nordic nations. Conversely, in countries that permit them to conduct economic activities, associations have strengthened their entrepreneurial dimension, following their engagement in welfare service delivery. This evolution has occurred notably in France and Belgium.

These parallel trends have resulted in a combination of the associative and cooperative forms[4] after their adjustment, to overcome their intrinsic limitations. In the case of cooperatives – oriented by definition to promoting their members' interests – the adaptation has aimed at enabling them to perform general-interest activities to the advantage of specific target groups or the entire community.

An additional key factor, which has played a role in both stimulating the widespread replication of social enterprises in different localities and facilitating the implementation of contracting-out policies, is the formal recognition of such organizations by means of national and European policies. This process, which is still in progress and has not yet led to a shared definition, has been furthered by the adoption of national laws specifically designed for social enterprise. Moreover, the recognition process has been supported by the European Commission with the Communication on the Social Business Initiative recently delivered with a view to contributing to the creation of a favorable environment for the development of social enterprises in Europe (European Commission, 2011).

However, in the majority of EU countries, social enterprises continue to be regulated by existing legal forms made available by the national legal system, which were not conceived for social enterprises. These include associations that are allowed to conduct economic activities with no restriction (e.g., in France and Belgium), cooperatives that are permitted to pursue general-interest goals (e.g., parent cooperatives providing childcare in Sweden), as well as companies for people with disabilities that were inherited from the communist era (e.g., in Slovenia and Poland).

Contextually, national legislation that is specifically designed to regulate social enterprises has substantially contributed to conceptual clarifications and has multiplied successful entrepreneurial models in key fields of interest to communities. Conceptual clarifications and regulations tailored specifically for social enterprises have been introduced principally by specific national legislation, which has adjusted existing legal forms by formalizing their empirical evolution in many instances. This recognition path primarily concerns the cooperative model, which is intrinsically distinguished by certain social connotations. This process started in the early 1990s, following the enforcement of law 381/1991 in Italy, where cooperatives' social function is recognized by the constitution, and such organizations are required by law to comply with a partial nonprofit distribution constraint. Traditional cooperative forms have evolved into *cooperativa sociale* (social cooperative) in Italy, *cooperativa de iniciativa social* (cooperative of social initiative) in Spain, *société coopérative d'intérêt collectif* (SCIC) (cooperative of collective interest) in France, solidarity cooperative in Portugal, social cooperative in Poland and Hungary, etc.

An alternative path has been the introduction of new legal brands for social enterprises. Specific legislation on social enterprise has been introduced in several EU countries: *société à finalité sociale* in Belgium (company with a social aim), CIC in the United Kingdom, social enterprise in

Italy, and social enterprise in Slovenia, with a view to supporting further the development of social enterprises. According to this recognition path, legal brands for social enterprises can be adopted by several/all legal forms, provided that they comply with key criteria that significantly coincide with the previously discussed characteristics of social enterprise.[5]

Contribution of Social Enterprises to Welfare and Economic Development

Evidence from countries where social enterprises play a role, such as Italy, the United Kingdom, and France, shows that such organizations make significant beneficial contributions to societal wellbeing, inclusion, and economic growth. They fill gaps in service delivery, increase the efficiency of the entire economic system, assume a role in generating social innovation, and contribute to employment creation.

Over the last decades, the landscape of European welfare states has undergone profound transformations. Despite the relevant amount of resources spent and reforms implemented, the welfare states have increasingly failed to cope with the emerging needs and growing problems of inequalities and poverty, on the one hand, and passive or opportunistic behaviors on the part of recipients, on the other hand (Organisation for Economic Co-operation and Development [OECD], 2009). Particularly noteworthy is the increasing inability of many welfare systems to meet the growing and increasingly diversified demands for social and general-interest services (Borzaga & Galera, 2012). Additionally, the bureaucratic approach of public welfare institutions, coupled with a scarce role for user participation, have played a part in generating beneficiaries' dependency on public aid rather than inducing self-help, which has nonetheless been averted by successfully tackling social exclusion (Evers, 1998; Giddens, 2007).

Social enterprises have emerged during the reformation process that has pervaded most European welfare systems. They have developed as an innovative response to welfare gaps, especially in EU welfare systems that were heavily based on cash benefits rather than service provision. In such countries, social enterprises have proven their ability to contribute to improving the welfare of local communities by complementing the public supply of general-interest services, including social, educational, and health services. They have thus turned into key welfare providers in several countries.

The initial social enterprise initiatives emerged spontaneously without being backed by dedicated policies. Following their consolidation, an important modality that has sustained social enterprises is the public entities' support for the production of general-interest services, thanks to a gradual paradigm shift that has favored collaborative relations among public agencies and private welfare providers.

In several EU countries, contracting out the production of general-interest services to social enterprises has thus implied a key shift to a more stable public engagement with social enterprises as social service providers. Social procurement has contributed to greater efficiency and a significant increase in the supply of services. However, by trying to assimilate social enterprise culture and managerial practices into the public one, the stable interaction of social enterprises with public policies has also generated isomorphic pressures, which have sometimes weakened the civic activism that marked the first social enterprise initiatives.

Nevertheless, evidence from countries where social enterprises are key providers of general-interest services suggests that such enterprises show some advantages in the production of general-interest services over public and for-profit enterprises. Advantages result from the governance model and ownership arrangement that characterize such organizations, which underpin a specific incentive structure. The inclusive governance and ownership structures presuppose the active involvement of all relevant stakeholders; through their engagement, users and volunteers are empowered and can control quality to ensure that it adequately meets existing needs. At the same time, social enterprises' incentive structure that is focused more on intrinsic, other-regarding motivations and preferences rather than extrinsic, self-regarding, and monetary motivations, allows the selection of workers and managers who are motivated by nonmonetary incentives, including the social benefits generated by the organization (Bacchiega & Borzaga, 2001, 2003; Ben-Ner & Putterman, 1998; Borzaga & Tortia, 2007). Furthermore, the engagement of various stakeholders attracts a mix of resources, including unexploited ones that otherwise would not address welfare and development goals. Such resources have a role in supporting stabilization and counterweighing social enterprises' low capitalization and difficulties in accessing the credit sector. The resulting improvement in efficiency terms translates to increased available resources that can be used to increase the supply of general-interest services.

An additional beneficial byproduct of many social enterprises is that their multi-stakeholder governance helps empower the local community in strategic decision making, enhances social cohesion, and fosters a more participatory democracy (Pestoff, 2008). Community involvement through social mobilization also contributes to positive changes in attitude, as communities become aware that they can take stock of their own situation and collectively solve their own problems. In other words, the social enterprise model provides the arena for effective solutions that can improve society, while ensuring that the social goals pursued address the general interest of the community rather than particularistic ones. Moreover, thanks to the interactions that they establish with other sectors, including public agencies and for-profit enterprises, social enterprises can have a role in transforming the social and economic system in which they operate, to the entire community's advantage (Galera, 2009).

Social enterprises are also a model of social innovation ahead of their time. With the evolution and diversification of needs, social enterprises have proven their ability to respond by developing new services and experimenting with new solutions to meet those needs better. They have also demonstrated their capacity to transform the "production process," replacing bureaucratic and hierarchical forms with participatory ones. The innovation power of social enterprises has proven to be robust in pioneering initiatives successfully, thanks to their ability to supply new products, define new production processes, or design new institutional arrangements. Nonetheless, innovation inevitably becomes less relevant when social enterprises start multiplying, entertain stable relationships with public authorities, and become a widespread evolutionary trend. In brief, while social entrepreneurship is by definition an innovative praxis to respond to unresolved social problems, social enterprises have neither proven to be necessarily innovative, nor is it desirable for them. Conversely, in addition to social enterprise's ability to generate social innovation, its capacity to replicate efficient models for managing general-interest issues and satisfying unmet needs matters.

Social enterprises also play a crucial role in job creation. Generally, social enterprises develop new activities and contribute to generating employment in the sectors where they operate – the social and community service sectors that show high employment potential. More specifically, some social enterprises aim for the work integration and training of disadvantaged workers with minimal opportunities to find jobs in traditional enterprises (Nyssens, 2006). Add to this, in a number of cases, they allow hiring hard-to-employ workers who seek for instance flexible jobs, like women with children, and they contribute to creating innovative models of industrial relations (Borzaga & Depedri, 2005; Borzaga & Tortia, 2007).

Indeed, the social enterprise model is also engaged in developing new forms of work organization, which can enhance workers' participation in decision-making processes. The employment capacity of social enterprises is especially important, given the high unemployment rates affecting particular segments of the population that are especially at risk of exclusion from the traditional labor market (i.e., women with children, youth, minority groups, disadvantaged people, immigrants, homeless people, and former prisoners) (Galera, 2009).

The beneficial impact of social enterprises is not recognized. On the contrary, there is a widespread belief that social enterprise development has offered an alibi to the public sector and privatization has contributed to worsening the quality of services and work. However, research so far conducted does not confirm the validity of such critics. Conversely, it corroborates the efficiency and effectiveness of social enterprises (Borzaga & Depedri, 2013).

CONCLUSION

The 2008 financial crisis further confirmed the Western social model's difficulties in dealing with both the increasingly diversified growth of societal needs and the unstable nature of the global economy. Indeed, the crisis put the implementation of common European and national policies at further risk. This situation is particularly true for rural and less developed areas, where general-interest services are becoming difficult to maintain on the basis of public budgets.

In this regard, it has become clear that to overcome the economic crisis, regenerate the landscape of the Western welfare states, and support smart, viable, and inclusive growth, a more sustainable business approach is required. This strategy necessarily implies a shift from a bipolar model, based on the predominant actions of the state and the market, to a pluralistic one, where different forms of enterprises and entrepreneurial behaviors coexist and play diverse roles (Sassmannshausen & Volkmann, 2013).

Against the background of overcoming conceptual confusion, we have identified the clear features of social enterprises vis-à-vis social entrepreneurship. Indeed, while social entrepreneurship initiatives pursue multiple goals to balance corporate profit with a commitment to social responsibility (Austin & Reficco, 2005; Baron, 2007; Boschee, 2006; Reis, 1999; Waddock & Post, 1991; Weerawardena & Sullivan Mort, 2006), social enterprises are created and structured to prioritize the pursuit of social aims. In essence, the principal distinction between social enterprises and social entrepreneurship is that the former generates value for social ends, and surplus is mainly used to enable reinvestment and sustainability of the business. Along these lines, social enterprise can be understood as a distinctive component of social entrepreneurship, which significantly contributes to strengthening its beneficial impacts on economic development and welfare. Social enterprise is indeed a new institutional instrument that can have a role in supporting growth and welfare.

However, in contrast to social entrepreneurship, social enterprises are precise legal entities that contribute to overcoming some of the typical limitations faced by public agencies and conventional enterprises when supplying general-interest services. Evidence from various EU countries shows that social enterprises can succeed in delivering innovative and personalized services to the advantage of local communities and vulnerable groups. Thanks to the engagement of committed entrepreneurs and workers, social enterprises have provided self-organized, concrete responses by promoting entrepreneurial initiatives and pooling a mix of resources. As such, social enterprises are contributing to bridging the gap between the demand and supply sides of general-interest services that are undersupplied or not supplied at all by public agencies and for-profit enterprises. Thus, social enterprises should be regarded as a vital institution for the future, given the growth in needs arising in society and the severe budget constraints affecting public finances.

Further research is nevertheless needed to explain better the structural features manifested by social enterprises and their sustainability. Advanced studies could also provide insights into how and to what extent social enterprises' limitations can be offset by more appropriate regulation and management, greater stakeholder engagement (as coproducers) and the intrinsic inclination of social enterprises to promote a dialogue between consumers and producers of goods and services (Pestoff, 2008).

NOTES

1. For instance, Young (2013) used the term social enterprise to refer to a variety of initiatives, ranging from social cooperatives, intersectoral partnerships, corporate social responsibility programs of for-profit corporations, and myriad combinations of all these forms.
2. The social dimension refers to the key objective pursued by social enterprises. The entrepreneurial and ownership-governance dimensions are related to the modality, whereby services and goods are produced and delivered.

3. Some organizational scholars (Pache and Santos) have recently contested the ability of the nonprofit constraint to build legitimacy, for instance, proving that some work integration social enterprises in France had chosen the for-profit legal status for legitimacy reasons (Pache & Santos, 2013). However, with this article authors' impression is that several authors tend to confuse the legal form with the profit aim. Indeed, empirical evidence from various countries proves that the legal status (for-profit company) often does not correspond with the aim pursued (for-profit aim).

4. This phenomenon has been taking place in other European countries as well and was first brought out by CECOP. See CECOP (1996). See also Conseil Supérieur de la Coopération, Le Statut Coopératif: support de l'Enterprise à but social, March 26, 1999, pp. 3–4.

5. For a more in-depth analysis of the legal evolution of social enterprise, see Galera and Borzaga (2009).

REFERENCES

Anheier, H. (2014). *Non-profit organizations*. London: Routledge.

Austin, J., & Reficco, E. (2005). *Corporate social entrepreneurship*. Working Paper No. 09–101. Harvard Business School.

Austin, J. E., & Reficco, E. A. (2005). with Austin, J. E. & Reficco, E. A. (2009). *Corporate social entrepreneurship* (June 30, 2009). Oekologisches Wirtschaften. Retrieved from http://ssrn.com/abstract=1427898

Austin, J., Stevenson, H., & Wei-Skillern, J. (2006). Social and commercial entrepreneurship: Same, different, or both? *Entrepreneurship Theory and Practice*, *30*(1), 1–22.

Bacchiega, A., & Borzaga, C. (2001). Social enterprises as incentive structures. In C. Borzaga & J. Deforny (Eds.), *The emergence of social enterprise* (pp. 273–295) London: Routledge.

Bacchiega, A., & Borzaga, C. (2003). The economics of the third sector: Towards a more comprehensive approach. In H. K. Anheier & A. Ben-Ner (Eds.), *The study of the nonprofit enterprise, theories and approaches*. Dordrecht: Kulwer.

Baron, D. (2007). Corporate social responsibility and social entrepreneurship. *Journal of Economics and Management Strategy*, *16*(3), 683–717.

Becchetti, L., & Borzaga, C. (2010). *The economics of social responsibility. The world of social enterprises*. London: Routledge.

Ben-Ner, A., & Putterman, L. (1998). *Economics, values, and organization*. Cambridge: Cambridge University Press.

Borzaga, C., & Defourny, J. (Eds.). (2001). *The emergence of social enterprises*. London: Routledge.

Borzaga, C., & Depedri, S. (2005). Inter-personal relations and job satisfaction: Some empirical results in social and community care services. In B. Gui & R. Sugden (Eds.), *Economics and social interaction: Accounting for personal relations*. Cambridge: Cambridge University Press.

Borzaga, C., & Depedri, S. (2013). When social enterprises do it better: Efficiency and efficacy of work integration in the Italian social cooperatives. In S. Denny & F. Seddon (Eds.),

Social enterprise. Accountability and evaluation around the world (pp. 85–101). London: Routledge.

Borzaga, C., & Galera, G. (2012). New opportunities for cooperatives in the changing landscape of the welfare systems. In J. Heiskanen, H. Henry, P. Hytinkoski, & T. Koppa (Eds.), *New opportunities for co-operatives: New opportunities for people, Mikkeli* (pp. 14–24). Finland: University of Helsinki.

Borzaga, C., & Tortia, E. (2007). Social economy organizations in the theory of the firm. In A. Noya & E. Clearence (Eds.), *The social economy. Building inclusive economies.* Paris: OECD Publications.

Boschee, J. (2006). Social entrepreneurship: The promise and the perils. In A. Nicholls (Ed.), *Social entrepreneurship. New models of sustainable social change* (pp. 356–390). Oxford: Oxford University Press.

CECOP. (1996). *Social enterprises: An opportunity for Europe.* First European conference on social co-operation, Research on social co-operation in Europe, Brussels.

Dees, G. (1998). *The meaning of social entrepreneurship.* Retrieved from http://www.caseat-duke.org/documents/dees_sedef.pdf

Defourny, J., & Nyssens, M. (2008). *Social enterprisein Europe: Recent trends and developments.* EMES Working Paper No. 08/01. Bergische Universitäet Wuppertal. Retrieved from http://www.emes.net/site/wp-content/uploads/WP_08_01_SE_WEB.pdf

Defourny, J., & Nyssens, M. (2014). Social co-operatives: When social enterprises meet the co-operative tradition. *Journal of Entrepreneurial and Organizational Diversity – JEOD, 2*(2), 11–33. doi:10.5947/jeod.2013.008

Eikenberry, A., & Kluver, J. (2004). The marketization of the nonprofit sector: Civil society at risk? *Public Administration Review, 64*(2), 132–140.

Euricse. (2013). La Cooperazione Italiana negli Anni della Crisi, 2° Rapporto Euricse.

European Commission. (2011). *Social Business Initiative: Creating a favourable climate for social enterprises, key stakeholders in the social economy and innovation.* Communication from the Commission to the European Parliament, the Council, the European economic and social Committee and the Committee of the Regions.

Evers, A. (1998). Consumers, citizens and co-producers. In G. Floesser & H. U. Otto (Eds.), *Towards more democracy in social services.* Berlin: Walter de Gruyter.

Galera, G. (2009). The re-emergence of social enterprises in the CEE and CIS. In S. Destefanis & M. Musella (Eds.), *Paid and unpaid labour in the social economy* (pp. 245–260). AIEL Series in Labour Economics. Heidelberg: Physica-Verlag.

Galera, G. (2010). Social enterprises and work-integration. In L. Becchetti & C. Borzaga (Eds.), *The economics of social responsibility* (pp. 105–122). London: Routledge.

Galera, G., & Borzaga, C. (2009). Social enterprise. An international overview of its conceptual evolution and legal implementation. *Social Enterprise Journal, 5*(3), 210–228.

Giddens, A. (2007). *L'Europa nell'Età Globale.* Roma-Bari: Laterza.

Hansmann, H. (1996). *The ownership of the firm.* Harvard: Harvard University Press.

Helm, S. T., & Andersson, F. O. (2010). An empirical validation of social entrepreneurship in the nonprofit sector. *Nonprofit Management and Leadership, 20*(3), 259–276.

Johnson, S. (2000). *Literature review on social entrepreneurship.* Edmonton: Canadian Centre for Social Entrepreneurship.

Kerlin, J. (2010). A comparative analysis of the global emergence of social enterprise. *Voluntas, 21,* 162–179.

Lee, M., & Battilana, J. (2013). *How the zebra got its stripes: Imprinting of individuals and hybrid social ventures.* Working Paper No. 14-005. Harvard Business School.

Light. (2006). Reshaping social entrepreneurship. *Stanford Social Innovation Review*, *4*(3), 46–51.

Mair, J., & Martì, I. (2006). Social entrepreneurship research: A source of explanation, prediction, and delight. *Journal of World Business*, *41*, 36–44.

Nicholls, A. (2006). Playing the field: A new approach to the meaning of social entrepreneurship. *Social Enterprise Journal*, *2*(1), 1–5.

Nyssens, M. (2006). *Social enterprise*. New York, NY: Routledge.

OECD. (2009). *L'Emploi public:un Etat des lieux*. Paris: OECD. Retrieved from http://www.oecdbookshop.org/oecd/display.asp?sf1=identifiers&st1=9789264055902

Pache, A.-C., & Santos, F. (2013). Embedded in hybrid contexts: How individuals in organizations respond to competing institutional logics. *Research in the Sociology of Organizations*, *39*, 3–35.

Pestoff, V. (2008). *A democratic architecture for the welfare state*. New York, NY: Routledge. ISBN: 0-415-47595-2 (hbk), 0-203-88873-1 (ebk)

Porter, M. (2011). *Rethinking capitalism*: Harvard Business Publishing. Available at http://blogs.hbr.org/2011/01rethinking-capitalism/

Reis, T. (1999). *Unleashing the new resources and entrepreneurship for the common good: A scan, synthesis and scenario for action*. Battle Creek, MI: W.K. Kellogg Foundation: 27.

Regulator of Community Interest Companies. (2012). Annual report 2011–2012. Community Interest Company Regulator, 2011–2012 Annual Report, Cardiff.

Roper, J., & Cheney, G. (2005). The meanings of social entrepreneurship today. *Corporate Governance*, *5*(3), 95–104.

Sabeti, H. (2011). The for-benefit enterprise. *Harvard Business Review*, *89*(11), 98–1040.

Santos, F. M. (2012). A positive theory of social entrepreneurship. *Journal of Business Ethics*, *111*, 335–351.

Sassmannshausen, S. P., & Volkmann, C. (2013). *A bibliometric based review on social entrepreneurship and its establishment as a field of research*. Scumpeter Discussion Paper 2013-003.

Somerville, P., & McElwee, G. (2011). Situating community enterprise: A theoretical exploration. *Entrepreneurship & Regional Development*, *23*(5–6), 317–330. doi:10.1080/08985626.2011.580161

Stiglitz, D. J. (2009). Moving beyond market fundamentalism to a more balanced economy. *Annals of Public and Cooperative Economics*, *80*(3), 345–360.

Valentinov, V. (2008). The economics of the non-distribution constraint: A critical appraisal. *The Annals of Public and Cooperative Economics*, *79*(1), 35–52.

Vamstad, J. (2012). Co-production and service quality: The case of cooperative childcare in Sweden. *Voluntas*, *23*, 1173–1188.

Waddock, S. A., & Post, J. E. (1991). Social entrepreneurs and catalytic change. *Public Administration Review*, *51*(5), 393–401.

Weerawardena, J., & Sullivan Mort, G. (2006). Investigating social entrepreneurship: A multidimensional model. *Journal of World Business*, *41*, 21–35.

Young, D. (2013, July 1–4). If not for profit, for what? Conference paper presented at the 4th EMES International Research Conference on Social Enterprise, Liège, Belgium.

Zahra, S. A., Gedajlovic, E., Neubaum, D. O., & Shulman, J. M. (2009). A typology of social entrepreneurs: Motives, search processes and ethical challenges. *Journal of Business Venturing*, *24*(5), 519–532.

PART III
ACCOUNTING AND ACCOUNTABILITIES FOR THE NON-PROFIT SECTOR

INTENTIONS, OBSERVATIONS, AND DECISIONS: METRICS IN INSURANCE CO-OPERATIVES

Louis Beaubien and Daphne Rixon

ABSTRACT

Purpose – *To examine metrics used for performance measurement, analysis, and decision-making by insurance cooperatives.*

Design and approach – *A documentary review and semi-structured interviews of three large insurance cooperatives form the basis of the study.*

Findings – *The analysis suggests insurance co-operatives metrics are consistent with investor-owned companies. These measures do not recognize the cooperative principles and values which consistent the formative basis of these insurance co-operatives.*

Practical implications – *The insurance co-operatives under examination do not engage in a comparison to other insurance co-operatives; rather comparisons are made against investor-owned companies. As this analysis is used in decision-making and strategy formulation, guiding the direction of the co-operatives the questions must be raised: does the co-operative*

Accountability and Social Accounting for Social and Non-profit Organizations
Advances in Public Interest Accounting, Volume 17, 113–127

ISSN: 1041-7060/doi:10.1108/S1041-706020140000017004

difference exist in the insurance sector and how (and what) performance analysis tools are used to assess their performance?

Originality – *There is a paucity of research in the area of metrics and analytics of co-operatives. As such this article expands the academic scope of examination of co-operatives in the context of financial and accounting operations. Additionally, it adds to the ongoing discussion in the academy focused on the nature of co-operatives and the nature of the co-operative difference.*

Keywords: Co-operatives; performance analysis; metrics; decision-making

INTRODUCTION

Co-operatives (Co-op) are a form of business that is distinct from the Investor Owned Companies (IOC) model. They are founded on the principles of collective ownership, with voluntary membership and democratic governance. While the co-op must operate under a financial imperative to ensure that it is able to be a sustainable economic enterprise, its primary purpose is to provide benefit to its membership (Birchall & Simmons, 2004). Members of co-ops are also customers and/or suppliers; as a result the economic actions of the firm must not act in such a fashion as to create a financial boon for the co-op, while at the same time impairing its members. Thus, co-ops act in a unique and "symbiotic" (Mazzarol, Limnios, & Reboud, 2013) relationship with customers and suppliers – where strategies and actions must be balanced to ensure satisfaction of both priorities.

Birchall and Simmons (2004) note that many co-ops utilize the co-operative principles as part of their mission, vision, and values statements, but there is little evidence that these sentiments are prescriptive in the operationalization of strategy. Hicks, Maddocks, Robb, and Webb (2007; see also Brown & Hicks, 2007) concur and extend this critique noting very few co-ops assess performance in relation to the principles. Given this variation in business practices, it is worthwhile asking, *How do cooperatives measure their performance?* And further, *Can Co-ops effectively attain their priority of fulfilling members' needs if they are not measuring activities in this area?*

The purpose of this article is to examine the metrics used for performance measurement, analysis, and decision-making by insurance co-operatives. Insurance co-operatives were selected for this study over other types of co-operatives in order to explore how co-operatives in the highly regulated financial services sector are influenced by the sector in which they operate. In addition, we were also interested in exploring if insurance co-operatives attempted to differentiate themselves from Investor Owned Companies (IOCs) in light of the financial crisis of 2008. In other words, how does the co-operative difference and the seven principles of co-operatives impact performance reporting of a regulated financial services co-operative in a post 2008 environment.

This article contributes to the literature by providing insight on the current practices of performance measurement in insurance co-operatives and theorizes how they have evolved. The discussion herein shall proceed as follows: The section "Co-operatives in the Literature" will review the extant literature on performance reporting, in particular how it relates to co-operatives; the section "Methodology" and "Case Study Findings: Discussion And Analysis" will discuss the methodology of the study and present the findings and analysis; and, the conclusions are presented in the section "Conclusion."

CO-OPERATIVES IN THE LITERATURE

Co-ops operate with a strong social purpose that is not always immediately measureable in financial terms. The "social purpose" is unique to each co-op and the context in which it is founded and is guided by the seven co-operative principles.[1] For example, a worker co-op may focus on providing gainful employment, training and education to a community. An alternative form of co-op might be a healthcare co-operative, which might focus on pooling resources to guarantee affordable, ready, and effective healthcare to its membership – something that might not be possible on an individual basis. However, this presents a third objective to which co-ops must be directed in addition to economic sustainability and member benefit.

Given the complicated rubric to which co-ops are matched, reliable ways to measure their success and performance are essential (Novkovic, 2008). Performance Analysis (PA) techniques, such as benchmarking are common, structured, and systematized and rely on the notion that an organization can identify a causal relationship between action and result, and by adjusting action, it can improve results (Dattakumar & Jagadeesh, 2003; Vera-Munoz, Shackell, & Buehner, 2007). However, despite widespread use, questions arise as to the accuracy of deemed "best practices" in PA, suggesting the causal relationships were not tested; the establishment of action-performance was not reliable; and, the resulting information was highly contextual (Ballou, Earley, & Rich, 2004; Banker, Potter, & Srinivasan, 2000; Ittner & Larker, 2003; Ittner, Larker, & Meyer, 2003; Maines et al., 2002).

Rixon and Ellwood (2011) point out common best-practice PAs cross over the threshold from IOCs to the public-sector, non-profit and charity organizations, and cooperatives. The choice of PA techniques and data is driven by the industry – both informal and formal factors (*ibid.*, Dattakumar & Jagadeesh, 2003). However, Taylor (2007; see also Parmenter, 2012; Sun, Salama, Hussainey, & Habbash, 2010) urge caution, citing agency effects may contribute to the choice of key performance indicators (KPI). Rather than serving as a true indicator of the organizations performance, they may be adopted and followed to satisfy the needs of particular agents rather than stakeholders and co-operative members. Leading the prevailing measures of success subject to the institutional influences of significant participants in the field, that is, the largest competitors (Beaubien, 2008; Moerman & Van Der Laan, 2005), and not necessarily what will provide the best information for decision-making (Malina & Selto, 2004). Given that Co-ops operate in many of the same industries as IOCs (Beaubien, 2011), this engenders the question: *How (and What) PA tools do co-ops use to assess their performance and does the co-op difference exist in the insurance sector?*

Lipe and Salterio (2000, 2002) argue a subjective perception of what information is "useful" is the most poignant influence in the selection and use of PA tools and measures. Ittner et al. (2003; see also Gibbs, Merchant, & van der Stede, 2004; Murphy & Oyer, 2001) suggest that a number of factors are relevant in PA tool selection including environmental and economic issues, as well as behavioral motivations and norms (e.g., the ability to achieve a measure and potential reward). While there is a documented bias toward economic and financial data in measure selection (Lambert, 2001; Liang, 2010), considerations such as the ability to use financial data as a proxy for non-financial data or the desire to avoid "too much" information also impact the decision of PA tool selection (Ittner et al., 2003).

Malina and Selto (2004) extend Kaplan and Norton's (2001) long-standing guidance for "balanced" approaches to performance measurement and analysis, including data on financial performance, growth and evolution, internal operations and stakeholder, and customer assessments. In an empirical study of a US manufacturing firm, the authors counter common practice of minimal and focused PA tools and assert organizations benefit from a greater diversity of measurements – both strategic and tactical in nature, both financial and non-financial in form. Vera-Munoz et al. (2007) suggest that this practice of linking industry benchmarks to decision-making can be helpful, but makes the implicit assumption that all market participants have similar goals and priorities. And further, measures that are incorrect or not aligned with strategic direction can have detrimental effects on the long-term success of the organization (Cavaluzzo & Ittner, 2004; Malina & Selto, 2004).

Passey (2005) states that by using the cooperative principles, a co-op, "differentiates itself from, and competes with, other types of organizations" (p. 29) – in other words, they are representative of the "co-operative difference." And, as by definition they represent the priorities of a co-op, they should be instructive on the strategic directions of the firm. (Novkovic, 2008; see also Novkovic, 2006; Spear, 2000) while there is general awareness of the co-operative principles it may be possible that because it is not a statutory requirement to report on the organization's performance vis-à-vis the co-operative principles, they do not do so. This may be in part due to the additional costs and effort required in such reporting, or it may be a result of familiarity with such reports being of added value as the "industry" has already established through, time and practice, what is expected in the form of reporting (Beaubien, 2008). Given the absence of influence of the co-operative principles in strategic reporting or planning, it may indicate a discontinuity between co-operatives and the "co-operative identity" (Hicks et al., 2007; Novkovic, 2006).

Hicks et al. (2007) point out that despite the nominal or stated importance of the co-operative principles, the principles are rarely seen explicitly in operating strategies and co-operatives are almost never measured against the ability to attain these principles. All this, despite ubiquitous mention of the co-operative principles in the mission, vision and value statements of these same organizations (see also: Birchall & Simmons, 2004; Brown & Hicks, 2007). Given this variation in business practices, it is worthwhile asking, *How do cooperatives measure their performance?* And further, *Can Co-ops effectively attain their priority of fulfilling members' needs if they are not measuring activities in this area?*

METHODOLOGY

Three insurance co-ops – two in North America (one in Canada and one in the United States) and one in the United Kingdom were adopted for this case study. The authors' motivation for choosing this industry was to examine whether the financial crisis of 2008 resulted in any attempts by co-operatives to emphasize their co-operative difference from Investor Owned Companies (IOCs). Since IOCs had come under significant public scrutiny as a result of the financial crisis, this might represent an opportune time to stress to the public that insurance co-operatives were significantly different from Investor Owned Companies.

One co-operative industrial sector was chosen to facilitate a comprehensive analysis through documentary reviews and semi-structured interviews with those involved in developing annual reports and various other reports such as sustainability and corporate social responsibility reports. The three focal organizations are among the largest in each of their respective countries.

The study was comprised of semi-structured interviews with 22 respondents and a documentary review of the KPIs published by the cooperatives spanning five years. The documentary review included annual reports, sustainability reports, corporate social responsibility reports, and websites. The KPIs were reported in various locations by each co-operative and the locations were not consistent from one co-operative to another. For example, one co-operative reported non-financial KPIs in its annual report, while another reporting similar KPIs in its corporate social responsibility report. To gain a better understanding of the documentary data, face-to-face interviews were held with members of senior management, ranging from managers and directors to vice-presidents of the focal organizations. Multiple representatives from each cooperative were interviewed since several departments contributed to the reports and were responsible to report on various aspects of the cooperatives' operations. The interviews were audio taped, transcribed and, coded using NVivo software.

CASE STUDY FINDINGS: DISCUSSION AND ANALYSIS

Over the five-year period covered in this study, many changes in non-financial reporting were observed. These changes were attributed to mergers and acquisitions and the resulting difficulty encountered in presenting comparable data. In addition, one insurance cooperative is part of larger co-op group that offered banking, investment services, and grocery stores. Consequently, the KPIs reflect its consolidated operations, rather than each line of business, with the exception of a few insurance-specific measures such as claims loss ratio, combined ratio, and capital adequacy.

KPIs reported by the cooperatives are depicted in Tables 1 and 2. As illustrated in Table 1, the majority of the KPIs are financial in nature. This is not surprising since insurance co-operatives are operating in the financial services sector. The KPIs reported by insurance co-operatives are largely unique to the financial services sector. According to Rixon (2013), credit unions also used similar KPIs. The literature review did not identify other studies on KPIs in the financial services sector. The significant number of financial KPIs reported by North American co-operatives relative to non-financial is explained by two respondents:

> The reality is your return on investment and your growth that sustains you ... if you don't have a reasonable return on investment, how do you sustain your business. (R1).
> Financial strength is critical, because if you don't have it, you can't do much of anything else. (R2)

Of the 14 financial KPIs depicted in Table 1, nine (64%) are specific to the insurance sector. The remaining financial indicators, comprised of dividend coverage ratio, shareholder net income, return on capital, net income and assumptions, are relevant for other industrial sectors and are also reported by Investor Owned Companies. The research found that insurance Co-ops strive to maintain comparable to the commercial sector for combined ratio, loss ratio, and expense ratio. These ratios measure efficiency and effectiveness in managing insurance claims. However, it could be argued that return on equity, return on capital, and net income for Co-ops might have a lower target than pure maximization of shareholder wealth. The minimum capital adequacy indicator is required by government regulators in North America and the United Kingdom. Of the KPIs listed in Table 1, only the minimum capital adequacy indicator is required by regulators.

Table 2 depicts the remaining KPIs which are grouped into non-financial categories including: staff profile; community investment; members; and environment. None of the KPIs in Table 2 are required by regulators.

A high-level examination of selected, investor owned insurance companies in Canada, the United States, and the United Kingdom that were comparable in terms of asset size found that the issue of regulation was discussed in the Management Discussion and Analysis and CEO letters in annual reports, but the actual metric was not publicly reported.

In addition to the IOCs examined, there were very few KPIs reported. The non-financial KPIs reported focuses on environmental measures such

Table 1. Financial Indicators.

Title	Description
Gross written premium	Component of revenue which represents the total insurance sales transactions
Return on equity	Ratio of net income to the average of opening and closing shareholders' equity excluding accumulated other comprehensive income
Combined ratio	Ratio of total expenses to net earned premium, expressed as a percentage
Loss ratio	Ratio of claims and adjustment expenses to net earned premium, expressed as a percentage
Expense ratio	Ratio of the total premium and other taxes, commissions, and agent compensation and general expenses to net earned premium, expressed as a percentage
Claims development	It represents the difference between any prior estimates in the claims costs and the claims costs actually paid on closed claims, plus any change in estimates for claims still open or unreported
Minimum capital test	Regulatory formula-driven, risk-based test of capital available over capital required (by government regulation)
Dividend coverage ratio	Measure of a company's liability to pay dividends due to its shareholders out of its current year earnings. It is calculated as a net income divided by dividends declared
Assets under management	Total assets that we manage to earn profits. It includes both assets on our balance sheet and segregated funds. It is an indicator of business volume
Shareholder net income	Portion of net income which will provide capital to support products or fund dividends to policyholders
Return on required capital (ROC)	Is the ratio of net income of a business segment to the average of opening and closing required capital
Net income	Refers to the income amounts that have been adjusted for income taxes and par for transfer to shareholders
New annualized premiums	Full year premium of new products sales
Assumption changes	Present value impact on actuarial liabilities due to changes in actuarial assumptions, changes to margin levels in actuarial liabilities, changes to actuarial methodologies, and error corrections made during the year

as greenhouse gas emissions, employee paper use, and corporate social responsibility which include the dollar amount of donations to various charities. Meanwhile, another investor owned insurance companies provided a description of its environmental and corporate social responsibility initiatives, but did not report quantifiable measures. Of the three countries examined in this case study, the United Kingdom provided the highest

Table 2. Non-Financial Measures.

Measure	Category
Number of employees	Staff profile
Employee turnover	Staff profile
Employee engagement	Staff profile
Community investment	Community investment
Percentage of pre-tax profit invested	Community investment
Staff volunteering	Community investment
Total members	Members
Tons of CO_2	Environment
Energy used	Environment
Renewable energy	Environment
Total mileage	Environment

number of non-financial KPIs, followed by Canada, with the United States reporting the lowest number of measures.

As illustrated in Table 2, the majority of the non-financial indicators are not specific to the insurance sector. For example, staff profile, community investment, members, and environment are applicable for all Co-ops.

The documentary review revealed that the choice of KPIs in the participant organizations was informed by their practice of comparing performance against IOC benchmarks (e.g., profitability) rather than a more customary measurement of a co-op's success such as education of the membership or support for other co-ops (Hicks et al., 2007). Respondents indicated that comparisons to co-op insurance organizations are difficult due to size and variation in operations. One respondent explained further they would "never think to compare ourselves to other Co-ops," rather, they compare to other financial services companies.

The extent of reliance on comparison to IOC benchmarks rather than Co-op benchmarks may be explained by management perceptions. Some of the respondents believed the KPIs used by cooperatives should be the same as those used by IOCs:

> [KPIs] they're exactly the same as the industry. There would be no reason for them to be different … .where I think you might find there's a difference is if you look at ROE or ROI. (R3)

The choice of benchmark may also have been influenced by the Co-op's perceptions of what constitutes a valid comparison. Respondents emphasized the importance of comparing to other cooperative benchmarks. They believed comparison of large co-ops with small co-ops would not be valid or reliable. Respondents contended that they had to compare IOC insurance companies because there was an insufficient number of insurance co-ops in similar size that could be sued for comparison purposes.

With respect to setting market prices, the determination of standards of production quality, and appropriate levels of profitability and return, IOCs are more influential in industries in which they compete with co-ops (Rixon, 2011). This position of primacy is often due to greater economic resources, their number (there are typically fewer cooperatives than IOC firms), and recognition in the marketplace by participants such as analysts and industry commentators. When asked how an insurance Co-op determined targets or benchmarks for their strategic plans, respondents indicated they acquire industry data from research companies and rating agencies such as JD Power and Gallop. Insurance benchmark data is available from trade associations such as the Canadian Life and Health Insurance Association, International Cooperative and Mutual Insurance Federation, and Insurance Institute for Highway Safety.

The examination of the three insurance Co-ops in this study suggests that while there is recognition of the Co-op principles, particularly in influencing organizational culture, they are not reflected in their operational KPIs. The participants in this study developed their strategies to satisfy performance measurements that are benchmarked against IOC organizations that have goals that are explicitly different from Co-ops (Hicks et al., 2007). Conversely, Cote (2000) argued that the methods of performance evaluation of Co-ops should be consistent and reflect the Co-op principles, despite the fact that contemporary studies show that Co-op members are not always familiar with what the principles of the cooperative are (e.g., Birchall, 1998). Thus, while Co-op principles may be valued explicitly, IOC principles are implicitly given greater value, as they are the governing components in the development of practice and strategy. This engenders the question: *do cooperatives give up their identity as a "cooperative" in the adoption of IOC appropriate performance indicators and benchmarks?*

While the financial KPIs detailed in Table 1 are representative of organizations operating in the insurance sector – both Co-op and IOC firms, most of the non-financial measures have representative elements that suggest an awareness of social issues that are consistent with Co-op principles, for example, tons of CO_2 produced, community investment, and number of members. However, it is important to recognize that non-financial measures such as tons of CO_2 produced, charitable donations, and shares outstanding are reported by IOCs. Staff volunteerism and engagement appear to be two forms of reporting that are unique to the Co-ops studied here.

Since only two measures out of 26 reflect Co-op principles, this is unlikely to substantively differentiate cooperatives from IOC firms.

Scott (2008) utilizes the term isomorphism as a foundational concept of Institutional Theory. He asserts organizational values, structures, and practices are socially legitimized by organizations that are deemed to be powerful and adopted by other organizations in a network through imitative pressures (see also, DiMaggio & Powell, 1983). Bernal, Pinzón, and Espejo (2005) discusses such imitative adoption in a study of public-sector organizations adopting double-entry accounting as a result of pressure to appear to be consistent with organizations perceived to be legitimate and correct, that is, the private sector. The adoption of standards and procedures is important as it influences day-to-day practice and thereby alters behavioral norms and values, which can alter the strategic direction and decision-making processes of an organization (Beaubien, 2008; DiMaggio & Powell, 1983).

The data in this case suggests that isomorphic pressures may be influencing insurance Co-ops in their adoption of IOCs commonly used PA tools and KPI, particularly as they do not reflect or address Co-op values. The adoption of practices, values, and regulations consistent with industry leading firms may foster the same appearance in other firms. This is commonly referred to as *normative isomorphism* and may provide Insurance Co-ops an air of acceptance which may advance business prospects by increasing business and a greater presence in the marketplace. However, it may also result in a shift away from the organization's core values in favor of the *norm*. Additionally, von Alberti-Alhtaybat, Hutaibat, and Al-Htaybat (2012) point out disclosure theory and argue that disclosure is the price paid for the benefit of limited liability. However there is an asymmetry of information between those within the organization, which make choices about the disclosures, and those outside the firm that might consume the information (or, in another facet of the firm). As these disclosures are voluntary, there is the potential for agency problems to arise (e.g., Taylor, 2007) and KPI are chosen and communicated for reasons other than impacting organizational performance.

In other words, more disruptive forms of isomorphism exist in the form of mimetic and coercive isomorphism. And, these forms may emerge at various times as isomorphic pressures alongside, following, or preceding normative isomorphism. For instance, *mimetic isomorphism* is the deliberate copying of another organization's (or, group of organizations') practices and values, as they are perceived to be "best practices" and will provide superior results. Rather than the somewhat passive alteration of the organization that occurs in normative processes, mimetic shifts represent conscious choices by the organization to step away from past practices and values in favor of a new and "more legitimate" set of behaviors.

In other words, mimetic pressures may be enacted by, and in turn enact normative pressures in process as various components of the organization change and adapt to particular KPI – all for different reasons. And additionally, coercive isomorphism may also be a component of the aggregate isomorphic pressures that is a channel for change. In contrast to the previous forms of isomorphism, which generally are internally motivated changes (Scott, 2008), *coercive isomorphism* is compliance for the sake of survival, "rather than the possible improvements to the organization that occur in the previous forms. For instance, insurance Co-ops adopt KPIs and benchmarks in association with industry practice in order to qualify for access markets to raise capital" (Beaubien & Rixon, 2012).

Respondents in the case study suggested that many of the goals of their organizations were chosen as a result of industry standard benchmarks, rather than internally developed priorities. As such, KPI reporting was adopted to provide feedback on strategies that were designed to attain these goals – goals developed by IOCs rather than Co-ops. As Kerr (1975) notes, it is unlikely that a strategy where "A" (fulfillment of the co-operative principles) is hoped for will be achieved if the only feedback comes from measuring "B" (goals developed by IOCs).

CONCLUSIONS

The research question posed at the outset of this article was: *How (and What) performance analysis tools do Co-ops use to assess their performance and does the Co-op difference exist in the insurance sector?* Through our analysis of three insurance Co-ops, the research found that performance is aligned with IOC firms in the same industry. This study contributes to the literature on Co-ops through its findings that insurance Co-ops use IOC benchmarks to evaluate performance. Moreover, the research extends the literature on cooperative benchmarking through its examination of the possible influences on why the Co-ops adopt IOC benchmarks to measure and evaluate performance.

The findings of this study provide considerable scope for further research. For example, it would be beneficial to examine how the adoption of IOC benchmarks has impacted the Co-op identity. Furthermore, it would also be worthwhile to conduct further research on other Co-op industrial sectors, to determine if these findings are unique to the insurance sector.

The Co-ops in this study have adopted practices and values more consistent with IOCs than with Co-op and it could be argued that this will influence to shape and structure their identity as something more similar to an IOC than a Co-op. Institutional Theory provides an interesting perspective from which to view the practices of an organization or industry. It is possible to focus the lens on macro processes such as isomorphic changes in organizations and to examine these changes at closer levels of abstraction – inspecting the individual and intertwined influences of normative, mimetic, and coercive pressures.

NOTE

1. Cooperatives are established to meet member and community needs, and are governed by seven guiding principles, including: voluntary and opened membership; democratic member control; member's economic participation; autonomy and independence; education, training and information; cooperation among cooperatives; and concern for community (ICA, 1995).

REFERENCES

Ballou, B., Earley, C., & Rich, J. (2004). The impact of strategic-positioning information on auditor judgments about business process performance. *Auditing: A Journal of Practice & Theory*, *23*(2), 71–88.

Banker, R., Potter, G., & Srinivasan, D. (2000). An empirical investigation of an incentive plan that includes non-financial performance measures. *The Accounting Review*, *75*(1), 65–92.

Beaubien, L. (2008). Constitutive practice and institutional change: Ethics and behavior. *Journal of Accounting and Organizational Change*, *4*(1), 47–66.

Beaubien, L. (2011). Cooperative accounting: Disclosing redemption contingencies for member shares. *Journal of Cooperative Studies*, *44*(3), 38–54.

Beaubien, L., & Rixon, D. (2012). Key performance indicators in co-operatives. *Journal of Co-operative Studies*, *45*(2), 51–69.

Bernal, M. C., Pinzón, P. A., & Espejo, C. (2005). Accounting regulation, inertia and organizational self-perception: Double-entry adoption in a Spanish casa de comercio accounting. *Business and Financial History*, *15*(2), 145–169.

Birchall, J. (1998). Co-operative values, principles and practices: A commentary. *Journal of Cooperative Studies*, *30*(2), 42–69.

Birchall, J., & Simmons, R. (2004). What motivates members to participate in co-operative and mutual businesses? *Annals of Public & Cooperative Economics*, *75*(3), 465–495.

Brown, L., & Hicks, E. (2007). Accounting for the social: Incorporating indicators of the cooperative difference into strategic planning. *CIRIEC conference*. Victoria, BC.

Cavaluzzo, K., & Ittner, C. D. (2004). Implementing performance measurement innovations: Evidence from government. *Accounting, Organizations and Society*, *29*(2), 243–267.

Cote, D. (2000). Cooperatives and the new millennium: The emergence of a new paradigm. In B. Fairbairn & N. Russell (Eds.), *Cooperative membership and globalisation*. Saskatchewan: Centre for the Study of Cooperatives.

Dattakumar, R., & Jagadeesh, R. (2003). A review of literature on benchmarking. *Benchmarking: An International Journal*, *10*(3), 176–209.

DiMaggio, P., & Powell, W. W. (1983). The iron cage revisited: Institutional isomorphism and collective rationality in organizational fields. *American Sociological Review*, *48*, 147–160.

Gibbs, M., Merchant, K., & van der Stede, W. (2004). Determinants and effects of subjectivity in incentives. *The Accounting Review*, *79*(2), 409–436.

Hicks, E., Maddocks, J., Robb, A., & Webb, T. (2007). Cooperative accountability and identity: An examination of reporting practices in nova scotia cooperatives. *Journal of Cooperative Studies*, *40*(2), 4–16.

International Cooperative Alliance (ICA). (1995). *International cooperative alliance: Statues*. Geneva: ICA.

Ittner, C. D., & Larker, D. F. (2003). Coming up short on non-financial measures. *Harvard Business Review*, (November), 88–95.

Ittner, C. D., Larker, D. F., & Meyer, M. W. (2003). Subjectivity and weighting of performance measures: Evidence from a balanced scorecard. *The Accounting Review*, *78*(3), 725–758.

Kaplan, R. S., & Norton, D. P. (2001). *The strategy-focused organization: How balanced scorecard companies thrive in the new business environment*. Cambridge, MA: Harvard.

Kerr, S. (1975). On the folly of rewarding A, while hoping for B. *The Academy of Management Journal*, *18*(4), 769–783.

Lambert, R. (2001). Contracting theory and accounting. *Journal of Accounting and Economics*, *32*(1–3), 3–87.

Liang, P. (2010). Equilibrium earnings management, incentive contracts, and accounting standards. *Contemporary Accounting Research*, *21*(3), 685–718.

Lipe, M. G., & Salterio, S. (2000). The balanced scorecard: The judgmental effects of common and unique performance measures. *The Accounting Review*, *75*(3), 283–298.

Lipe, M. G., & Salterio, S. (2002). A note on the judgemental effects of the balanced scorecard's information organization. *Accounting, Organizations and Society*, *27*(6), 531–540.

Maines, L., Bartov, E., Fairfield, P., Hirst, E., Innaconi, T., Mellett, R., ... Vincent, L. (2002). Recommendations on the disclosure of non-financial measures – A commentary. *Accounting Horizons*, *16*(4), 353–362.

Malina, M. A., & Selto, F. (2004). Choice and change of measures in performance measurement models. *Management Accounting Research*, *15*(4), 441–469.

Mazzarol, T., Limnios, E. M., & Reboud, S. (2013). Co-operatives as a strategic network of small firms: Case studies from Australian and French co-operatives. *Journal of Co-operative Organization and Management*, *1*(1), 27–40.

Moerman, L., & Van Der Laan, S. (2005). Social reporting in the tobacco industry: All smoke and mirrors? *Accounting, Auditing & Accountability Journal, 18*(3), 374–389.

Murphy, K. J., & Oyer, P. (2001). *Discretion in executive incentive contracts: Theory and evidence.*

Novkovic, S. (2006). Cooperative business: The role of cooperative principles and values. *Journal of Cooperative Studies, 39*(1), 5–15.

Novkovic, S. (2008). Defining the co-operative difference. *The Journal of Socio-Economics, 37*(6), 2168–2177.

Parmenter, D. (2012). *Key performance indicators for government and non profit agencies: Implementing winning KPIs.* Hoboken, NJ: Wiley.

Passey, A. (2005). Cooperative principles as "action recipes": What does their articulation mean for cooperative futures? *Journal of Cooperative Studies, 38*(1), 28–41.

Rixon, D. (2011). Are cooperative principles reflected in key performance indicators? A case study of insurance cooperatives. *International workshop on accounting for cooperatives.* Valencia, Spain.

Rixon, D. (2013). *Credit union performance reporting in North America.* Madison, WI: Filene Research Institute.

Rixon, D., & Ellwood, S. (2011). Reporting for public sector agencies: A stakeholder model. In S. Osborne & A. Ball (Eds.), *Social accounting and public management: Accountability for the public good.* London: Routledge.

Scott, W. R. (2008). *Institutions and organizations.* Thousand Oaks, CA: Sage.

Spear, R. (2000). Reasserting the cooperative advantage project – Overview. *Journal of Cooperative Studies, 33*(2), 95–101.

Sun, N., Salama, A., Hussainey, K., & Habbash, M. (2010). Corporate environmental disclosure, corporate governance and earnings management. *Managerial Auditing Journal, 25*(7), 679–700.

Taylor, J. (2007). The usefulness of key performance indicators to public accountability authorities in east Asia. *Public Administration and Development, 27*(4), 341–352.

Vera-Munoz, S. C., Shackell, M., & Buehner, M. (2007). Accountants' usage of causal business models in the presence of benchmark data: A note. *Contemporary Accounting Research, 24*(3), 1015–1038.

von Alberti-Alhtaybat, L., Hutaibat, K., & Al-Htaybat, K. (2012). Mapping corporate disclosure theories. *Journal of Financial Reporting and Accounting, 10*(1), 73–94.

THE EFFECTS OF THE ACCOUNTING RECLASSIFICATION OF MEMBERS' SHARES IN COOPERATIVES: AN APPROACH

Fernando Polo-Garrido

ABSTRACT

This study addresses the effects of the accounting reclassification of members' shares in Spanish cooperatives motivated by the new accounting standards. The study reports the results of semi-structured in-depth interviews with experts. The accounting reclassification from equity to liability of members' shares has effects even if there is no actual material change in terms of the members' shares. Thus cooperatives are incentivised to modify their statutes in order to retain their equity accounting classification, even when this modification is not desired. The evidence is obtained from qualitative methods and a generalization using quantitative methods would be interesting if data were available. The present study provides a starting-point for further research into the use of lending technologies in the financing of cooperatives and the use of accounting information in granting bank finance to cooperatives, thereby contributing to the study of the use of accounting information by capital providers.

Accountability and Social Accounting for Social and Non-profit Organizations
Advances in Public Interest Accounting, Volume 17, 129–149

ISSN: 1041-7060/doi:10.1108/S1041-706020140000017005

There is very little literature on the effects of equity-liability accounting reclassification motivated by a change in an accounting standard. The study takes advantage of the recent accounting standard change in Spain which may be considered as a 'natural experiment' and contributes to the literature on the effects of accounting standards.

Keywords: Members' shares; cooperatives; effects of accounting standards; equity; liability; lending technologies

BACKGROUND

Cooperatives have special characteristics that differentiate them from other firms. The aim of this type of company is not to obtain a profit, but to meet the economic and social needs of the members through business activities.

Moreover, this type of company plays an important role in the business fabric of Spain. According to the Ministry of Labour and Immigration, in 2013 there were about 21,412 cooperatives in Spain, employing 286,771 workers registered with the Social Security. Indeed, cooperatives are an important social and economic player throughout Europe; for example, there are 250,000 co-operative enterprises in the European Union, owned by 163 million citizens (1 in 3 EU citizens) and they employ 5.4 million people (EU, 2014).

Furthermore, the European Economic and Social and Committee points out that protecting and preserving the diversity of enterprise types are especially important for both ensuring the success of the single market and maintaining the European social model. To this end it is necessary that the legal framework regarding competitiveness policies foster diversity of form for enterprises and takes into consideration the characteristics of each form (European Economic and Social Committee [EESC], 2009). There is also significant interest focused on the stronger resilience of the cooperative firm when compared to Investor-Owned Firms (e.g., Birchall & Ketilson, 2009; CICOPA, 2010).

There has been considerable debate surrounding the equity-liability classification and its effect on cooperatives mainly triggered by the International Accounting Standards 32 and its unsuitability for cooperatives (e.g., Beaubien, 2011; Detilleux & Naett, 2005; López-Espinosa, Maddocks, & Polo-Garrido, 2009, 2012; Polo-Garrido, 2005), but the particular aim of this study is to assess the possible impact of the reclassification of members' shares in cooperatives from equity to liabilities brought about by the new accounting standards. Therefore, the present study is related to the current line of literature on the (economic) effects of accounting standards. Although the issue of the effects of accounting standards is not a new topic (e.g., the seminal work of Zeff, 1978), interest in the issue is currently increasing significantly, both in academic circles (e.g., Haller et al., 2012; Trombetta, Wagenhofer, & Wysocki, 2012)[1] and among accounting bodies (e.g., European Financial Reporting Advisory Group [EFRAG], 2011).

In addition, this study provides evidence regarding the use of accounting information by providers of capital to cooperative firms. A recent study financed by the European Financial Reporting Advisory and the Institute of Chartered Accountants of Scotland, considering this information to be essential, has called for more descriptive evidence on information gathering and the processing of activities of capital providers, particular non-equity investors (Cascino et al., 2013). Our study shows the different information needs of the capital providers once the cooperative model has been properly understood. Consequently, this study also relates to the different needs of the various users of accounting information.

In view of the possible negative effects of this accounting reclassification, the national law on cooperatives and the regional laws have been modified to accommodate, as well as the 'traditional' members' shares which are redeemable when the member leaves the cooperative, other contributions whose redemption can be refused unconditionally by the cooperative. These latter contributions would retain their classification as equity under the new accounting standards. The legal modifications establish options for configuring the set of rules by which the members' shares are to be governed, the cooperatives can opt for the former or the latter.

Since the great majority of cooperative enterprises do not have access to the capital markets, the main source of external funding is bank finance. In this context, if accounting information plays an important role in the credit technologies used by the financial institutions, the accounting reclassification will affect access to finance as well as its cost, and cooperatives will have incentives to modify their statutes by incorporating a regime of members' shares that will retain the classification of members' shares as equity; if on the contrary accounting information does not play an important role in the credit technologies used, the cooperatives will not have any incentives to modify their capital regime, in fact, just the contrary, given that the change is incentivised merely by the accounting reclassification and is of no interest in itself. The cooperative world has seen this change as problematic as it affects the very characteristics of this type of firm.

This is what is called a 'natural experiment' and we have found no similar studies regarding the impact on access to bank finance of an accounting reclassification similar to the one described. Despite the importance of distinction between equity and liability to users of accounting information (Clark, 1993), we found only two related antecedents, both of which study the effects in the capital market. One is the article of Scott, Wiedman, and Wier (2011) which provides evidence from Canadian firms. The introduction of new and more restricted accounting standards in 1996 prohibited the equity classification of anything other than the conversion option in convertible bonds in shares. This provoked the decline of the use of hybrid instruments in corporations with high leverage, but not so in trusts, where the principal motivation for their use was that they provided more financial flexibility. Another is the working paper of Levi and Segal (2014), who document how the reclassification from equity to financial liabilities of hybrid financial instruments by virtue of the Statement of Financial Accounting Standard no 150 has decreased the issue of such financial instruments, indicating just how the accounting classification of the financial instrument affects its use.

Due to the complexity of the research problem, in which several factors can interact, and the scarcity of previous studies dealing with similar problems, a qualitative research approach will be undertaken as outlined in the methodology section later on. In the section which follows, we review the accounting reform process undergone in Spain with special reference to cooperatives. The section 'Credit Technologies' provides an introduction about credit technologies. The section 'Methodology' sets out the methodology followed, the section 'Results and Discussion' presents the results and their discussion and the section 'Conclusion' lays out the conclusions.

THE ACCOUNTING REFORM PROCESS IN SPAIN – REFERENCE TO COOPERATIVES

The introduction into our accounting system of International Financial Reporting Standards concluded with the passage of the law on reform and adaptation of commercial legislation in matters of accounting in pursuit of international harmonization based on European Union norms.

This process of reform of the mercantile norms in accounting matters has modified the basic body of regulations (Commercial Code, Law on Public Limited Companies and Law on Limited Liability) and has also developed a new General Accountancy Plan that is in consonance with the International Financial Reporting Standards. Based on the current IAS 32 and of its interpretation IFRIC 2, members' shares in cooperatives would be reclassified as liabilities.

The current General Accounting Plan (PGC) establishes, in line with IAS 32, in its Measurement Standard 9, 'Credit Technologies', that the instruments issued shall be classified as financial liabilities:[2] 'provided that in accordance with their economic reality they constitute for the firm a contractual obligation, direct or indirect, to deliver cash or another financial asset, or to exchange financial assets or liabilities with third parties in potentially unfavourable conditions, such as a financial instrument that provides for its obligatory repurchase by the issuer, or that grants to the holder the right to demand of the issuer its redemption on a determinate or determinable date and for a determinate or determinable amount, or to receive a predetermined remuneration whenever there are distributable profits. In particular, certain redeemable shares and non-voting shares'.

Conscious of the possible impacts that these changes would have, as early as 2007, the law on reform and adaptation of commercial legislation in matters of accounting modified the national law on cooperatives, introducing the possibility of a new regime of members' shares that would retain their classification as equity, as is explained below.

The accounting reform in relation to cooperatives concludes in Order EHA/3360/2010, of 21st December, which approves the norms on accounting aspects of cooperative societies. These norms were drawn up on the basis of a document drawn up by a group of experts working in the Institute of Accounting and Audit of Accounts (ICAC).

The purpose of these norms is for cooperative societies to be able to have available to them accounting standards that will permit them to continue to supply financial information in the framework of the PGC and the PGC for Small and Medium Enterprises, in accord with the International Financial Reporting Standards adopted by the European Union, but without abandoning to any great extent the special regulation approved in 2003.

The first of the norms on the accounting aspects of cooperative societies establishes that 'the corporate capital of a cooperative society, as defined in the law, is constituted by the contributions, obligatory and voluntary, made for that purpose, whether monetary or non-monetary in nature, at the time of the setting up or at a later time, either by incorporating new members or as a consequence of subsequent resolutions to increase capital or voluntary contributions, and corresponds to the members' shares subscribed in accordance with the law'. 'Members' shares whose redemption in the event of cessation of membership may be refused unconditionally by the Governing Board or the Annual Meeting shall have the consideration of equity, as established by the applicable law and the Statutes of the cooperative, provided that they do not compel the cooperative society to pay an obligatory remuneration to the member or participants and the return is discretional'.

These new accounting criteria have led to the modification of the laws on cooperatives in order to introduce a new regime of capital contributions that will retain their equity classification.

The main modifications introduced by the laws on cooperatives consist of the introduction of contributions whose redemption in the event of cessation of membership may be refused unconditionally by the Governing Board. This right to refuse may be applicable to the entirety of the corporate capital, or partially, that is to a part of the corporate capital, that is the statutes may provide that when in an accounting year the amount of the return of contributions exceeds the percentage of capital established in the statutes, any new redemptions will be conditional upon a favourable resolution of the Governing Board. In addition the statutes may provide that the capital contributions of any new members joining a cooperative must preferentially be made through acquisition of the members' shares whose redemption has been requested due to their holders' cessation of membership and refused by the cooperative. This acquisition shall be made in the same order as the requests of this type were made, and in the case of requests made on the same date, shall be distributed in proportion to the amount of the contributions.

CREDIT TECHNOLOGIES

As remarked above, with the introduction of the new accounting standards a change has occurred in the classification of the sources of finance of firms, principally of cooperatives. This reclassification affects equity figures and therefore the solvency outlook of a firm and may affect access to bank financing. This aspect will, in our opinion, depend to a large extent on the credit technology used by the financial entities.

Banks currently use different credit technologies when evaluating whether or not to grant finance to firms. Udell (2004), for example, enumerates six different categories of loan techniques: credit based on financial statements, relationship credit, loans to micro-firms with credit scoring, asset-based credit, factoring and commercial credit.

One of the technologies used by financial entities is the economic-financial method. This technology is based on an analysis of the firm's financial statements by means of ratios that indicate the trend and situation of the firm in relation to the sector and to other competing firms. This method is suitable for application to high-value operations.

Another credit technology that uses financial information is credit scoring. This technology embraces all the statistical models and techniques that help lenders to make decisions linked to the granting of credit. Credit scoring implies the processing of the data on the firm and its owner by means of statistics. The result is a score or statistic summarising the borrower's future behaviour with regard to the loan (Feldman, 1997; Mester, 1997).

Another method that has been gaining importance in recent years is relationship banking. The basis of this new trend is that a close relationship between banks and borrowers can be economically beneficial.

This technology relies on analysis of the information possessed by the financial institution as a result of its previous relations with the client. It does not have a structured methodology, but through the historical information on the relationships between the bank and the client aims to find a response adequate to the desired level of risk.

Petersen and Rajan (1994) provided evidence on the benefits of relationship banking in small businesses. The main benefit was to increase the availability of financing, as well as lesser benefits in the price of credit.

Boot (2000) considers that, according to most theories, relationship banking is likely to be even more valuable for smaller firms.

According to Berger and Udell (2006), lending technologies are often categorized into two types: transactions lending based primarily on 'hard' quantitative data, and relationship lending based significantly on 'soft' qualitative information.

Therefore, the possible effect of the accounting reclassification of members' shares will depend on whether the technology used is based primarily on 'hard' information (and within this, accounting information) or on 'soft' information.

METHODOLOGY

As pointed out before, due to the complexity of the research problem, several factors can interact and the scarcity of previous studies tackling similar problems mean that the research problem is not sufficiently framed. All these reasons justify the use of a qualitative research methodology.

From among the qualitative research methodologies, we have opted for the method of interviews (Arksey & Knight, 1999; Wengraf, 2001). From all the different types of interviews we have chosen to use in-depth interviews. With the in-depth interview, the interviewer wants to know what is important and significant for the respondent, wishes to reach an understanding of how he/she sees and interprets the situation. Therefore, the use of in-depth interview is appropriate in this research as we want to know the thinking behind the interviewee's responses (Gray, Walters, Bebbington, & Thomson, 1995; Larrinaga-Gonzalez, Carrasco, Caro, Correa, & Páez, 2001).

Some advantages of the in-depth interview are that it is a very valid technique when one has little information on a subject and wants to make an exploratory study; it allows valuable information to be obtained; and, as only the interviewer and the respondent are present there is a free exchange of information without any kind of pressure (e.g., social pressure if a group session is carried out).

The in-depth interview can be performed in two ways (Sarabia Sánchez, 1999):

(1) *Free, non-structured interview*: no specific guidelines are followed for the interview and it is simply monitored that the respondent does not stray too far from the subjects of study.
(2) *Semi-structured interview*: the interviewer uses a script with the subjects or general lines to be dealt with in the interview, controlling the process of information gathering more directly.

We use the semi-structured interview, in order to enquire more specifically about aspects which are, a priori, of greater interest. Other studies in accounting have also used in-depth interviews, for example, Arquero et al. (2009), Brav, Graham, Harvey, and Michaely (2005), Hjelstrom and Schuster (2011) and Lillis (1999) among others, and they have also been used in many other fields such as marketing (Wright, 1996).

Based on the research topic a script on the a priori main aspects was prepared. The main aspects and their justification are outlined below.

- Which statutory clauses, besides the right of the member to redeem shares, could affect accounting reclassification?

  The purpose of this item is multiple. First, to check this crucial point with the expert, second to get additional information, such as if these clauses are common or unusual in cooperative practice, and finally it allows the experts to express their opinions, that is, if they agree or disagree with the new accounting standards and for what reasons.
- How might the accounting classification of member's shares as equity or liability affect the cooperative? Would it affect access to financing? Would it affect the cost of financing? What is the role of accounting information in the financing of cooperatives?

  This item is the central point of our research. We expect that the accounting classification of members' shares will have an impact on cooperative financing. The possible impact will depend on the role of accounting information; therefore, the last question is explorative in this issue and tries to find out information regarding the current situation.
- Are debt covenants commonly used?

  The finance literature justifies the use of debt covenants as instruments to reduce agency costs in lending contracts (Beatty, Ramesh, & Weber, 2002). They are defined as financial conditions established by the financial entity that must be met for the loan to be maintained, as if they are used it is evident that the reclassification of capital will have effects on financing which has already been granted and therefore on the financing and its cost. Nevertheless, they are relatively new and little is known about the current extent of their use in Spain, particularly in financing to cooperatives.
- Do the potential effects affect all cooperatives alike or would there be differences depending on the type of cooperative (agricultural, worker ownership, etc.) size, or other factors?

  Berger and Udell (2006) suggest that lending based on borrower financial statements is reserved for relatively informationally transparent firms, and an important aspect of the information environment is the accounting infrastructure (strong accounting standards and credible independent accounting firms) and credit granting in Small and Medium Enterprises is not fundamentally based on the analysis of financial statements. We expect that the use of financial statements by financial institutions will depend on the size of the firm. Therefore, the possible effect of the accounting classification will depend on the size of the cooperative.

Although there is a branch of literature on cooperative financing, mainly focused in agricultural cooperatives of the United States (e.g., Cobia & Peterson, 2000; Dhal & Dobson, 1976; Illiopoulos, 2003; Jones, 1986; Royer, 1992; Vansickle & Ladd, 1983), to the best of our knowledge there is no previous literature which specifically addresses financing and the type of cooperative, that is, whether the different role of the economic participant member under each type of cooperative when carrying out transactions with the cooperative as a worker, supplier or customer could affect cooperative financing. Therefore this is a relatively new field. Finally, an open question on another possible factor is considered.

- What limitations does accounting information present with regard to access to finance? How could it be improved? What additional information could be reflected in financial statement notes to improve the interpretation?

  This item is a continuation of the previous one on the role of accounting information. We seek authoritative opinions from experts on how to improve accounting information.
- Are there other factors specific to cooperatives that may affect access to financing other than the accounting reclassification of members' shares, such as the assessment of transactions between members and the cooperative?

  Although previously this has been very poorly addressed, the cooperative model does have an impact on the net income figures. We think that this could affect the estimation of future cash flows and assessment of risk in the cooperative firm.
- Given the possible effects outlined above, amendments to the laws governing cooperatives permit options when configuring the members' shares, from the traditional redeemable members' shares to those which are fully refusable by the cooperative, including the partially refusable by the cooperative. Do you think cooperatives will change their traditional redeemable members' shares? Which option do you think will be most used? What factors might explain the choice of option (size, sector, corporate governance issues, etc.)?

This item also features at the heart of our research. As we expect that the accounting classification of members' shares will have an impact on cooperative financing, we therefore expect that cooperatives will perceive incentives to modify their statutes in order to retain equity accounting classification. As well as checking our hypothesis, this item has an exploratory purpose, that being to estimate which options would be more popular and what factors could motive the choice of a particular option over others.

Some additional items have been included for risk analysts and similar professionals:

- Financial institutions in granting loans use what are known as lending technologies, which ones are the most commonly used by your organization? Do you also use them for SMEs?[3]
- Do you use relationship banking and credit scoring?

Both items are exploratory and their purpose is to find out information concerning current banking practices.

The interviewees are experts in the field and belong to different collectives, the aim being to obtain a broader vision.

The panel of interviewees is made up of

- An auditor, partner of a second tier auditing firm, specialised in the cooperative sector.
- A business consultant and part-time university associate professor, specialised in accounting and tax for cooperatives.
- The managing director of a mutual guarantee company. This mutual guarantee company operates only within the social economy sector, that is, mainly cooperatives. She was previously a financial director of one of the biggest worker cooperatives in Spain, and previous to that, an auditor specialised in the cooperative sector.
- The managing director of a cooperative bank who had previously held senior positions in the representative organization of the Spanish cooperative bank.
- The financial director of a major agricultural cooperative.
- The financial director of a major worker cooperative.
- An accounting professional at a federation of worker cooperatives who is in charge of the accounting and tax advisory services to cooperative members.

A total then, of seven in-depth interviews were carried out. Therefore, we have set up a purposive sampling based on the expertise of the interviewees and the variety of their backgrounds. The range of interviewees enabled us to identify possible differences between the opinions of each professional group.

The interviews were audio taped and summarized in a structured data display in order to be analysed systematically.

RESULTS AND DISCUSSION

In this section we will describe the main results and the discussions prompted by the in-deep interviews.

With regard to the statutory clauses and the question of which of these, besides the right of the members to redeem shares, could affect accounting reclassification, five of the seven experts commented specifically on the issue, the managing director of the cooperative bank and the managing director of the mutual guarantee company being less forthcoming on this topic. They were aware of all the characteristics of the members' shares which could affect the accounting classification in addition to the right of the member to redeem their shares. Their answers allowed us to confirm our previous perception that mandatory return is quite rare and none of the participants were aware of even a single such case. On the other hand, they did know of some cases of mandatory interest (remuneration), but this was seldom used.

On the issue of possible effects of the accounting reclassification of the members shares from equity to liability, all the experts considered that this reclassification would hinder access to financing for the cooperatives.

The experts considered that the larger-sized cooperatives and those in which the members' shares were an important percentage of the equity and liabilities (B side balance sheet) would have more difficulties to access financing, mainly because in these the financing operations would be for larger amounts, in consonance with the size of the firm, and the relationship with the financial entity would be more distant.

In general, with the possible exception of indirect consequences, the effects of the accounting reclassification would not be felt differently by different types of cooperative. That is, various respondents highlight that agricultural cooperatives may be more affected, as the members' shares are usually high, while in other cooperatives, such as worker cooperatives, capital is not as important as, for example, the labour provided by the members. Other respondents consider that access to financing will depend on the behaviour, the strategy or the way of operating of the cooperative.

By this, they mean that it will depend on the self-financing policy of the cooperative, and closely related to this is the policy of the cooperative in establishing the price of the product provided by the members because of how this affects the net income and, consequently, the self-financing of the cooperative.

They agree that this reclassification will affect the granting of finance, since the credit entities use various tools into which they introduce financial data from the balance sheet and from the profit and loss account and which provide them with a score, on which they base their decisions to grant financing or otherwise. The auditor, business consultant and financial directors of the cooperatives consulted all concurred that risk analysts from financial entities based their decision on the accounting information contained in the balance sheet and the profit and loss account.

However, the point of view of the general director of the cooperative bank is different; he explains that the first thing the financial entity does is to calculate a credit score, but the decision whether or not to grant financing is influenced by other credit technologies, such as relationship banking, that is the financial entities base their decision on their knowledge of the cooperative, and the closeness of their relationship with the cooperative. Evidently, if this relationship does not exist, as will be the case of a cooperative that is a new customer, the financial entity has no data or clear references, and therefore, what matters is the data contained in financial statements.

The views of the managing director of the mutual guarantee company on this point are particularly interesting. Currently, the finance supervisors are demanding the use of techniques of credit scoring for mutual guarantee companies. Accounting data are inputs in these techniques, therefore the accounting reclassification affects the score provided for these techniques (for instance, the solvency ratio). The accounting classification of the members' shares is not the only aspect to be considered differently, the figure of net income has to be interpreted taking into account the transactions of the cooperative with the members and the method used to establish 'prices' for those transactions. They understand the cooperative model and from this knowledge they can adapt the resulting score from the standard techniques. To this end, they take account of other aspects such as the possible existence of 'voluntary' member shares, if there are voluntary reserves, the historic generation of margins, the quantity of advance wage payments in worker cooperatives or the quantity of 'purchases' from members by the cooperatives (for instance in agricultural cooperatives). As the managing director said, there are 23 mutual guarantee companies in Spain and her company is the only one which operates with cooperatives and other entities inside the, so-called, 'social economy', because no other companies understand the cooperative model and thus are unable to adapt the scoring, nor are able to ascertain the business risk in cooperative firms.

Taking into account the views of the managing director of the mutual guarantee company, we can understand the contrasting views of the managing director of the cooperative bank with the rest of the participants. As may be logically supposed, the cooperative bank is better placed to understand the cooperative model and to take into account other variables besides the initial score, such as past records from long relationships.

As we have mentioned, it is important to know whether debt covenants are used. We were told that this tool is not very usual either in operations with cooperatives, or with other types of firms. In some cases this tool has been used by the financial entity in refinancing operations, but when obtaining initial finance it is not usual for the financial entity to use these clauses. On the other hand, the managing director of the mutual guarantee company described some limited practices of covenants in big cooperatives. Mainly, the covenants consist in establishing that the redemption of members' shares is subject to the previous full or partial repayment of the loan.

All experts agree that adding additional information to the notes of the financial statements will not enhance the interpretation of the balance sheet or of the profit and loss account, because as outlined above, the end users of the accounting information in the case that concerns us, the financial entities, look at the accounting data and do not analyse the notes in detail.

This will involve, in the best of cases, a greater effort on the part of the cooperatives, as it will be they who, when requesting financing, try to explain to the financial entities the reclassification of members' shares as liabilities and the effects that this change has produced in their company balance sheets.

Furthermore, it may also affect the image that the cooperatives present to suppliers, customers and even to new members.

The laws on cooperatives permit various options for configuring capital: the traditional redeemable members' shares; members' shares whose redemption is completely refusable by the cooperatives; partly refusable redemption; or modifying the transfer regime for members' shares. For this reason it would be interesting to find out which options cooperatives will choose and when they will do so.

As to the path that the cooperatives will take, there is no consensus. One group considers that the redemption of members' shares should be 100% refusable.

On the other hand, others have opted in the statute to set a percentage (5% or 6%) of the capital at the start of each year whose redemption may not be refused, the rest (95% or 94%) remaining as equity.

Other cooperatives, however, will not modify their statutes. This has been detected in the case of certain large cooperatives. In particular those that are self-financing to a high degree and do not need to seek bank finance, that have not modified their statutes, and more generally in small workers' cooperatives that have little capital, approaching or at the legal minimum. Generally, financial entities ask for personal guarantees from the members in order to grant financing to the cooperative. The Financial Director told us an anecdotal but illustrative case concerning a cooperative which considered not modifying its statutes, but when this cooperative needed to ask for a bank loan, it had to urgently modify its statutes so as to be granted the loan.

The need for personal guarantees was also highlighted by the managing director of the mutual guarantee company, who mentioned that the financial support line of a government bank always requested additional personal guarantees from the members in the case of cooperatives. For instance, in a worker cooperative of close to 400 members, the joint personal guarantee of all 400 members was necessary for the loan to be granted. This proved to be such a hurdle that very few loans were granted to cooperatives, therefore making this support line inadequate.

Another observation is that there is a general perception that the cooperatives have not been faithfully represented by the changes in accounting standards. Some experts have suggested that a probabilistic model based on historical data might have been more suitable for classifying members' shares.

It was also stated that modifications in the statutes may generate conflict within the cooperative, for example, between younger members and older members, when the latter, closer to retirement, are more reluctant to give the cooperative the unconditional right to refuse redemption.

Moreover, one respondent, among other comments, declared that the new accounting standards and the modifications of the laws on cooperatives could, in future, bring about a fall in the creation of new cooperative firms due to the increased complexity of the regulation of cooperatives.

Regarding the two additional questions put to financial sector experts about the most commonly used lending technologies, the following feedback was received. The use of both credit scoring and relationship banking was confirmed and of particular interest were the comments of the managing director of the mutual guarantee company. She stated that the economic and financial crisis have provoked a breakdown in relationship banking to the extent that relationship banking currently plays a far less significant role in the credit granting process. The new capital requirements of the banks in conjunction with the recent concentration process motivated by the financial crisis, has brought about, on the one hand, a more important role for credit scoring and, on the another hand, a greater distance between the loan applicant and the centre of decision-making in the credit granting process. The latter being clearly detrimental to the role of relationship banking.

CONCLUSIONS

This study contributes to the literature on the effects of accounting standards, taking advantage of the recent accounting standard change in Spain which may be considered as a 'natural experiment'. Despite the importance of equity-liability distinction to the users of financial statements, there is a lack of studies on equity-liability accounting reclassification motivated by a change in an accounting standard.

The principal conclusion that we can draw from the in-depth interviews is that the experts unanimously consider that this reclassification will have a negative effect on the access of cooperatives to financing. This would appear to indicate that the accounting change has real and damaging effects despite not changing the reality which the accounts aim to represent, that is, there is no change in the characteristics of the financial instrument, in this case the members' shares.

Another point on which all the experts agree is that additional information in the notes of the financial statements does not offer sufficient improvement to offset the potentially negative effects of the accounting reclassification of members' shares.

The study also points out that the accounting reclassification also affects other users of the accounting information such as suppliers, customers and potential new members, and thereby their potential or current relation with the cooperative can be affected.

In addition, the accounting change occurs simultaneously with one of the most severe financial crises in history. Therefore the cooperatives have strong incentives to modify their statutes. By contrast, there is no consensus among experts about which of the options of modifying the statutes will be the most popular choice, or if there will be differences between different types of cooperatives in this regard.

This study brings to light other effects of the accounting classification change in equity or liability and the modifications of the statutes; first it would appear to underline intergenerational differences between members, with young members, faced with a more distant membership horizon being more favourable to changing the statutes. Moreover, the creation of new cooperatives may be discouraged because of the increase in the complexity in the regulation of cooperatives and entrepreneurs may end up opting for other kinds of legal entities.

These findings relates with the widely known fact that the IAS 32 clashes with the first Cooperative Principle 'Voluntary and open membership' (Polo-Garrido, 2004), in other words, the capital of a cooperative is intrinsically variable and cooperatives adopted the capital variable rule because of the 'dual status' principle (Detilleux & Naett, 2005), that is, the member as both economic participant and capital provider. The IFRIC 2 is seen as a compromise solution and would allow the cooperative to classify members' shares as equity '*... without fundamentally altering their specific characteristics*' (Detilleux & Naett, 2005). Although this is a controversial issue, as Beaubien (2011) points out: '*in fact it pushes co-operatives further down a path they should not travel*'. The forced introduction of the unconditional right, which is new for the majority of cooperatives, heralds certain dangers, such as the risk of misappropriate use and the loss of a powerful members' disciplinary tool on the management (Llewellyn, 2004).

It could be argued that IASB seeks to ensure financial stability by strict equity-liability rules of classification. But IAS 32 and IFRIC 2 have been shown not to be an adequate solution. The long history of cooperatives and, in particular, the recent financial crisis have proven that the cooperatives are more stable than Investor-Owned Firms irrespective of the right of the member to redeem shares. In addition, the amendment of IAS 32 in 2008 which allows for equity classification of certain puttable instruments (International Accounting Standard Board [IASB], 2008) weakens the argument that IASB seeks to ensure stability. Moreover, it shows again how Standards Setters fails to understand the very nature of cooperatives, as members' shares fall beyond the scope of that amendment due to the capped interest on the net assets of the cooperative.

On the other hand, as has already been pointed out, the accounting change and the resulting cooperative law and statutes amendments add complexity which discourages the creation of cooperatives, which is in stark contrast to the promotion of cooperatives by the European Union. The reclassification of members' shares from equity to liability raises an important question. Could the members be seen merely as creditors? What is more, the reclassification points out the need to consider the different requirements of the members in their role as accounting information users, requirements which are largely absent in the accounting literature and would constitute an interesting line of research.

In addition to accounting issues, other interesting insights can be made. With regard to credit technologies the study pointed out the importance for the financial entities to understand the cooperative model. This understanding is essential to enhance the application of relationship banking in the financing of cooperatives. This highlights the role of cooperative banking and other protagonists as they understand the cooperative model better, even more so when new requirements for banking capital and the mergers in the banking sector have brought about a decline in relationship banking. Therefore, the use of accounting information by capital providers to cooperative entities is, without doubt, an interesting line to follow in the future.

Finally, with regard to the effects of the accounting reclassification, an expansion of the study using quantitative methods, once data is available, would be interesting in order to generalize the findings.

NOTES

1. See the Special Issue: 'The effects of Accounting Standards', of the Journal 'Accounting in Europe', Volume 2, number 2, 2012.
2. Either in their entirety, or in one of their parts when they are compound financial instruments.
3. Note that the vast majority of cooperatives are SMEs.

ACKNOWLEDGEMENT

This work is part of the research Project 'Información contable, financiación, resistencia a la crisis y cooperativas' (Accounting information, finance, resilience to the crisis and cooperatives entities), financed by the research and development support Programme (PAID-06-12) of the Universitat Politècnica de València.

REFERENCES

Arksey, H., & Knight, P. (1999). *Interviewing for social scientist* (p. 208). London, UK: Sage Publications.

Arquero Montaño, J. L., Donoso-Anes, J. A., Jiménez-Cardoso, S. M., & González González, J. M. (2009). Análisis exploratorio del perfil demandado para administración y dirección de empresas: Implicaciones para el área contable. *Revista de Contabilidad, 12*(n.2), 180–214.

Beatty, A., Ramesh, K., & Weber, J. (2002). The importance of accounting changes in debt contracts: The costs of flexibility en debt calculations. *Journal of Accounting Economics, 33*(2), 205–227.

Berger, A., & Udell, G. F. (2006). A more complete framework for financing of small and medium enterprises. *Journal of Banking & Finance, 30*, 2945–2966.

Beaubien, L. (2011). Co-operative accounting: Disclosing redemption contingencies for member shares. *Journal of Co-Operatives Studies, 44*(2), 38–44.

Birchall, J., & Ketilson, L. H. (2009). *Resilience of the cooperative business model in time of crisis*. Italy: International Labour Organization.

Boot, A. W. A. (2000). Relationship banking: What do we know? *Journal of Financial Intermediation, 9*, 7–25.

Brav, A., Graham, J. R., Harvey, C. R., & Michaely, R. (2005). Payout policy in the 21st century. *Journal of Financial Economics, 77*, 483–527.

Cascino, S., Clatworthy, M., García Osma, B., Gassem, J., Imam, S., & Jeanjan, T. (2013). *The use of information by capital providers*. Academic review literature. Institute of Chartered Accountants of Scotland and European Financial Reporting Advisory, p. 83.

CICOPA, International Organisation of Industrial, Artisanal and Service Producers' Co-operatives (2010). *Cooperative enterprises in industry and services prove their strong resilience to the crisis*. Retrieved from http://www.cecop.coop/IMG/pdf/Report_on_crisis_2010EN.pdf

Clark, M. W. (1993). Entity theory, modern capital structure theory, and the distinction between debt and equity. *Accounting Horizon, 7*(3), 14–31.

Cobia, D. W., & Peterson, C. H. (2000). Managing capital structure. In *Cooperatives: An economic and management perspective*. Manhattan, KS: Arthur Capper Cooperative Center, Kansas State University.

Detilleux, J. C., & Naett, C. (2005). Cooperatives and international reporting standards: The case of IAS 32. *Revue Internationale de L'Economie Sociale, 295*, 1–13.

Dhal, W., & Dobson, W. D. (1976). An analysis of alternative financing strategies and equity retirement plans for farm supply cooperatives. *American Journal of Agricultural Economics, May, 58*(2), 199–208.

European Economic and Social Committee. (2009). *INT/447 diverse forms of enterprise*. Opinion of the European Economic and Social Committee on the Diverse forms of enterprise (own-initiative opinion).

European Financial Reporting Advisory Group. (2011). *Considering the effects of accounting standards*. Brussels: European Financial Reporting Advisory Group.

European Union. (2014). *Co-operatives. Importance of the sector*. Retrieved from: http://ec.europa.eu/enterprise/policies/sme/promoting-entrepreneurship/social-economy/co-operatives/index_en.htm#h2-1

Feldman, R. (1997, September 19–25). *Small business loans, small banks and a big change in technology called credit scoring*, Federal Reserve Banks of Minneapolis, The region.

Gray, R., Walters, D., Bebbington, J., & Thomson, I. (1995). The greening of enterprise: an exploration of the (non) role of environmental accounting and environmental accountants in organizational change. *Critical Perspectives on Accounting*, *6*(3), 211–239.

Haller, A., Nobes, C., Cairns, D., Hjelstrom, A., Moya, S., Page, M., & Walton, P. (2012). The effects of accounting standards – A comment. *Accounting in Europe*, *9*(2), 113–125.

Hjelstrom, A., & Schuster, W. (2011). Standards, management incentives and accounting practice – Lessons from the IFRS transition in Sweden. *Accounting in Europe*, *8*(1), 69–88.

Iliopoulos, C. (2003, October). Long-term financing in US and European Agricultural Co-operatives: Emerging methods for Ameliorating Investment Constraints. *NCR-194 conference*, Kansas City.

International Accounting Standard Board. (2008). *Amendments to IAS 32 Financial Instruments Presentation and IAS 1 Presentation of Financial Financial Statements*. Puttable Financial Instruments and Obligation Arising on Liquidation.

Jones, B. L. (1986). A model of cooperative finance: Comment. *American Journal of Agricultural Economics, February*, *68*(1), 170–172.

Larrinaga-Gonzalez, C., Carrasco, F., Caro, F. J., Correa, C., & Páez, J. M. (2001). The role of the environmental accounting in organizational change: An exploration of Spanish companies, *Accounting, Auditing and Accountability Journal*, *14*(2), 213–239.

Levi, S., & Segal, B. (2014). The impact of debt-equity reporting classifications on the firms' decision to issue hybrid securities. *European Accounting Review*, (March), (Forthcoming). Retrieved from http://ssrn.com/abstract=861685

Lillis, A. M. (1999). A framework for the analysis of interview data from multiple research sites. *Accounting and Finance*, *39*, 79–105.

Llewellyn, D. T. (2004). *Issues in the governance of mutuals in the finance sector*. Retrieved from http://62. 164.176.164/d/myners_llewellyn.pdf

López-Espinosa, G., Maddocks, J., & Polo-Garrido, F. (2009). Equity-liability distinction. The case for co-operatives. *Journal of Financial Management and Accounting*, *20*(3), 274–306.

López-Espinosa, G., Maddocks, J., & Polo-Garrido, F. (2012). Co-operatives and the equity-liabilities puzzle: Concerns for accounting standards setters. *Accounting Horizons*, *26*(4), 767–787.

Mester, L. (1997). What's the point of credit scoring? Federal reserve bank of Philadelphia. *Business Review*, (September/October), 3–16.

Petersen, M. A., & Rajan, R. G. (1994). The benefits of r lending relationships. Evidence from small business data. *The Journal of Finance*, *49*(n.1), 3–37.

Polo-Garrido, F. (2004). Accounting principles versus co-operative principles: Influence in the co-operative identity. In *International co-operative alliance research conference on* The future of Co-operatives in a growing Europe. Segorbe, Spain, May 6–9.

Polo-Garrido, F. (2005). Co-operative entities and the international financial reporting standards. *28th Annual Congress of European Accounting Association*. Göteborg, May 18–20.

Royer, J. S. (1992). Cooperative principles and equity financing: A critical discussion. *Journal of Agriculture Cooperation*, *79*, 79–82.

Sarabia Sánchez, F. J. (1999). Metodología para la investigación en marketing y dirección de empresas, editorial Pirámide.

Scott, T. W., Wiedman, C., & Wier, H. A. (2011). Transaction structuring and Canadian convertible debt. *Contemporary Accounting Research, 28*(3), 1046–1071.

Trombetta, M., Wagenhofer, A., & Wysocki, P. (2012). The usefulness of academic research in understanding the effects of accounting standards. *Accounting in Europe, 9*(2), 127–146.

Udell, G. F. (2004). El crédito a las PYME: Delimitación en una perspectiva global. *Papeles de Economía Española, 101*, 80–98.

Vansickle, J. J., & Ladd, G. W. (1983). A model of cooperative finance. *American Journal Agricultural Economics, May, 65*(2), 273–281.

Wengraf, T. (2001). *Qualitative research interviewing*. London: Sage.

Wright, L. T. (1996). Exploring the in-depth interview as a qualitative research technique with American and Japanese firms. *Marketing Intelligence & Planning, 14*(6), 59–64.

Zeff, A. (1978). The rise of economic consequences. *Journal of Accountancy, 146*(6), 56–63.

PART IV
SOCIAL ACCOUNTING FOR THE NON-PROFIT SECTOR

TOWARD AN INTEGRATED ACCOUNTABILITY MODEL FOR NONPROFIT ORGANIZATIONS

Michele Andreaus and Ericka Costa

ABSTRACT

Purpose – *By contributing to the burgeoning debate regarding "for what" nonprofit organizations should be accountable, this article aims to develop and present an Integrated Accountability Model (IAM) that considers three dimensions of accountability.*

Methodology/approach – *After highlighting the limits of conventional accounting for NPOs and reframing the role of profit within them, the article presents a complete literature review on "to whom" and "for what" NPOs have to be accountable while further developing the IAM of integrated accountability.*

Findings – *The integrated accountability model developed in this article proposes three categories of NPO accountability: (i) the economic and financial dimension or the capability/ability to be economically sustainable in the long term; (ii) the mission-related dimension or the* raison d'être *of an NPO, that is, the purpose for which the NPO has been set up, its mission; and (iii) the social-related dimension or the relationship*

Accountability and Social Accounting for Social and Non-profit Organizations
Advances in Public Interest Accounting, Volume 17, 153–176

ISSN: 1041-7060/doi:10.1108/S1041-706020140000017006

with the stakeholders, that is the impact of NPO activities on its stakeholders in terms of the social contract between them.

Originality/value – *Broadly, this article makes a contribution to the literature on accountability for NPOs. In particular it sheds light on two points: the importance of separating the mission-related dimension from the social-related one and the potential to open avenues for expansion of the IAM model to for-profit organizations.*

Keywords: Accountability; NPOs; economic and financial dimension; mission-related dimension; social-related dimension

INTRODUCTION

The nonprofit sector is an important and rapidly growing part of the European and US economies (Anheier, 2009). It includes several organizational forms, such as cooperatives, nongovernmental organizations (NGOs), social enterprises and associations (Defourny & Nyssens, 2010). The worldwide emergence of the nonprofit sector has been recognized in the promotion of social values and civil integration while creating a strata of global civil society that often can influence the practices and policies of national and international governments. The increased significance of nonprofit organizations (NPOs) has necessitated urgent attention be given to the transparency and accountability mechanisms able to measure the impact of NPO activities on society at large (Ball & Osborne, 2011).

Even though the concept of accountability has been widely discussed in academic literature (Edwards & Hulme, 1996; Gray, Adams, & Owen, 1996; Kearns, 1994), it remains a complex and multifaceted concept requiring further investigation, especially with reference to NPOs (Gray, Dillard, & Spence, 2011). Indeed, NPO accountability cannot solely be connected to or based on its economic and financial performance because this information could be misleading. NPO accountability cannot be reduced only to economic and financial aspects; it also has to consider the relationship with the stakeholders, and undoubtedly, the NPO's ability to reach its determined objectives, which are by definition not only financial but also relevant to the social dimensions of people's lives.

Scholarly descriptions of accountability are not uniform, and there is no unique approach to NPO accountability. However, there exists a relatively high level of agreement as to the basic questions relating to the accountability framework: *who should be held accountable, to whom, for what, how*, and *with what consequences* (Acar, Guo, & Yang, 2012). Many researchers have used one or more of these questions in their studies on accountability (Ebrahim, 2009; Kearns, 1994; Najam, 1996). However, two of these questions have attracted (and still attract) the attention of a considerable number of scholars: *accountability to whom* (e.g., Ebrahim, 2003), *accountability for what* (e.g., Quarter, Mook, & Armstrong, 2009) or both of them combined (e.g., Acar et al., 2012).

The "accountability to whom" question deals primarily with stakeholders affected by the NPO activities, namely donors, funders, beneficiaries, workers, volunteers and the members themselves. By addressing the "accountability for what" agenda, scholars have reported on issues, categories and drivers in depth by identifying and describing the core area(s) to which the NPO should be accountable.

Within the aforementioned two questions of "to whom" and "for what" NPOs have to be accountable, this article aims to contribute to the second question by addressing an integrated accountability framework. This integrated framework will include three main areas of disclosure: (i) the economic and financial dimension or the capability to be economically sustainable in the long term; (ii) the mission-related dimension or the *raison d'être* of an NPO, that is, the purpose for which the NPO has been set up, its mission; and (iii) the social-related dimension or the relationship with the stakeholders, that is the impact of NPO activities on its stakeholders in terms of the social contract between them.

From a methodological point of view, the article presents a review of the literature regarding possible conceptual frameworks for designing accountability perspectives in NPOs and then it develops a model of integrated accountability for NPOs.

The remainder of the article is structured as follows: The first section explains the inadequacy of applying the conventional accounting framework to NPOs before moving into "Interpreting the Role of Profit in NPOs," which explores the different roles of profit in NPOs including its fundamental role as a means to driving the organization's economic activity. "Putting Stakeholders at the Core" introduces the concept of relational accountability for NPOs, which is related to stakeholder theory and the social contract perspective. "A Complex and Multifaceted Accountability System for NPOs" then points out the need to enlarge the accountability framework to multi-directional accountability before introducing accountabilities models. Finally, the article discusses an integrated accountability model (IAM), which brings together three fundamental dimensions of NPOs' daily management, namely the economic, mission-related and social-related dimensions. Based on this discussion, conclusions then are drawn.

THE LIMITS OF CONVENTIONAL ACCOUNTING IN NPOS

The primary roles for accounting information are as applicable in the non-profit sector as in the for-profit sector. In a nonprofit context, donors want to be kept informed regarding the use of their financial contribution, which (hopefully) should be employed in effective and efficient ways. Similarly, in a for-profit organization, funders are interested in comprehending the efficiency and effectiveness of fund use.

This demand for accounting information has two primary theoretical foundations (Hofmann & McSwain, 2013): firstly, an information asymmetry emerges between the organization (nonprofit or for-profit) and its stakeholders and secondly, an agency problem occurs from the property and the managers (both nonprofit and for-profit organizations). The combination of information asymmetry and agency problems creates an increasing demand for accountability, which primarily responds with ex post accounting information, providing motives and opportunities for financial disclosure management.

When NPOs deal with financial accounting and draw up the conventional financial statement and balance sheet, they usually adopt formats that have been designed for for-profit organizations. Indeed, the conventional accounting framework historically has been designed to identify, gather, measure and report economic and financial data (profit or loss) in order to support managerial decision-making. Thus, conventional accounting frameworks primarily reflect the need of stockholders to be informed regarding the organization's economic and financial performance.

This traditional approach to accounting has attracted criticisms that call into question its assumptions. Such criticisms highlight the inability of the traditional approach to consider the inconsistencies, injustices, invisibilities and inequalities of modern western life, and thus, to deliver social change (Gray, 2002; Mathews, 1997). "Critical accounting" scholars argue that accounting should serve as an intermediary between (and within) *organizations* and *society*, thus considering its role within the societal context in a broader sense (Lehman, 1992). According to critical theorists, accounting should be grounded on the principles of *democracy* and *accountability*; in other words, organizations have to provide accountability not only to shareholders, but also to a wide range of stakeholders affected by the organization's activities (Gray et al., 1996). Moreover, accountability for a broad range of stakeholders must go beyond a financial orientation and include social impacts as well. The basis for making organizations accountable becomes the empowerment of the democratic process of accountability.

When applied to NPOs, the conventional accounting framework becomes even more meaningless because of the multi-stakeholder nature of these organizations and their roles within society in promoting and fostering the well-being of the people they serve. NPOs do not aim at the maximization of shareholder wealth; they operate in society by seeking to enhance social value (Ebrahim, 2003; Moore, 2000).

With regard to NPOs, various studies have pointed out the limitations of conventional accounting (Reheul, Caneghem, & Verbruggen, 2014; Vermeer, Raghunandan, & Forgione, 2009) by also highlighting the function and effects of accounting and reporting in such organizations. Palmer and Vinten (1998) detail three main approaches to accounting for NPOs: (i) positivist, where accounting is used to describe what happens in the real world (Watts & Zimmerman, 1979; Whittington, 1986); (ii) critical, which embraces a historical, economic and policy context for accounting (Power & Laughlin, 1996); and finally, (iii) interpretive, where accounting is seen as a symbolic mediator between various social groups in order to arrive at a negotiated social order (Ryan, Scapens, & Theobald, 1992).

These approaches, in different ways and with different epistemic methods, question traditional conventional accounting for NPOs, which remains too exclusively focused on financial measurements (Reheul et al., 2014). Financial measurements emphasize NPO financial performance and evaluate how the funds are acquired or spent. However, as highlighted by Maddocks (2011), financial measurements present only an incomplete picture of the organization because information regarding success, performance and impact are often missing or underdeveloped.

Epstein and McFarlan (2011) describe the critical importance of considering both financial and nonfinancial measures when assessing NPOs. They argue that financial and nonfinancial measures are closely related because, on the one hand, financial resources are meaningless if not employed to achieve the mission. On the other hand, it is not possible to achieve a social purpose without efficient employment of financial resources. Epstein and McFarlan (2011) thus emphasize the role of financial resources and profit within the nonprofit sector.

INTERPRETING THE ROLE OF PROFIT IN NPOS

NPOs focus on creating social value and their mission is not oriented to economic value but wealth for public good. However, this focus does not exclude NPOs from needing to undertake strategies to guarantee an adequate level of net income earnings; on the contrary, NPOs must continually create economic value to survive over time. The creation of economic value ensures that the NPO will be able to continue its mission to create social value over time.

For-profit organizations consider profit as the vehicle to assess their activities, which by definition are oriented to the creation of economic and financial wealth. In NPOs, the role of profit differs because it represents a means and not an ends in itself (Dees, 1998). In other words, in NPOs profit is a vehicle to the achievement of socially oriented purposes, that is the mission and thus, it can be interpreted as a constraint required for the efficient achievement of social value.

Mission performance assessment is essential for NPOs because of its role in the board's decision-making; however, mission performance is difficult to measure and often has a long-term perspective. At the same time, financial performance is somewhat meaningless and often demands immediate attention and a short-term focus (Epstein & McFarlan, 2011). Therefore, the competing demands to measure both social value creation and financial aspects make NPOs "double bottom line" organizations (Dart, Clow, & Armstrong, 2010) as they pursue social and economic value simultaneously (Dees & Economy, 2001).

Since profit in NPOs is a constraint that organizations have to respect in order to pursue their primary socially oriented purposes, what does *efficiency* and *effectiveness* mean for NPOs?

Efficiency "requires revenues covering operational and capital costs with downsized margins in order to limit distortions such as the deadweight loss" (Le Lannier & Porcher, 2014, p. 557). Efficiency is not an absolute concept because it refers to the relationships between inputs and outputs, which in turn, depend upon the characteristics of the environment in which NPOs operate to deliver their services.

Effectiveness reflects the ability to realize strategies and activities aimed at achieving and maximizing social value creation. The monitoring and assessment of NPOs' effectiveness links strategically to the evaluation of organizational success, which is not measurable by financial accounting. Even though financial accounting and financial data certainly represent one key criteria in determining NPO efficiency, they are unimportant when considering effectiveness and this implies meeting the social needs the NPO has been designed to address (Bagnoli & Megali, 2011). Effectiveness thus depends upon beneficiaries' perceptions regarding the services from which they are benefitting, which are by definition intangible and difficult to measure.

Manetti (2014) proposes several nuanced views in defining effectiveness for NPOs:

- "in relation to a standard (quality);
- as the gap between actual service provided and the end-user's perception of its quality (external effectiveness);
- as a correlation of results achieved with those expected (internal effectiveness);
- in comparison with services provided by alternative agents (relative effectiveness);
- by measurement against the situation that would have occurred if services had not been provided (impact)" (p. 449).

In short, since effectiveness in NPOs cannot be evaluated by conventional accounting measurements, the need has emerged to enlarge the required accountability systems. These systems should be anchored not only in economic and financial performance, but also in the social impact for a variety of stakeholders (Ebrahim, 2009, 2010).

PUTTING STAKEHOLDERS AT THE CORE

The inadequacy and meaningless of the conventional accounting framework for NPOs has been highlighted by different authors and as a result there has been an urgent call for a better/clearer understanding of the concepts and meanings of accountability in NPOs (Gray et al., 2011).

Generally, Gray et al. (1996) define accountability as "the duty to provide an account (by no means necessarily financial) or reckoning of those actions for which one is held responsible. In other words, accountability involves two responsibilities or duties: a) responsibility to undertake certain actions; b) responsibility to provide an account for these action" (p. 38). In order to encourage an efficient and sensible approach to accountability, SustainAbility (2003) lists several potential drivers for accountability:

morality where accountability is right in principle; performance (accountability improves effectiveness); political space (accountability increases credibility and thus influence); and wider democratization (accountability of NGOs improves democracy in society) (Gray, Bebbington, & Collison, 2006, p. 337).

Accountability can be conceived of as a relational concept primarily based on a stakeholder approach, according to which any organization has the moral duty to answer to stakeholders upon whom their actions and strategies have (or may have) an impact (Ebrahim, 2005; Edwards & Hulme, 1996; Najam, 1996; Unerman & O'Dwyer, 2006; William & Taylor, 2012).

Closely related to the concept of accountability, therefore, is the stakeholder perspective. In his well-known definition of stakeholders, Freeman (1984) refers to them as "any group or individual who can affect or is affected by the achievement of an organization's objectives" (p. 46). The managerial perspective of stakeholder theory goes a step beyond neoclassical profit maximization because it calls for fiduciary responsibility towards all the stakeholders, owners or not, because of their legitimate interests (Donaldson & Preston, 1995). Indeed, most of the normative basis of stakeholder theory[1] considers business organizations as a means to coordinating and balancing stakeholders' requirements (Evan & Freeman, 1988). In order to manage, coordinate and balance different stakeholders' claims, the organizations rely on an implicit or explicit "social contract" (Donaldson & Dunfee, 1994) that should manage and govern the relationship between the business and society: "The firm-as-contract view holds that legitimate stakeholders are identified by the existence of a contract, expressed or implied, between them and the firm. Direct input contributors are included, but environmental interests such as communities are also believed to have at least loose quasi-contracts (and, of course, sometimes very specific ones) with their business constituents" (Donaldson & Preston, 1995, p. 85).

The concept of a social contract is also linked to legitimacy theory (Lindblom, 1993) because the social contract is used to represent the multitude of stakeholders' expectations while ensuring legitimate operation within the norms of society (Sinclair & Bolt, 2013). If society does not consider the organization legitimate, a *legitimacy gap* occurs, and organizations have to deliver different strategies to bridge the gap. Therefore, the existence of a social contract among business and society, which is closely linked to the concept of organizational legitimacy, demands the discharge of social accountability (Gray, Owen, & Maunders, 1988).

A COMPLEX AND MULTIFACETED ACCOUNTABILITY SYSTEM FOR NPOS

Through this discussion of stakeholder theory and organizations-as-a-contract, it becomes clear that accountability must be considered as a relational concept. In the relational approach to accountability, organizations are required to explain and take responsibility for their actions to stakeholders. Therefore, identification of stakeholders is a key element within relational accountability (Unerman & O'Dwyer, 2006), and consequently one of the first questions arising from this perceptive is *to whom* organizations should be or are held accountable.

Several studies state that NPOs are accountable to multiple actors: (i) to patrons, (ii) to clients, and (iii) to themselves as organizations (Ebrahim, 2005, 2009, 2010; Edwards & Hulme, 1996; Kearns, 1994; Najam, 1996). NPOs' accountability to the patron, or upwards accountability (Najam, 1996), usually refers to relationships with donors, foundations, and governments and are related to how NPOs spent the received funds for designated purposes. The accountability to clients, or downwards accountability, involves the relationships with people for whom NPOs provide services. Finally, accountability to themselves refers to the internal accountability of NPOs. Ebrahim (2005) argues that this kind of accountability "includes an NGO's responsibility to its mission and staff, which includes decision makers as well as field-level implementers" (p. 60).

These theoretical models also make evident that in developing this "multi-demands" accountability system NPOs should satisfy the competing claims of multiple stakeholders and thus NPOs have to prioritize their stakeholders within their own aims and expectations (Brown & Moore, 2001; William & Taylor, 2012). However, many practitioners and scholars have expressed concerns regarding the "difficulties [NPOs] face in prioritizing and reconciling these multiple accountabilities" (Edwards & Hulme, 1996, p. 968), especially in cases where accountability is "skewed to the most powerful constituency." In prioritizing stakeholders and stakeholders' claims, Unerman and O'Dwyer (2006) stressed the importance of also considering the stakeholders or rather the individuals, communities and/or regions who are indirectly (not just directly) impacted by NPO activities.

The applications of the *to whom* models and frameworks of accountability reveal that NPO accountability currently is strongest to boards and donors and weakest to communities and beneficiaries (Costa, Ramus, & Andreaus, 2011; Epstein & McFarlan, 2011; Murtaza, 2012). Murtaza

(2012) stresses the urgency of reconsidering current approaches to NPO accountability and strengthening accountability to communities in order to better achieve the two most important purposes of accountability, namely "converting acceptable performance into excellence and ensuring greater justice in the global economy and polity" (p. 123).

In rethinking the role of accountability *to whom*, several scholars have proposed a strategic approach to accountability in which they shed light on different areas that need to be covered by NPO accountability systems (Avina, 1993; Bagnoli & Megali, 2011; Brown & Moore, 2001; Moore, 2000). Avina (1993) has defined functional-strategic accountability by focusing on the two components where functional accountability focuses on short-term change in organizations, while strategic accountability focuses on long-term organizational change. Further, he notes that functional accountability is related to resource use and immediate impacts of social and political change, while strategic accountability focuses on the impacts of organizational activity on the environment and society.

Reflecting on the strategic worthiness of international NGOs' accountability, Moore (2000) proposes a "strategic triangle" to bolster leaders' calculations involving social value creation, sustainable support by donors and founders and organizational survival. Using this approach, Brown and Moore (2001) proposed a multilevel accountability model aimed at linking and balancing these three dimensions simultaneously because each of these issues can be seen as demanding accountability. They stated that "in this sense, the choice of organizational strategy is a negotiated deal among the stakeholders to whom an INGO owes accountability. A successful strategy would be one that aligns these different kinds of accountability" (p. 587).

When investigating social enterprises, Bagnoli and Megali (2011) propose a model of accountability for NPOs in which a three-level accountability process is developed: the social effectiveness dimension or the ability to achieve social goals, the institutional dimension or the respect of legal and self-imposed rules and the economic and financial dimension or the evaluation of performance and long-term sustainability.

Most of these accountability frameworks place the NPO mission at their core (Moore, 2000), but they somehow fail to consider mission as an explicit driver for accountability (Costa, 2014; Epstein & McFarlan, 2011; William & Taylor, 2012). Because accountability involves ensuring that the various informative needs of stakeholders are met, the NPOs' accountability framework should explicitly consider the NPO's mission as a category for which it must be answerable.

Considering the issues discussed in the previous sections regarding the role of profit for NPOs and the development of a "silent" social contract among different stakeholders, the next section contributes to the current debate concerning "*for what*" NPOs should be accountable. We now turn to present an integrated accountability framework for NPOs with the intent of contributing to the productive discussion of these accountability approaches.

TOWARD AN INTEGRATED ACCOUNTABILITY MODEL (IAM) FOR NPOS

NPOs are mission-oriented and multi-stakeholder organizations and as a result in the previous paragraphs we analyzed different accountability models that offer interesting insights regarding meeting the demands for accountability from different stakeholders. We analyzed and discussed the fact that donors or funders are not the primary stakeholders in NPOs like shareholders are in for-profit organizations. In addition, alignment with organizational objectives does not singularly guarantee the achievement of the organization's goals, or the satisfaction and consequent support of stakeholders. In fact, long-term survival of an NPO is based on its ability to maximize its social value as defined in the organizational mission and as perceived by the multiple stakeholders influencing and influenced by the NPO (Costa et al., 2011).

Therefore:

- Accountability cannot be focused only on the economic and financial dimensions (*efficiency*). These measurements certainly remain important, and NPOs devote significant effort to measuring their performance in relation to donor funds and budget achievement (Costa et al., 2011; Murtaza, 2012), but measuring organizational success focuses primarily on achieving the mission.
- Economic and financial dimensions, therefore, have to be integrated with measures that relate to achieving mission success (*effectiveness*). In for-profit organizations, the economic and financial dimensions and the mission dimension align but in NPOs, there are at least two stand-alone bottom lines. The first considers the *economic-financial* dimension of the activity, while the second relates to the *mission* dimension. The combination of economic and financial performance with the information

regarding mission achievement allows organizations to have a more informed view of their performance and a better understanding of the manner in which they affect the served communities (Epstein & McFarlan, 2011).

- Finally, by adopting a relational approach to accountability (Brown & Moore, 2001; Ebrahim, 2005; Edwards & Hulme, 1996; Najam, 1996; Unerman & O'Dwyer, 2006), NPOs also have to be answerable/accountable to all the stakeholders who are directly or indirectly affected by the organization's activity.

These three dimensions of accountability – economic and financial, mission-related and social-related – are interrelated. Therefore, in this article, we suggest an IAM for NPOs in order to avoid an "add-on" approach (Gray, 2002) in which some of this information is added to other existing organizational information. The IAM, which will be presented in detail later, is not intended to create a new set of instruments and reporting tools but rather, it should spontaneously emerge as an integration of instruments that are currently employed by NPOs in their daily management but not linked to each other. The intention is also to clarify possible reporting instruments which currently exist within the NPOs and which could be used to build a complete IAM accountability overview.

The IAM model considers three drivers of accountability for NPOs:

- *The economic and financial dimension* is a means to an end because NPOs have to be economically and financially sustainable over the long term in order to guarantee mission achievement over time. This dimension provides information regarding how the financial resources have been obtained or how they have been generated and employed.
- *The mission-related dimension* refers to accountability for the coherence of NPOs activities with the mission benchmark values. This dimension takes into account the objectives met through the mission statement. Unerman and O'Dwyer (2006) considers this dimension "identity accountability" since it "represents a means by which managers (or activists) running organizations take responsibility for shaping their organizational mission and values" (p. 356).
- Finally, *the social-related dimension* refers to the NPO's relational accountability to stakeholders by providing them with information needed to react to the organization's actions. This dimension meets the stakeholder's informative needs emerging from the "silent social contract" set up between the NPO and its stakeholders. NPOs thus have to

be accountable to all stakeholders who are directly or indirectly affected by the NPO's activity, not just the primary or financial stakeholders.

The IAM model is presented in Fig. 1.

The Economic and Financial Dimension

Economic and financial efficiency calls for the NPO to develop, implement and oversee a coherent economic and financial strategy to which organizations devote significant effort. In NPOs, this dimension represents more of a "constraint" than a purpose because they constantly have to guarantee proper economic and financial equilibrium in order to be sustainable in the long run and, therefore, also able to pursue the institutional dimension, that is, the mission. The more efficient an organization, the more economic and financial resources it has to direct to reach its mission. Because of the importance of economic and financial resources in supporting social services, without "healthy" NPO economic and financial management, it is impossible to reach the desired social outcomes. A lack in the economic and financial equilibrium could produce a dangerous situation which could

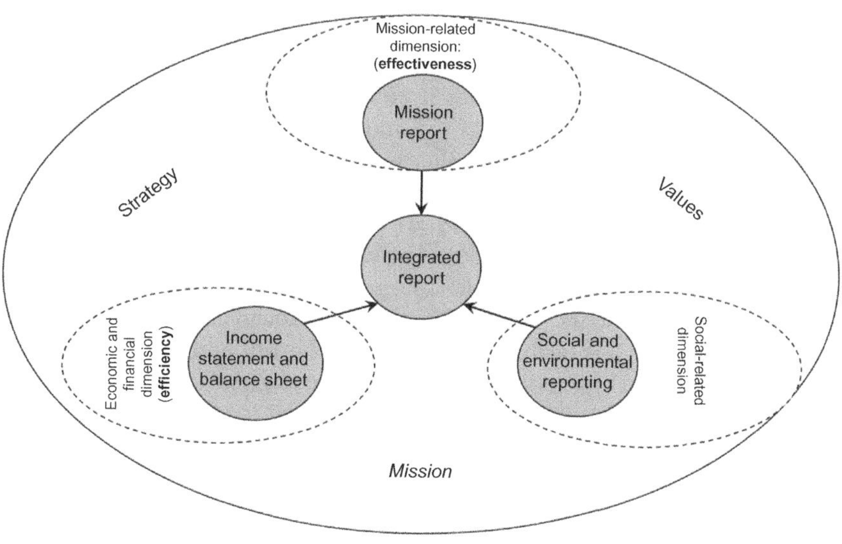

Fig. 1. The Integrated Accountability Model (IAM) for NPOs.

foster serious financial instability or heavy economic losses in the long run. Such imbalances eventually could destroy equity and compromise the NPO's survival. Therefore, the economic and financial dimension has to be considered a constraint in guaranteeing long-term NPO stability.

Within the broad conceptualization of NPOs (Defourny & Nyssens, 2010), the economic and financial dimension is where the most differences between social enterprises, social cooperatives, charities and NGOs emerge. By definition, social enterprises and social cooperatives are entrepreneurial activities that directly operate in the market as providers of health, social, educational and cultural services. On the contrary, NGOs and charities do not operate on the market and their activities mainly depend on external financial support. Therefore, two possible models for evaluating the economic and financial efficiency of NPOs can be suggested.

The first one refers to social enterprises and social cooperatives and contains three different levels of disclosure:

1. The economic disclosure
2. The financial disclosure
3. The investment-liabilities-equity disclosure

The *economic disclosure* refers to costs and revenues received for the delivered social services. This information is recorded primarily by the income statement with two ends: on the one hand, it measures and reports on the efficiency between inputs and outputs (getting the most out of resources) while on the other hand, it enables a first analysis of the value added of NPOs. The value added "is a much broader definition of wealth. [...] Value added looks beyond the wealth (profit) created for shareholders and includes the wealth for a wider group of stakeholders such as employees, creditors, government, and the organization itself" (Mook, Richmond, & Quarter, 2003, p. 286). The value added represents the wealth created by NPOs and distributed to a large group of stakeholders. It therefore reveals and represents "something about the social character of production, something which is occluded by traditional profit and loss accounting" (Burchell, Clubb, & Hopwood, 1985, p. 388). However, the value added and its statement are not flawless since the starting point for this type of analysis is based on the income statement, which is exclusively able to gather, elaborate, measure and report information that can be monetized. Mook et al. (2003) have proposed an Extended Value Added Statement (EVAS) that also includes social inputs which normally do not involve financial transactions.

The *financial disclosure* is based on the financial equilibrium or the equilibrium between invested capital and sources of collateral. This goal can be accomplished by defining a satisfactory financial statement which generally does not require special adaptations of the conventional statement used in the for-profit organizations. It follows the indications given by national and international accounting bodies.

Finally, similar considerations apply to the *investment-liabilities-equity disclosure* which makes reference to the capital information or the statement of financial position. It reports on the makeup of organizational investments, liabilities and equity at the end of the financial year. For this kind of analysis, conventional accounting frameworks can be applied.

The role of economic and financial dimension is somewhat different for NGOs and charities. NGOs and charities do not work for or produce goods and services for the market; rather, they deliver social services through external support from donors, governments and fundraising activities. Therefore, since the added value statement mainly involves how created value is employed, in NGOs and charities, there is no self-creation of value. Instead, the employment of financial resources is made available by external sources. Consequently, except in rare cases, the information is primarily of a financial nature and must be addressed by showing how funding is used. In these cases, the conceptual framework upon which the value-added statement is based is not coherent with the peculiarities of NGOs and charities and requires adaption. There are three main areas that should be considered (see Fig. 2):

(a) the funding area aimed at reporting how the organization is funded;
(b) the management area where management costs are summarized; and
(c) the destination area where remaining resources are accounted for, not only in relation to the activities carried out but also to the distribution of these resources to the organization's stakeholders.

The first part of the IAM model illustrates the critical importance and complexity of the economic and financial dimension: "Without financial resources, there's no mission. Conversely, all of the financial resources in the world are irrelevant if the company isn't focused on a well thought out mission" (Epstein & McFarlan, 2011, p. 28). Therefore, NPOs cannot be accountable only on their financial efficiency. They simultaneously have to consider their effectiveness in meeting organizational purposes, that is, the mission.

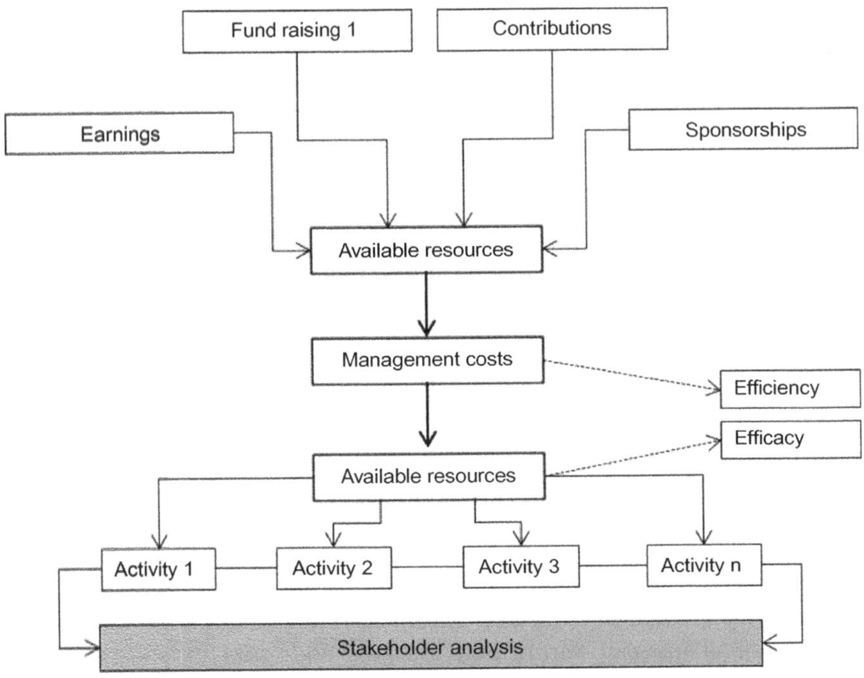

Fig. 2. The Economic and Financial Dimensions in NGOs and Charities.

The Mission-Related Dimension

The mission-related dimension refers to evaluating the effectiveness of the NPO's activities for members and beneficiaries. As Epstein and McFarlan (2011) put it, "To measure its effectiveness, a nonprofit must ask itself, 'Are we really delivering on our mission, not just meeting budget, and are we getting maximum impact from our expenditures?'" (p. 28).

An NPO's mission defines the set of values that the organization intends to produce for its stakeholders and for the broader society and refers to an "identity accountability" (Unerman & O'Dwyer, 2006) according to which "managers (or activists) running organizations take responsibility for shaping their organizational mission and values, for whether (and, if so, how) to open themselves to public or external scrutiny, and for assessing their performance in relation to their goals" (p. 356). Since the mission prominently represents the very core of NPO activities (Ebrahim, 2010) – similar to the position that maximization of shareholder wealth occupies for for-profit organizations – it should be the metric that is used in evaluating and effectively assessing past performance and future activities. The mission-related dimension has informative significance closely linked to effectiveness in a narrow sense, vis-à-vis the organization's performance. For an NPO, this dimension cannot be measured in economic or financial terms since creation of social value is its reason to exist. Broadly, the missions of NPOs are set out in substantive rather than financial terms. These missions focus on particular societal problems that the NPOs seek to ameliorate or on desirable social conditions that the NPOs seek to encourage.

The mission statement is also related to values and principles that form the foundation of the NPO (Moore, 2000; Unerman & O'Dwyer, 2006). These values, together with the purposes that NPOs aim to achieve, become the NPOs' *visions*; thus, visions, missions and goals are strictly related. All three can be formulated broadly or narrowly, abstractly or concretely. However, they are frequently more substantive than for-profit organizations because they are not anchored to maximization of economic wealth (Moore, 2000), but present answers to various societal needs, which by definition are not financial in nature. Money may be needed to accomplish these goals but the ultimate goals are neither economic nor financial.

Fig. 3 represents a possible "strategic pyramid" which exemplifies the relationship between vision, mission and goals.

The vision and the mission statement therefore represent the starting point when defining the operational goals of NPOs. For example, a possible *vision* for an NPO could be "*to become the reference point for voluntary activities in the community reference group.*" This vision could then generate the following *mission* statement: "*to sustain, promote and certify voluntary activity as well as organizations and their activities.*"

The vision and mission have both to be long-term oriented and adaptable to change. First, the long-term view of vision and mission statements requires the ability to cope with uncertainty and changing circumstances. Nonprofit managers are unlikely to know how best to pursue their goals but repeated trials and critical scrutiny can lead to new insights and solutions (Ebrahim, 2010). Second, NPOs often feel that their identity rests on remaining committed to their original mission and they might lose legitimacy from members and beneficiaries when changing their mission due to changes in social conditions, resulting in a so-called "mission drift" (Moore, 2000).

Not only vision and mission statements but also organizational goals and strategies are subject to adaptation as managers learn more about the

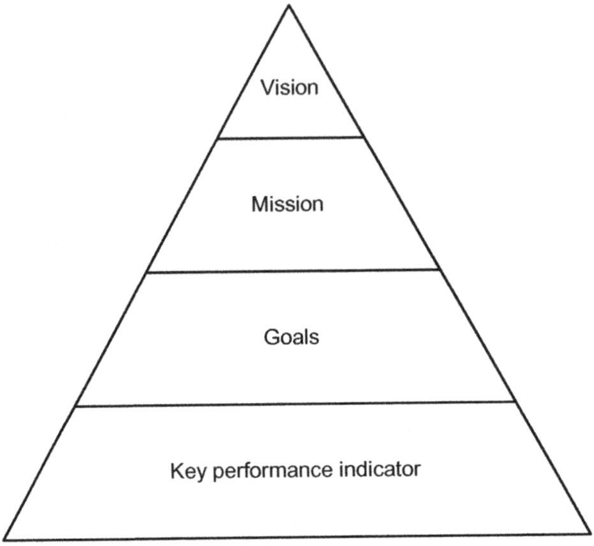

Fig. 3. The Strategic Pyramid of NPOs.

social problems that they are trying to understand and solve: "A central managerial challenge becomes putting in place processes that can engender systematic critical reflection and adaptation, while remaining focused on solving social problems" (Ebrahim, 2010, p. 10).

The strategic pyramid presented in Fig. 3 makes it clear that after defining the vision, mission and goals, NPOs need to consider key strategic indicators, or indicators to define preventive action and measure final outcomes. These indicators cannot fall within a conventional annual report since neither the vision nor the mission and goals can be based on economic and financial metrics.

The Social-Related Dimension

While the economic and financial dimension focuses on evaluating *efficiency* in managing NPOs, and the mission-related dimension concerns the *effectiveness* of reaching their objectives, the social-related dimension refers to the relational attitude of accountability, according to which NPOs have to engage in deliberative dialogue with all stakeholders. While the mission-related dimension refers to the internal dimension of accountability – to make NPOs answerable to themselves while pursuing their declared social aims (Ebrahim, 2010; Unerman & O'Dwyer, 2006) – the social-related dimension considers the external approach to accountability. This approach is primarily based on the existence of an implicit social contract between NPOs and their various stakeholders.

Private and public funders demand that NPOs be accountable for the efficiency and impacts of the social services they have funded. *Beneficiaries* press NPOs to be accountable for the development of their social welfare and for delivery of social services. *Workers* expect NPOs to guarantee their job while maintaining job quality. *Volunteers* demand to be involved in project design while receiving professional growth opportunities. *Communities* require NPOs to focus their energies on better understanding the societal impacts on the local contexts/environments (see Table 1). In short, different stakeholders call upon NPOs to account for their activities (Brown & Moore, 2001).

Even if an NPO's mission is oriented towards the creation of social value, it does not mean that NPOs are automatically accountable to, and

Table 1. The Accountability Expectations of NPO Stakeholders.

Workers	Involvement in management Job quality Protection of workers Equal opportunity Career progress
Members	Nonprofit institutional goals Democratic management Representation on the Board(s) No capital gains
Volunteers	Professional growth Involvement Reciprocal duties Transparency and accountability
Beneficiaries	Type of activity Level of professional response Transparency and disclosure
Funding bodies	Financial trustworthiness Transparency
Public bodies	Type of activity Social cost-benefit analysis
Community	Type of activity Transparency and disclosure Social cost-benefit analysis

thus responsible for, the broad variety of stakeholders and society as a whole. Focusing on the mission-related dimension could lead NPOs to overlook the accountability expectations of other stakeholders, which would result in not respecting the social contract between them.

NPOs have to consider the information needs of all stakeholders involved in their activity in order to satisfy their expectations and claims. Providing such information allows the NPO to maintain its legitimacy within its society of operation (Sinclair & Bolt, 2013). This consideration means that accountability to all the varied stakeholders does not represent the NPO's purpose – the creation of social value. Rather, accountability becomes a necessary constraint for strengthening the relationship with the stakeholders. As such it represents a necessary but deficient condition necessary for long-term effectiveness for without legitimacy from all stakeholders, NPOs assume the risk of a weakened ability to achieve the mission statement which is, by definition, socially oriented.

For example, even if an NPO does not place the well-being of certain stakeholders (e.g., the workers) as its ultimate aim, it has to support their demands for accountability. Indeed, NPOs have to be aware that workers are not really committed to the mission of the organization: "It is not true that they love the mission so much that they are willing to work long hours at low pay for the sake of the cause. They are really no different than those who work for for-profit firms. They, too, are motivated by the crass desire to stay employed. The evidence for such an indictment is that when the choice came down to staying true to their original mission or assuring their financial survival, they opted for financial survival" (Moore, 2000, p. 192).

CONCLUSIONS AND FURTHER DEVELOPMENT

This article has intended to contribute to the academic debate regarding NPO accountability by fostering the adoption of an IAM which identifies the three foremost areas of accountability for NPOs.

First, by questioning the application of the conventional accounting framework for NPOs and exploring its limitations, the article calls for attention to the critical importance and the complexity of the *economic and financial dimension* of accountability for NPOs (Epstein & McFarlan, 2011). NPOs cannot ignore strategies which are able to guarantee economic and financial stability in the long term because they have to constantly create economic value – and be accountable for it – in order to survive over time and to ensure that they can continue with their mission. When analyzing the efficiency of NPOs' economic and financial resources, the fact that the purpose of NPOs cannot be reduced simply to profit maximization or economic and financial wealth has to be taken into account because the purpose is linked to benefit maximization for the beneficiaries of NPOs' activities and for the broader community. NPOs' economic and financial performance cannot be measured with the traditional indicators used in the for-profit sector because the "bottom line" does not allow for the correct interpretation of real performance in these types of organizations.

Second, NPOs have also to consider an internal dimension of accountability, which refers to the ability to be accountable and transparent regarding the values and principles summarized in the mission statement. The IAM presented in this article considers the *mission-related dimension* as one explicit driver for accountability (Moore, 2000). The evaluation of mission performance is urgent for NPOs because it assists managers in delivering strategies that increase NPO effectiveness.

Finally, in light of the relational approach to accountability (Unerman & O'Dwyer, 2006), the IAM model described in this article makes it clear that NPOs cannot be considered as accountable (or responsible) a priori because of their orientation to pursuing social value. In order to be accountable and transparent to all stakeholders, NPOs have to respect the silent social contract that embodies stakeholders' claims and expectations for accountability. In doing so, NPOs answer the social-issue dimension of accountability.

These different dimensions of accountability should not be considered as "add-ons" (Gray, 2002) or as the sum of different, unrelated pieces. These dimensions have to come together consistently in order to address the accountability challenges of NPOs.

Future research could investigate whether or not the IAM model also is applicable to for-profit organizations because the primary roles for accounting information are as applicable in the nonprofit sector as in the for-profit sector. Broadly, there is considerable similarity in the core nature of accountability in for-profits and NPOs. Other research could investigate the possibility of transferring what we know about accountability in the nonprofit sector to the for-profit one. However, the underlying differences in mission, philosophy, structure and values between the two sectors – are considerable and one must bear in mind that the IAM presented in this article should be adapted accordingly.

NOTE

1. Rowan (2001) argues that the normative approach to stakeholder theory plays a significant role because of its applicability to empirical research and managerial scenarios. However, "purely normative approaches to business ethics, built on traditional moral theories such as consequentialism, Kantian deontology, and virtue ethics, are too detached from the real world to offer managers any real guidance in particular situations" (p. 379).

REFERENCES

Acar, M., Guo, C., & Yang, K. (2012). Accountability in voluntary partnerships: To whom and for what? *Public Organization Review*, *12*, 157–174.

Anheier, H. K. (2009). What kind of nonprofit sector, what kind of society? Comparative policy reflections. *American Behavioral Scientist*, *52*(7), 1082–1094.

Avina, J. (1993). The evolutionary life cycles of non-governmental development organizations. *Public Administration and Development*, *13*, 453–474.

Bagnoli, L., & Megali, C. (2011). Measuring performance in social enterprise. *Nonprofit and Voluntary Sector Quarterly*, *40*(1), 149–165.

Ball, A., & Osborne, S. P. (Eds.). (2011). *Social accounting and public management. Accountability for the common good.* New York, NY: Routledge.

Brown, L. D., & Moore, M. H. (2001). Accountability, strategy and international nongovernmental organizations. *Nonprofit and Voluntary Sector Quarterly*, *30*, 569–587.

Burchell, S., Clubb, C., & Hopwood, A. G. (1985). Accounting in its social context: Towards a history of value added in the United Kingdom. *Accounting, Organizations and Society*, *10*(4), 381–413.

Costa, E. (2014). Social reporting for Italian social enterprises. Did the Italian legislator miss an opportunity? In Z. Hoque & L. Parker (Eds.), *Performance management in nonprofit organizations: Global perspectives* (pp. 93–131). New York, NY: Routledge.

Costa, E., Ramus, T., & Andreaus, M. (2011). Accountability as a managerial tool in nonprofit organizations: Evidence from Italian CSVs. *Voluntas: International Journal of Voluntary and Nonprofit Organizations*, *22*(3), 470–493.

Dart, R., Clow, E., & Armstrong, A. (2010). Meaningful difficulties in the mapping of social enterprises. *Social Enterprise Journal*, *6*(3), 186–193.

Dees, J. G. (1998). *The meaning of social entrepreneurship.* Working Paper. Stanford University – Graduate School of Business, Stanford, California.

Dees, J. G., & Economy, P. (2001). Social entrepreneurship. In J. G. Dees, J. Emerson, & P. Economy (Eds.), *Enterprising nonprofits: A toolkit for social entrepreneurship* (pp. 1–18). New York, NY: Wiley.

Defourny, J., & Nyssens, M. (2010). Conceptions of social enterprise and social entrepreneurship in Europe and the United States: Convergences and divergences. *Journal of Social Entrepreneurship*, *1*(1), 32–53.

Donaldson, T., & Dunfee, T. W. (1994). Toward a unified conception of business ethics: Integrative social contracts theory. *The Academy of Management Review*, *19*(2), 252–284.

Donaldson, T., & Preston, L. E. (1995). The stakeholder theory of the corporation: Concepts, evidence, and implications. *The Academy of Management Review*, *20*(1), 65–91.

Ebrahim, A. (2003). Making sense of accountability: Conceptual perspectives for northern and southern nonprofits. *Nonprofit Management & Leadership*, *14*(2), 191–212.

Ebrahim, A. (2005). Accountability myopia: Losing sight of organizational learning. *Nonprofit and Voluntary Sector Quarterly*, *34*(1), 56–87.

Ebrahim, A. (2009). Placing the normative logics of accountability in "Thick" perspective. *American Behavioral Scientist*, *52*(6), 885–904.

Ebrahim, A. (2010). *The many faces of nonprofit accountability*. Working Paper No. 10-069. Harvard Business School.

Edwards, M., & Hulme, D. (1996). Too close for comfort? The impact of the official aid on nongovernmental organizations. *World Development*, *24*(6), 961–973.

Epstein, M. J., & McFarlan, F. W. (2011). Measuring the efficiency and effectiveness of a non-profit's performance. *Strategic Finance*, *93*(4), 27–34.

Evan, W. M., & Freeman, R. E. (1988). A stakeholder theory of the modern corporation: Kantian capitalism. In T. L. Beauchamp & N. E. Bowie (Eds.), *Ethical theory and business* (3rd ed., pp. 97–106). Englewood Cliffs, NJ: Prentice Hall.

Freeman, R. E. (1984). *Strategic management: A stakeholder approach*. Boston, MA: Pitman.

Gray, R. (2002). The social accounting project and accounting organizations and society privileging engagement, imaginings, new accountings and pragmatism over critique? *Accounting, Organizations and Society*, *27*, 687–708.

Gray, R., Adams, C., & Owen, D. (1996). *Accounting and accountability: Changes and challenges in corporate social and environmental reporting*. Upper Saddle River, NJ: Prentice Hall.

Gray, R., Bebbington, J., & Collison, D. (2006). NGOs, civil society and accountability: Making the people accountable to capital. *Accounting, Auditing and Accountability Journal*, *19*(3), 319–348.

Gray, R., Dillard, J., & Spence, C. (2011). A brief re-evaluation of "The Social Accounting Project". In A. Ball & S. P. Osborne (Eds.), *Social accounting and public management. Accountability for the common good* (pp. 12–22). New York, NY: Routledge.

Gray, R., Owen, D., & Maunders, K. (1988). Corporate social reporting: Emerging trends in accountability and the social contract. *Accounting, Auditing and Accountability Journal*, *1*(1), 6–20.

Hofmann, M. A., & McSwain, D. (2013). Financial disclosure management in the nonprofit sector: A framework for past and future research. *Journal of Accounting Literature*, *32*, 61–87.

Kearns, K. P. (1994). The strategic management of accountability in nonprofit organizations: An analytical framework. *Public Administration Review*, *54*(2), 185–192.

Le Lannier, A., & Porcher, S. (2014). Efficiency in the public and private French water utilities: Prospects for benchmarking. *Applied Economics*, *46*(5), 556–572.

Lehman, C. R. (1992). *Accounting's changing roles in social conflict*. London: Paul Chapman.

Lindblom, C. K. (1993). The implications of organisational legitimacy for corporate social performance and disclosure. Paper presented at the Critical Perspectives on Accounting Conference, New York, NY.

Maddocks, J. (2011). Debate: Sustainability reporting: A missing piece of the charity-reporting jigsaw. *Public Money & Management*, *31*(3), 157–158.

Manetti, G. (2014). The role of blended value accounting in the evaluation of socio-economic impact of social enterprises. *Voluntas: International Journal of Voluntary and Nonprofit Organizations, 25*, 443–464.

Mathews, M. R. (1997). Twenty-five years of social and environmental accounting research is there a silver jubilee to celebrate? *Accounting, Auditing and Accountability Journal, 10*(4), 481–531.

Mook, L., Richmond, B. J., & Quarter, J. (2003). Integrated social accounting for nonprofits: A case from Canada. *Voluntas: International Journal of Voluntary and Nonprofit Organizations, 14*(3), 283–297.

Moore, M. H. (2000). Managing for value: Organizational strategy in for-profit, nonprofit and governmental organizations. *Nonprofit and Voluntary Sector Quarterly, 29*, 183–208.

Murtaza, N. (2012). Putting the lasts first: The case for community-focused and peer-managed NGO accountability mechanisms. *Voluntas: International Journal of Voluntary and Nonprofit Organizations, 23*, 109–125.

Najam, A. (1996). NGO accountability: A conceptual framework. *Development Policy Review, 46*, 339–353.

Palmer, P., & Vinten, G. (1998). Accounting, auditing and regulating charities – towards a theoretical underpinning. *Managerial Auditing Journal, 13*(6), 346–355.

Power, M., & Laughlin, R. (1996). Habermas, law and accounting. *Accounting, Organisations and Society, 21*(5), 441–465.

Quarter, J., Mook, L., & Armstrong, A. (2009). *Understanding the social economy: A Canadian perspective*. Toronto: University of Toronto Press.

Reheul, A. M., Caneghem, T., & Verbruggen, S. (2014). Financial reporting lags in the non-profit sector: An empirical analysis. *Voluntas: International Journal of Voluntary and Nonprofit Organizations, 25*, 352–377.

Rowan, J. R. (2001). How binding the ties? Business ethics as integrative social contracts. *Business Ethics Quarterly, 2*(2), 379–390.

Ryan, B., Scapens, R. W., & Theobald, M. (1992). *Research method and methodology in finance and accounting*. London: Academic Press.

Sinclair, R., & Bolt, R. (2013). Third sector accounting standard setting: Do third sector stakeholders have voice? *Voluntas: International Journal of Voluntary and Nonprofit Organizations, 24*, 760–784.

SustainAbility. (2003). *The 21st century NGO: In the market for change*. London: SustainAbility, The Global Compact, UNEP.

Unerman, J., & O'Dwyer, B. (2006). Theorising accountability for NGO advocacy. *Accounting, Auditing and Accountability Journal, 19*(3), 349–376.

Vermeer, T., Raghunandan, K., & Forgione, D. (2009). Audit fees at US non-profit organizations. *Auditing: A Journal of Practice & Theory, 28*(2), 289–303.

Watts, R. L., & Zimmerman, J. L. (1979). The demand for and supply of accounting theories: The market for excuses. *The Accounting Review, 54*(2), 273–305.

Whittington, G. (1986). Financial accounting theory: An over-view. *The British Accounting Review, 18*(1), 4–41.

William, A. P., & Taylor, J. A. (2012). Resolving accountability ambiguity in nonprofit organizations. *Voluntas: International Journal of Voluntary and Nonprofit Organizations, 24*, 559–580.

STEWARDSHIP THEORY: APPROACHES AND PERSPECTIVES

Massimo Contrafatto

ABSTRACT

This article focuses on the lesser-used notion of stewardship and stewardship-ism. Stewardship is a concept that has inspired the activities of several organizations whose mission is to preserve, protect and maintain natural, social and economic assets for the benefit of stakeholders and communities. As observed by Contrafatto and Bebbington (2013), stewardship has some resonance with current policy agendas that attend to the issues related to sustainable development, corporate social responsibility and accountability. Most of the existing works on stewardship provide several perspectives with the focus being either on normative foundations of stewardship or on its organizational and managerial implications. In particular, the stewardship-related literature offers a range of conceptions and approaches ranking from a relatively narrow view of the resources, sources and time frame of stewardship to very broad specification. In this article, the management, organization and accounting literature is analysed to propose a map of current theorizing on stewardship. In particular, drawing on the methodological approach adopted by Lowndes (1996), four theoretical vignettes have been proposed to illustrate different variants and approaches in stewardship

Accountability and Social Accounting for Social and Non-profit Organizations
Advances in Public Interest Accounting, Volume 17, 177–196

ISSN: 1041-7060/doi:10.1108/S1041-706020140000017007

framework. Each vignette provides a set of conceptual constructs, ideas and views to understand stewardship and stewardship-inspired behaviour. The variety of approaches/perspectives on stewardship, as illustrated from the analysis undertaken in this article, provides an opportunity for deeper theory-based understanding of social and organizational dynamics. In particular, it is argued that the richness of perspectives, focus and levels of analysis could offer insights to conceptualize, see and make sense of some of the challenges that are posed by a desire for promoting transition towards more sustainable ways of organizing our society.

Keywords: Stewardship and stewardship-ism; stewardship theory; stewardship and sustainable development

INTRODUCTION

In early 2014, grave flooding affected many cities, towns and villages in the areas of South-West England causing death, considerable destruction and long-lasting damage to properties, infrastructure and the surrounding natural landscape (BBC, 2014a). For many commentators, this flow of floods had been even more severe than those that had hit England over the last few years and notably in 2007. Sadly, this is not an isolated episode. Indeed, similar catastrophic events have affected, over time, and with differing magnitude, several other countries and areas across the world (from South to North and from West to East). In Italy, for example, in October 2011 the world-renowned Cinque Terre (i.e. Five Lands), in the coastal area of Liguria, was hit by massive flooding and landslides that provoked death, destruction and almost the complete annihilation of the Unesco Heritage towns of Monterosso and Vernazza (SKY, 2012). These events together with other climatic-related catastrophes, which regularly harm different parts of our planet, in one way or another, re-propose to the public the issues related to climate change, global warming and human beings' responsibility for such phenomena. Whether and the extent to which these disastrous events are attributable to man-made greenhouse (and other atmospheric-related) effects is still something of heated debate. Unsurprisingly, among the scientific community, there is no definitive, uncontested and categorical answer to these concerns. Scientists have tried to detect the cause-effect relationship between human activities and changes in the current climate and have often used different adjectives and phrases to depict such relationships: 'not at all', 'hard to say', 'not a simple yes or no', 'impossible to detect so far', 'likely' and/or 'certain' (BBC, 2014b). I am neither a scientist nor a climatologist, and I certainly do not propose to speak as if I were, but simply as a commentator, I feel we might pose the questions in a different way.

Rather than asking whether there is a definitive causal relationship between human activities and current climate events (and changes), and the extent to which the latter are determined by the former, perhaps the questions could be framed more broadly. More specifically: (1) can our current way of living, organizing and acting be excluded, with certainty, from not being an influencing factor in the natural equilibrium of our Planet? Put differently, (2) is there any evidence or sign that humanity (and human activities) are in some way deteriorating the capacity of our planet to sustain in the future? If any such signs exist, (3) do we[1] actually have any right at all to act as if we are the only owners and beneficiaries of our planet? (4) What are our responsibilities, as individuals and/or community, in order to ensure the well-being of our (current or future) societies and the world in which we live? In other words, (5) how should our socio-economic-legal system be organized and what responsibilities should be incorporated for achieving sustainable development?[2] Finally, (6) what are the responsibilities of organizations (and corporations), given their prominent role in the current system of organizing our society (Gray, 2010, 2013), for the way in which business and economic operations are conducted?

Some of the issues related to the corporate responsibilities for a sustainable transformation will be discussed in this article. In particular, the focus of the analysis will be on the lesser-used concept of stewardship and stewardship theory. Drawing on the methodological approach adopted by Lowndes (1996), the existing literature on stewardship is analysed to propose a map of current theorizing. The variety of approaches and perspectives on stewardship that emerge from the analysis could offer important insights to conceptualize (and attend to) some of the challenging aspects related to sustainable development (hereafter SD) and the (un)sustainability of current society and business undertakings.

This article is organized as follows. In the next section, stewardship theory is reviewed by taking into consideration the way in which the notion of stewardship has been conceptualized in the finance, management, organization and accounting literature. Based on the analysis undertaken in the following section, a classification of the different strands of the stewardship-research is proposed. Finally, some concluding remarks about how and the extent to which stewardship could represent a potent framework for promoting transition towards a sustainable way of organizing our society are offered.

STEWARDSHIP: UNDERSTANDING CURRENT THEORIZING

Stewardship is not a novel concept in finance, management and accounting literature nor in the organizational domain. As Contrafatto and Bebbington (2013) note, the notion of stewardship has motivated the activities of several organizations (in different contexts, sectors and geographical areas) whose mission is to protect, maintain and enhance natural, social, cultural and economic resources for the benefit of stakeholders, communities and society at large. At first glance, stewardship appears to be a potent concept that has some resonance with current policy agendas that, at the macro and more organization-focused levels, attend to global issues such as SD, corporate social responsibility and accountability. Although pertinent to the concepts of corporate social responsibility and (social) accountability, the notion of stewardship has not been substantially developed in the current management, accounting and social accountability literature, nor have the adopted organizational practices been studied in great depth (Contrafatto & Bebbington, 2013). Gaps exist in the definition, scope and conceptualization of the role and nature of stewardship. As noted by Hernandez (2012), 'although many have theorized about stewardship theory, none have provided a precise definition [and conceptualization] of stewardship' (p. 173). Most of the existing theoretical work provides different, and in some cases alternative, perspectives with the focus being either on normative foundations of stewardship (e.g. Enderle, 1997; McCuddy & Pirie, 2007) or on its organizational and managerial implications (e.g. Caldwell, Hayes, Karri, & Bernal, 2008; Davis, Schoorman, & Donaldson, 1997; Hernandez, 2008, 2012; Van Puyvelde, Caers, Du Bois, & Jegers, 2012). Overall, the existing literature provides a wide range of conceptions and approaches ranking from a relatively narrow view of the resources, sources and time frame of stewardship to much broader specification (Contrafatto & Bebbington, 2013). Drawing on and expanding upon the work of Contrafatto and Bebbington (2013), these different approaches and perspectives will be discussed below.

Before considering in more detail how stewardship has been conceptualized in the literature, a preliminary definition will be proposed to offer a general background. The MacMillan dictionary defines stewardship as 'the way in which someone *organizes* and *looks after* something' (MacMillan, 2007, emphasis added). A few considerations can be made from this preliminary definition. First, stewardship involves a set of guiding-principles for someone's behaviour. Second, stewardship-based behaviour implies a 'looking after', that is a taking care and protecting something belonging to someone else. Third, the object of this taking care behaviour is 'something', that is, resources that for different reasons possess a relative importance for others. Stewardship is a notion that has some historical pedigree (particularly in the Middle Ages) as it referred to the 'means [undertaken] to *protect* a kingdom while those rightfully in charge were away or more often to *govern for* the sake of an underage king' (Block, 1993, p. xx, emphasis added). In the Middle Ages, the steward played a 'vital role ... [...] because he was an officer who managed the interest of an estate on behalf of his employer [i.e. the King and/or Lord]' (Contrafatto & Bebbington, 2013, pp. 40–41). As we will see later on, in the contemporary understanding of stewardship and the role of stewards, some of this historical heritage is still evident. In one way or another, the notion of stewardship still appears to be rooted in its historical background, as it represented a noble practice whose purpose was to look after, protect and govern on behalf of others who were the only legitimate owners/beneficiaries.

In the following sub-section, the existing finance, management and accounting literature is analysed in order to propose a map of current theorizing. Drawing on the methodological approach adopted by Lowndes (1996), the analysis is conducted through *vignettes* to provide illustrative depictions of the way in which stewardship has been described and conceptualized in the different disciplines. Each vignette represents no more than a theoretical 'snapshot' (Lowndes, 1996, p. 184) of stewardship, its features and foundations. As such, each vignette provides a 'tool box of ideas' (*ibid.*, p. 184) and conceptual constructs to understand stewardship and stewardship-driven behaviour. The stewardship-related vignettes are described in the following sub-sections.

Stewardship-Related Theoretical Vignettes

From the illustrative analysis of the literature undertaken in this article, four vignettes are elaborated to represent different variants/approaches to stewardship theory. In describing each of these variants, attention will be devoted to differences in terms of (i) focus and locus of analysis; (ii) definition and terminology used; (iii) role of stewardship and/or steward; and (iv) underlying theoretical assumptions.

The Traditional Accounting and Finance Approach: Stewardship as a Synonym of conventional accountability/responsibility

In this approach, stewardship is regarded as a synonym of accountability as normally conceived in the conventional finance and financial accounting literature. This is the view that is held, for example, by Gjesdal (1981) and O'Connell (2007) who analyse stewardship (and stewardship reporting in particular) drawing on a narrow agency framework.[3] From this perspective, as argued by Gjesdal (1981) and O'Connell (2007), there is a 'stewardship demand for information', in the form of financial accounts and reporting, because this information is an essential component for evaluating and controlling the actions of managing the (mainly) financial and economic resources on behalf of the owners (i.e. stockholders).[4] In other words, as observed by Rosenfield (1974), this demand for information is fundamental for reporting 'on the control and use of the resources by those accountable for their control and use to those whom they are accountable' (p. 126). Hence, in the traditional financial 'accounting literature [this] stewardship objective is usually taken as an axiom' (Gjesdal, 1981, p. 209); there is a stewardship demand for information because the use of such information represents a Pareto-optimal solution for the organization and interested parties. In this approach, the focus of analysis is on the information provided by financial statements with stewardship being the conceptual framework that is used to justify the provision of such information. Robb (2012) makes similar considerations in the context of cooperative organizations, when he maintains that stewardship lies 'at the heart of cooperative accounting' (p. 20) and the provisions of financial statements, from these organizations, is primarily grounded on the need (of the Board) to 'account to members for the way in which the resources entrusted have been used' (*ibid.*, p. 24). In essence, stewardship is conceptualized as a synonym of accountability as normally understood in the conventional financial accounting literature (Contrafatto & Bebbington, 2013; O'Connell, 2007). As such, it represents a fundamental mechanism to regulate *efficiently* and *effectively* agency relationships between agents and the principal in the use and control of the entrusted (financial and economic) resources.

Similar considerations emerge in the conventional finance literature, where stewardship is envisaged as an essential mechanism for financial decision-making. This is the view held, for example, by Ali (2012) who also adopts an implicit agency framework to discuss the notion of stewardship and, in particular, its prominent role in ensuring the integrity, stability and soundness of financial institutions and markets. Stewardship-based behaviour is defined as the conduct undertaken by an agent (e.g. financial intermediaries/institutions) who *diligently* and *dutifully* manages others' economic resources and finances on their behalf. The agent-steward is described as a responsible, respectful, accountable and efficient 'caretaker [...] of [the] properties owned by another' (Ali, 2012, p. 207). In so doing, stewardship behaviour and stewards' conducts become the 'cornerstone' (*ibid.*, p. 209) for sound, efficient and well-functioning financial markets. As argued by Ali (2012), 'the effects of failed stewardship [would be] far-reaching, touching not only on the soundness of the financial markets but on the reputation of [the] jurisdiction itself' (p. 209). In other words, stewardship behaviour is envisaged as an accountable, responsible and diligent way of acting and conducting business through which to ensure the effectiveness, reputation, solidity and ultimately the existence of financial institutions and finance jurisdiction itself.

The Theological Perspective: Stewardship as a Normative Foundation for Business Undertakings

The theological perspective provides the broadest conception of stewardship. This is the approach adopted, for example, by Enderle (1997) and McCuddy and Pirie (2007), who embrace a Judeo-Christian perspective to conceptualize the notion of stewardship and theorize its role in driving organizational and business undertakings. Enderle (1997), in particular, grounds his analysis on the perspective of the Christian Environmental Stewardship for discussing and 'understanding [issues related] to corporate environmental responsibility' (p. 173). Stewardship is proposed as a normative framework for corporate environmental responsibility and represents a contribution towards the search of a common ethical ground on which to base the central issues about environmental responsibility. As observed by Enderle (1997) the notion of Christian Environmental Stewardship is introduced by the biblical text of 'Genesis', to which it is necessary briefly to refer to help understand its underpinnings. At the basis of Judeo-Christian tradition there is the belief that the world is a creation of God, who is the only creator of all creatures and visible/invisible things. God loves all his creatures, which are made in his image. As such, all creatures (human and non-human) have a divine right to life. Within the creation, God has given men and women a privileged role: to be (and act as) stewards within God's world and for God's will (Enderle, 1997, p. 177). Hence, stewardship represents the spiritual conduct of humanity to be a steward. Stewardship is not ownership nor domination; rather it is the act of *serving* God and his creation. Being a steward entails acting 'in service' (*ibid.*, p. 177) of someone and for something which one believes in. From the perspective of Christian Environmental Stewardship, stewardship thus 'involves *respect* and *care* for all human and non-human beings and rules out their total instrumentalization' (Enderle, 1997, p. 178, emphasis added). According to Enderle (1997), Christian Environmental Stewardship represents a powerful normative ethical ground for justifying and understanding any corporate social responsible behaviours in undertaking business and commercial activities.

A similar view is held by McCuddy and Pirie (2007), who draw on a Judeo-Christian theological perspective to discuss the role of stewardship as a normative foundation for decision-making in finance and economics. McCuddy and Pirie (2007) see stewardship (and stewardship behaviour) as grounded on theological underpinnings since that in 'acting as stewards, principles of spirituality are necessarily invoked' (p. 958). These principles of spirituality, thus, represent the pillars of stewardship, which is described as a 'protective restraint, a taking care of resources through nurturing and thrifty management of their use' (McCuddy & Pirie, 2007, p. 961 who quote Leopold, 1998, p. 228). As such, stewardship involves a duty for taking care, nurturing and conservation of resources. According to the Judeo-Christian tradition (as seen above), this duty of being steward lies with human beings. As emphasized by McCuddy and Pirie (2007) stewardship:

(i) Is the responsibility of human beings for all 'things of spirit' (i.e. all things which are the creation of God);
(ii) Involves sharing, rather than exploiting, with others;
(iii) Entails acting in service of God;
(iv) Benefits all current and future humankind.

Based on these premises, thus, stewardship is defined as acting in such a way that: (a) 'benefit[s] ourselves and the people currently around us; (b) provide[s] the potential for benefiting and sustaining future generations' (*ibid.*, p. 962). According to McCuddy and Pirie (2007), at the core of stewardship (and stewardship behaviour) there is a fundamental idea of service with the purpose of bringing welfare:

> [r]eturning to the notion of stewardship, in general, we can conclude that it clearly revolves around service to humankind. This service benefits [all] human beings (others and ourselves) – both in the current generation and in future generations. (p. 963)

What seems to emerge is that stewardship per se combines an orientation towards others' benefits with one's self-interest now and in the future. In other words, from this view, stewardship (and stewardship behaviour) is driven by both selflessness (i.e. focus on others) and selfishness (i.e. focus on oneself). McCuddy and Pirie (2007) introduces the term of self-fullness to attempt to reconcile the two apparently contradictory concepts of selflessness and selfishness. In the way in which it is conceptualized, self-fullness does 'involve the simultaneous pursuit of reasonable[5] self-interest and reasonable concern for the common good ... [...]. Self-fullness involves pursuing one's self-interest in the form of fully developing and utilizing one's capabilities ... [...]. As such, self-fullness is an essential precursor for stewardship' (pp. 960–961). These considerations seem to be particularly relevant for non-profit organizations. For instance, it would be useful to investigate how and to what extent the concept of 'self-fullness' could provide an effective theoretical lens to understand the motives and rationales, which drive managers and employees of socially responsible organizations (e.g. social enterprises, charities, community-based organizations, etc.) towards the search for objectives that are wider than simple economic and financial ones.

In conclusion, what seems evident from the above review, is that the theological perspective enlarges the focus of analysis and broadens the range of resources (including natural, social and spiritual) to be stewarded as well as the subjects to whom one is responsible, by involving all human beings, all non-human creatures and creation itself. Stewardship is, thus, conceptualized as the normative-theological foundation on which to ground models of thinking and organizing economics and business undertakings in a social and environmental responsible way.

The Management and Organization Perspective: Stewardship as an Effective/Efficient Model of Governance and Organizational Leadership

As Contrafatto and Bebbington (2013) note, somewhere between the two extremes described above there is a perspective that is held mostly in management/organization literature, where the potential of stewardship as an alternative model of governance, managerial motivation and organizational leadership is discussed (e.g. Caldwell et al., 2008; Davis et al., 1997; Hernandez, 2008, 2012). Stewardship, which is fundamentally defined as 'the attitudes and behaviours that place the long-term best interests of a group ahead of personal goals that serve an individual's self-interests' (Hernandez, 2008, p. 122), represents the conceptual framework for an *alternative* governance model that is able to explain (and regulate) the relationships between managers, shareholders and other stakeholders (Davis et al., 1997). In particular, stewardship and stewardship-behaviour presuppose that 'organizational actors take personal responsibility for the effects of organizational actions on [other] stakeholder welfare' (Hernandez, 2008, p. 122). Thus, stewardship-based behaviours entail a relationship-centred and others-oriented way of acting whose purpose is ultimately to promote and '[protect] others' long term welfare. Accordingly, stewardship behaviours are a type of prosocial action, intended to have a positive effect on other people' (Hernandez, 2012, pp. 174–175). Hernandez (2012), who provides a detailed theoretical model to explain the dynamics and factors that drive stewardship behaviours, discusses the underlying theoretical elements of stewardship. First, stewardship entails a covenantal-type relationship that links several subjects at different levels of analysis. Second, at the basis of this relationship there is a sort of moral commitment according to which individuals feel obliged to act in certain ways to pursue a valued end cause for the benefit of others involved in the relationship. In particular, for organizations, it implies an obligation towards this valued end and for employees a commitment to promote the ability of the organization to pursue this valued end. Stewardship, therefore, reflects an ongoing sense of obligation to others based on the intention to uphold the covenantal relationship in the long term (Hernandez, 2012). As explained by Hernandez (2012), this sense of obligation is grounded on two psychological elements, that is, (i) cognitive and (ii) affective. The cognitive dimension describes an individual' willingness to 'subjugate his or her personal interests to act in protection of others' long term welfare' (*ibid.*, p. 174). However, the affective component represents the emotional elements, which link stewards to their beneficiaries, according to which individuals are willing to uphold this self-sacrificial behaviour. In contrast to the theological perspective, this type of obligation appears to be willingness-based and driven by an a-spiritual ethos; it is a willing decision that is based on considerations that seem to be devoid of any spiritual underpinnings. Although, the focus of stewards and stewardship behaviour is 'others and not [just] self' (Hernandez, 2008, p. 121), stewards/managers are described as 'self-actualizers' (Davis et al., 1997), who adopt a pro-organizational and collectivistic (Van Puyvelde et al., 2012) behaviour in order to realize his/her full potential and to maximize their personal utility/benefits. It is through this pro-organizational/collectivistic conduct that the manager/steward is able to align his/her personal interests with the objectives of other stakeholders and, as such, to ensure long-term wealth of the organization and stakeholders themselves. From this perspective, the steward/manager acts by integrating different stakeholders' interests with the purpose of generating long-term economic and social benefits (Caldwell et al., 2008). As noted by Caldwell and Karri (2005), at the basis of stewardship theory there is the 'fundamental assumption [...] that the maximization of long-term economic wealth will ultimately serve to be in the best interests of the principals and the various stakeholders collectively, in addition to maximizing social welfare and the long-term economic benefit to society' (p. 251). These considerations resonate with the non-profit literature, which has specifically focused on the governance mechanisms of non-profit organizations[6] (e.g. Caers et al., 2006; Van Puyvelde et al., 2012). Van Puyvelde et al. (2012), for example, adopt insights from stewardship theory to expose a more comprehensive and extended governance and managerial model to investigate the complex principal-agent relationships, (which involve donors and board of directors; managers and employees; etc.), of the non-profit organizations. According to Van Puyvelde et al. (2012), a stewardship-infused model of governance provides a more effective way to substantiate and explain the behaviour of agents/stewards (e.g. the board in principal-agent relationship with the donors), who are intrinsically motivated to act in a collectivistic and collaborative way so as to pursue the long-term social/economic outcome of the organizations.

In conclusion, the management and organization perspective on stewardship is based on a broader principal-agent framework where managers act as stewards by performing a collectivistic and pro-organizational behaviour in order to achieve the objectives of organizations. In this approach, if on one hand the spectrum of subjects involved in the relationship is wider than that seen in the conventional finance and financial accounting approach, on the other hand this is more restricted than the theological perspective. Similar considerations could be made about the time frame of the analysis, the assets entrusted and sources of stewardship. The underpinning time frame is clearly longer than that considered in the narrow traditional agency theory, though still being within the temporal boundaries of the business and organizational activities. With regard to the assets to be stewarded and the sources of duties for stewardship, these are broader than those established in law or contract.

The Social Accounting Approach: Stewardship as an Extension of Social Accountability

As far as social accountants have been interested in stewardship, the focus of examination has been on understanding whether and the extent to which the notions of stewardship and social accountability are theoretically linked as well as the relevance that this may have for issues related to SD (e.g. Contrafatto & Bebbington, 2013). At first glance, the notion of stewardship appears to have much in common with the concept of social accountability (for a conceptualization, see Gray, Owen, & Adams, 1996). Both concepts are, indeed, centred on the relationship between two (or more) subjects (respectively described as accountee/principal and accountor/steward), where the accountor/steward has a duty of taking decisions/actions on behalf of and for the interests of others (Contrafatto & Bebbington, 2013). The relationship between these two parties involves the existence of some *responsibilities:* the responsibilities that the accountor/steward holds for managing and preserving others' resources/assets (Contrafatto & Signori, 2012). Although there are similarities, the concept of stewardship has not to be considered per se a synonym for social accountability. With regard to this, for example, Contrafatto and Bebbington (2013) maintain that stewardship should be seen as 'a special case of accountability where the asset[s] to be looked after, the time scale on which care is being exercised, and the range of stakeholders forming part of the stewardship relationship are all broader than the relationships most often identified within the accountability-focused social accounting literature' (p. 45). The same authors, who analysed stewardship and the stewardship-driven activities of a social economy organization, concluded that stewardship represents a particular type of social accountability. Stewardship is metaphorically a 'plus form' of social accountability. As such, a stewardship framework enlarges the scope, focus and time frame of reference compared to what is generally considered within social accountability literature. In other words, from this perspective, stewardship is conceptualized as an extension, rather than an alternative, of social accountability in several respects. First, stewardship involves a longer 'generational time frame' (Contrafatto & Bebbington, 2013, p. 51) and, as such, it extends the time length of analysis beyond that which is usually discussed in social accounting literature. Second, stewardship enlarges the scope and focus of analysis as it takes into consideration a wider set of resources (including natural, cultural heritage, community-based and tradition-related assets) and range of stakeholders (including ancestors, the Estate and future generations) for which, and to whom, a steward is responsible for. Finally, stewardship conceptualization seems to be grounded on a distinctive ethos. Contrafatto and Bebbington (2013) suggest that behind the concept of stewardship, as envisaged in their case study, there is an idea of maintaining, nurturing and preserving the resources that have been entrusted. This emphasis and ethos on nurturing, respecting and preserving are important aspects for understanding this approach. From this perspective, the steward is not only the keeper but also the nurturer who is emotionally involved in looking after others' resources. In some ways, stewardship behaviour is motivated by a taking care attitude towards the subjects and things forming part of the relationship.

Summary
It can be observed from the previous discussion that the various conceptions of stewardship, which emerge from existing literature, do not constitute an organic theoretical whole. Differences in terms of definition, interpretation, focus and perspectives arise from an analysis of the different approaches within the stewardship framework. In the following sub-section, the four vignettes described above are synthesized in a table.

Stewardship-Related Vignettes: Theoretical Appraisal

The four vignettes that have been proposed to describe the different approaches in *stewardship-ism* depict distinguishable, though not necessarily contrasting, variants of stewardship, steward and stewardship-behaviour. Overall, they provide the lens for visualizing and understanding the core assumptions and elements about stewardship and stewardship-driven behaviour by emphasizing one or other of these elements. Table 1 synthesizes the four vignettes that have been proposed.

CONCLUDING REMARKS

In this article, an illustrative analysis of the existing finance, management and (social) accounting literature on stewardship has been conducted to investigate the way in which stewardship has been conceptualized in these different disciplines. The purpose of this article was to provide a deeper theoretical understanding of stewardship-ism so as to offer insights to conceptualize how and the extent to which stewardship could inform humanity's *modus operandi* that is oriented to SD. Drawing upon the methodological approach adopted by Lowndes (1996), four theoretical vignettes have been proposed to illustrate alternative variants and approaches in the

Table 1. Stewardship-Related Theoretical Vignettes.

	Stewardship as a Synonym of Conventional Accountability/ Responsibility	Stewardship as a Normative Ground for Organizational and Economic Undertakings	Stewardship as an Effective/ Efficient Model of Governance and Organizational Leadership	Stewardship as an Extension of Social Accountability
Focus of analysis	Stewardship demand for information and stewardship behaviour for decision-making.	The role of a theological-inspired conception of stewardship in organizational, economic and financial decision-making.	Stewardship as foundation of an alternative model of management, control and motivation into organizations.	The extent to which the notion of stewardship could be theoretically linked to the concept of social accountability and the relevance that this has on sustainable development-issues.
Definition of stewardship	Stewardship is the responsibility and accountability of agents (e.g. corporate executives, financial institutions, etc.) for managing diligently and dutifully others' economic/financial resources on their behalf.	Stewardship is the human acting, in service of God and creation itself, with the purpose of providing benefits to all human and non-human beings now and in the future.	Stewardship entails the attitude and behaviour of individuals to willingly subordinate personal goals to the protection of others' long-term best interests.	Stewardship represents a special case of social accountability, that is, a 'plus-form' accountability that entails an attitude to look after, take care and nurture others' resources.
Steward	Steward is a responsible/ accountable agent who diligently, dutifully and efficiently manages others' properties.	Steward is a spiritual-inspired carer and nurturer who respectfully acts in service of and for God's will and his creation.	Steward is a pro-social (and organizational) collectivistic actor whose behaviour is aimed to promote and ensure others' (e.g. other stakeholders) welfare and benefits.	Steward is an accountable and emotionally involved carer, nurturer and preserver of resources (e.g. ecological, cultural and tradition related) for current and future generations.

Purpose of stewardship	Stewardship information and behaviour for ensuring principals' control and integrity/soundness of financial/economic markets.	To provide the normative-ethical grounds for social and environmental responsible behaviours and decision-making.	Stewardship-based managerial and governance models as a way for maximizing organizational performance, for creating long-term wealth and for ensuring the interests of principals and agents themselves.	Stewardship for inspiring and driving economic and organizational transformations towards sustainable development.
Theoretical underpinnings	Based on a Neo Classic Economics agency framework, according to which individuals act as rational, self-serving actors who seek to maximize their interests. Governance and control mechanisms are put in place to regulate self-oriented behaviours of agents.	Based on a Judeo-Christian infused theological perspective, according to which human beings act as respectful and self-fullness actors in service of God's will for taking care and nurturing all (human and non) beings and inanimate things created by God.	Based on a broader principal- agent perspective of organizational governance, according to which managers/stewards act as collectivistic self-actualizers to maximize, through organizational achievement, their utility.	Based on an enlarged social accountability framework, according to which managers and organizational representatives have wider responsibilities, rather than generating only economic results, to current and future stakeholders and society.

stewardship framework. The four vignettes are: (i) stewardship as a synonym of agency-theory based accountability/responsibility; (ii) stewardship as a normative/theological ground for economic and social undertakings; (iii) stewardship as an efficient/effective model of governance and organizational leadership; (iv) stewardship as a deeper, wider and extended social accountability. As Lowndes (1996) notes, each vignette represents no more than a 'snapshot' (p. 184) that is intended to depict the concept/role of stewardship and stewards, their features and theoretical foundations (see Table 1 for an overview of the vignettes).

A series of conclusions can be drawn from the theoretical analysis undertaken in this article. First, stewardship-ism does not seem to be a single and organic body of theory, but comprises several strands of arguments, positions and implications. Each strand of research, although the focus on stewardship as motivating rationale for individual and/or organizational behaviours, is informed by diverse underlying philosophical/methodological assumptions and appears to be inspired by distinctive research agendas. Differences in terms of definition/conceptualization, focus of analysis, role and purpose of stewardship-based behaviour emerge.

Second, the variety of approaches/perspectives on stewardship, not necessarily competing or contrasting, should not be seen as a limitation but rather as an opportunity for generating deeper theory-based understanding of social and organizational dynamics. In particular, it is argued that the richness of perspectives, focus and levels of analysis could offer insights into, and help make sense of, some of the challenges that are posed by a move towards SD. As noted by many commentators (e.g. Bebbington, O'Dwyer, & Unerman, 2007; Gray, 2010, 2013), SD is a notion that [challenges] the very heart of everything that we assume about business, [society] and modernity' (Gray, 2013, p. 316)[7] and that requires fundamental 'societal change[s]' (Bebbington, 2007, p. 226) in the current way of organizing our life. The first change that is required in order to start a transition towards a more sustainable society and economics would be in the way of thinking about SD and in the prospects from which to observe/conceptualize SD-related challenging issues.[8] Stewardship, in particular in the way in which it has been conceptualized in the normative/theological and social accountability traditions, has the potential to provide alternative views to those held, for example, within mainstream corporate social responsibility literature, because 'stewardship links more readily to sustainable development' (Contrafatto & Bebbington, 2013, p. 51).

A SD-compatible way of organizing society and conducting business would need an ecological-centred view/approach that is able to reconcile socio-organizational and eco-systems (Bebbington et al., 2007). Bebbington et al. (2007, pp. 345–346) explain that two aspects are intrinsic to the notion of SD, respectively: (1) an attention on an ecological space, its carrying capacity and the ability of the system to endure; (2) an onus to ensure some form of eco-socio justice with regard to the access to natural resources as well as to the social/economic benefits that come from the use of these resources. From this perspective, thus, SD demands an ethos and attitude to preserving, keeping and nurturing (rather than exploiting, consuming and damaging) the ecological resources of our planet (Gray, 2010). Such an ethos would be inspired by a moral, ethical and spiritual, though not necessarily religious, commitment to act with respect, fairness and justice towards others things (resources, human and non-human beings). As seen above, in the concept of stewardship there is a strong emphasis on 'looking after' and 'protecting' on behalf of *others*, who are not able to do this themselves. In one way or another this emphasis on 'others' rather than 'us' is a key aspect of stewardship. This is particularly emphasized, as seen above, in the theological/normative and social accountability approaches, where the *others group* is wider and includes subjects and entities (e.g. future generations, ancestors, non-human beings, etc.) which are not generally considered in the management and organizational literature. In addition, in the theological and social accountability traditions on stewardship, the time frame of reference would be generational (and intergenerational) and include resources (e.g. built heritage, traditions, divine things) that are respectively much longer and wider than seen in much of the business and organizational literature. Finally, the steward is envisaged as the keeper, who acts as an emotionally inspired guardian of others' entrusted resources. These observations have strong resonance with the notion of SD and related challenging issues/demands. In particular, it could be argued that stewardship has the potential to provide a strong foundation to inspire ways of organizing humanity and undertaking economic actions so that a SD transition might be achieved. For instance, stewardship (with the emphasis on 'others'; 'preservation' and 'protection'; 'fairness and justice', etc.), could provide the guiding principles for the supra-national and national governing bodies (e.g. EU; UN) that are concerned at a macro level with elaborating and introducing regulations about extending the responsibilities and accountability of organizations (including, for profit, public and non-profit) for their economic and business undertakings. In addition, stewardship principles could be adopted to guide professional bodies (e.g. accounting bodies), which, at a more organizational level, are involved in providing rules (e.g. accounting standards) to help to manage, control and report the organizations' economic activities and the effects of such activities.

NOTES

1. The pronoun 'we' is used in a generic sense to indicate 'us' who are living in the current time period. However, the term could be widely used to refer to any human community who live (or will live) in a specific context and period.

2. Drawing on the Brundtland Report published by the United Nations World Commission on Environment and Development (UNWCED) in 1987, in this article Sustainable Development is defined as a 'development which meets the needs of the present without compromising the ability of the future generations to meet their own needs' (United Nations World Commission on Environment and Development [UNWCED], 1987, p. 8. See also Bebbington, 2001).

3. The agency theory, which is essentially based on an economics paradigm, represents a theoretical framework that explains how and why actors behave (or do not behave) in their organizational/social undertakings. According to the agency theory, individuals act as 'rational actors who seek to maximize their self-interest' (Hernandez, 2012, p. 172). Hence, individuals/agents are oriented fundamentally to self-serving and tacitly take actions that pursue their own benefits regardless of the impacts on others, including the principal (Jensen & Meckling, 1976). In order to control such self-serving behaviours, organizations internally adopt control, evaluation and governance mechanisms to 'ensure agent-principal interest alignment' (Davis et al., 1997, p. 23. See also, Hernandez, 2012; Jensen, 1983).

4. As noted by O'Connell (2007, p. 215), in the financial accounting and reporting literature stewardship is considered to be one of the two objectives of financial reporting together with the provision of information, which is useful for decision-making (for further discussion see also Birnberg, 1980).

5. What a 'reasonable self-interest' represents and how it should be defined/identified is not explained and discussed further by McCuddy and Pirie (2007). However, it is clear that such issues would need further specification and clarification, which is beyond the scope of this article.

6. For a more detailed analysis of this literature, see Caers et al. (2006).

7. Gray (2010) explains that sustainability (and sustainable development) are not easy to define, but rather they represent contested, complex and elusive concepts. Understanding sustainability, its ontological/epistemological pedigree and its interactions with the life and existence of our planet is *a sine qua non* for any discourse about the (un)sustainability and sustainable development of our current society. These issues are not dismissed. However, they are not central to this article. For a more nuanced, in-depth and contextual understanding of sustainability and sustainable development and their complex interactions with humanity and modernity refer to Gray (2010, 2013).

8. For further discussion, see for example Milne and Gray (2007).

ACKNOWLEDGEMENTS

I would like to thank John Ferguson, Sara Moggi, the two anonymous reviewers and especially the guest editors, Ericka Costa, Lee D. Parker and Michele Andreaus, for their advice and helpful comments on earlier drafts of this article.

REFERENCES

Ali, S. (2012). Re-defining stewardship? *Journal of Financial Crime*, *19*(2), 207–212.

BBC. (2014a). Retrieved from http://www.bbc.co.uk/news/uk-26111598 (about event). Accessed on February 26, 2014.

BBC. (2014b). Retrieved from http://www.bbc.co.uk/news/science-environment-2622253 (about the uncertainty of climate change) (David Shukman). Accessed on February 26, 2014.

Bebbington, J. (2001). Sustainable development: A review of the international development, business and accounting literature. *Accounting Forum*, *25*(2), 128–157.

Bebbington, J. (2007). Changing organizational attitudes and culture through sustainability accounting. In J. Unerman, J. Bebbington, & B. O'Dwyer (Eds.), *Sustainability accounting and accountability*. London: Routledge.

Bebbington, J., O'Dwyer, B., & Unerman, J. (2007). Postscript and conclusions. In J. Unerman, J. Bebbington, & B. O'Dwyer (Eds.), *Sustainability accounting and accountability*. London: Routledge.

Birnberg, G. (1980). The role of accounting in financial disclosure. *Accounting, Organizations and Society*, *5*(2), 71–80.

Block, P. (1993). *Stewardship: Choosing service over self-interest*. San Francisco, CA: Berrett-Koehler.

Caers, R., Du Bois, C., Jegers, M., De Gieter, S., Schepers, C., & Pepermans, R. (2006). Principal-agent relationships on the stewardship-agency axis. *Nonprofit Management & Leadership*, *17*(1), 25–47.

Caldwell, C., Hayes, L., Karri, R., & Bernal, P. (2008). Ethical stewardship: The role of leadership behaviour and perceived trustworthiness. *Journal of Business Ethics*, *78*, 153–164.

Caldwell, C., & Karri, R. (2005). Organizational governance and ethical systems: A covenantal approach to building trust. *Journal of Business Ethics*, *58*, 249–259.

Contrafatto, M., & Bebbington, J. (2013). Developing techniques for stewardship: A Scottish study. In L. Mook (Ed.), *Accounting for social value*. Toronto: University of Toronto Press.

Contrafatto, M., & Signori, S. (2012). Responsabilità, accountability e sostenibilità aziendale: Alcune riflessioni. In *Saggi di storia delle discipline aziendali e delle dottrine economiche*. Scritti in onore di Antonio Amaduzzi professore emerito. Rome: RIREA.

Davis, J. H., Schoorman, F. D., & Donaldson, L. (1997). Toward a stewardship theory of management. *Academy of Management Review*, *22*(1), 20–47.

Enderle, G. (1997). In search of a common ethical ground: Corporate environmental responsibility from the perspective of Christian environmental stewardship. *Journal of Business Ethics*, *16*, 173–181.

Gjesdal, F. (1981). Accounting for stewardship. *Journal of Accounting Research*, *19*(1), 208–231.

Gray, R. (2010). Is accounting for sustainability actually accounting for sustainability … and how would we know? An exploration of narratives of organisations and the planet. *Accounting, Organizations and Society*, *35*, 47–62.

Gray, R. (2013). Sustainability + accounting education: The elephant in the classroom. *Accounting Education*, *22*(4), 308–332.

Gray, R., Owen, D., & Adams, C. (1996). *Accounting & accountability: Changes and challenge in corporate social and environmental reporting*. London: Prentice-Hall.

Hernandez, M. (2008). Promoting stewardship behaviour in organizations: A leadership model. *Journal of Business Ethics*, *80*, 121–128.

Hernandez, M. (2012). Toward an understanding of the psychology of stewardship. *Academy of Management Review*, *27*(2), 172–193.

Jensen, M. (1983). Organizational theory and methodology. *Accounting Review*, *58*, 319–338.

Jensen, M., & Meckling, W. (1976). Theory of the firm: Managerial behavior, agency costs, and ownership structure. *Journal of Financial Economics*, *3*, 305–360.

Leopold, A. (1998). Stewardship. In *Encyclopedia of applied ethics* (Vol. 4). San Diego, CA: Academic Press.

Lowndes, V. (1996). Varieties of new institutionalism: A critical appraisal. *Public Administration*, *74*(Summer), 181–197.

MacMillan. (2007). *Macmillan English dictionary for advanced learners*. Oxford: A&C Black Publishers.

McCuddy, M., & Pirie, W. (2007). Spirituality, stewardship, and financial decision-making: Toward a theory of intertemporal stewardship. *Managerial Finance Review*, *33*(12), 957–969.

Milne, M., & Gray, R. (2007). Future prospects for corporate sustainability reporting. In J. Unerman, J. Bebbington, & B. O'Dwyer (Eds.), *Sustainability accounting and accountability*. London: Routledge.

O' Connell, V. (2007). Reflections on stewardship reporting. *Accounting Horizons*, *21*(2), 215–227.

Robb, A. (2012). Stewardship: The core of cooperative accounting. *Journal of Co-Operative Accounting and Reporting*, *1*(Summer), 19–27.

Rosenfield, P. (1974). Stewardship. In *Objectives of financial statements selected papers* (Vol. 2). New York, NY: AICPA.

SKY. (2012). Retrieved from http://tg24.sky.it/tg24/cronaca/2012/10/25/alluvione_cinque_terre_un_anno_dopo_disastro.html. Accessed on February 26, 2014.

United Nations World Commission on Environment and Development. (1987). Our common future (The Brundtland Report). Oxford: Oxford University Press.

Van Puyvelde, S., Caers, R., Du Bois, C., & Jegers, M. (2012). Nonprofit organizations: Integrating agency theory with stakeholder and stewardship theories. *Nonprofit and Voluntary Sector Quarterly*, *41*(3), 431–451.

AN INTEGRATED SOCIAL ACCOUNTING MODEL FOR NONPROFIT ORGANIZATIONS

Laurie Mook

ABSTRACT

The purpose of this article is to develop a nonprofit integrated social accounting (NISA) model that takes into account the particular objectives of nonprofit organizations (achieving their mission and remaining viable as an organization), their specific characteristics (e.g., the engagement of volunteers), and their economic, social and environmental impacts. The conceptual framework includes defining social accounting, setting the boundaries of the reporting entity, identifying the objectives of nonprofit reporting, identifying the users of the accounts and their information needs, and considering the questions that have to be answered in order to know if the organization is achieving its goals. From the conceptual framework, the NISA model is developed, incorporating four elements: (1) economic and human resources; (2) economic, social and environmental value creation; (3) internal systems and processes; and (4) organizational learning, growth and innovation. Overall, the model provides a mechanism to address both functional and strategic accountability concerns of the organization, its effectiveness

Accountability and Social Accounting for Social and Non-profit Organizations
Advances in Public Interest Accounting, Volume 17, 197–221

ISSN: 1041-7060/doi:10.1108/S1041-706020140000017008

and efficiency, and to drive behavior through feedback and readjustment. In this way, accounting plays an important role in shaping the 'reality' of the organization.

Keywords: Social accounting; nonprofit organizations; balanced scorecard; expanded value added; accountability

INTRODUCTION

Nonprofits are self-governing organizations formed to serve the public or a membership (Salamon, 1996). As a group, they have been called the nonprofit sector, not-for-profit sector, voluntary sector, third sector, independent sector, and nongovernmental sector (usually known as NGOs). They are also considered, together with cooperatives and social enterprises, part of the social economy (Quarter, 1992). There are a myriad of such organizations, from those geared toward serving the larger public, such as education and human services organizations, to those oriented toward a membership, such as professional associations and self-help groups. Their common feature is that they have primarily social goals and at the same time must remain viable (McLaughlin, 2009). Traditional accounting helps monitor financial viability, but does not consider the social goals of these organizations. Social accounting, on the other hand, is a tool that can be used to integrate and manage these two bottom lines. Social accounting can be defined as "a systematic analysis of the effects of an organization on its communities of interest or stakeholders, with stakeholder input as part of the data that are analyzed for the accounting statement" (Mook, Quarter, & Richmond, 2007, p. 2).

Social accounting is a fairly new development in the accounting world, first appearing in the corporate sector in the mid-1950s. Since then, external demand for social and environmental responsibility in reaction to unsafe and unfair labor practices and concerns over environmental degradation have led many corporations to adjust their business practices and report accordingly. Small- and medium-sized enterprises (SMEs) are increasingly considering social and environmental factors in their operations, spurred not only by reduced costs and increased efficiency, but also by the ability to attract and motivate top employees (Kechiche & Soparnot, 2012). Indeed, it is safe to say that social and environmental reporting is on the rise. An international survey of the top 100 companies in 41 countries found that 71 percent produced corporate responsibility reports, while in 1993 this number was 13 percent (in 10 countries) (KPMG, 2013; Larrinaga-González, 2007). The largest online database of corporate responsibility and sustainability reports (primarily of for-profit organizations, but also including cooperatives and public agencies) now considers this type of reporting as mainstream, when only 10 years ago it could be considered a niche market (Corporate Register, 2013).

In this article, we are dealing with social accounting for nonprofit organizations, which arguably has some differences to social accounting for the for-profit sector. Whereas for-profit sector social accounting is "a response by principally economic organizations to demonstrate that they are not purely economic," social accounting for nonprofit organizations developed "to justify their pursuit of social and environmental goals in economic terms" (Gray, Dillard, & Spence, 2011, p. 13). Many nonprofits have been reporting their social impact on their annual reports for a long time. However, monetized social accounting statements (assigning a monetized value to nonmonetary items) for nonprofit organizations only started in the mid-1990s (Mook, 2013). Some of the pioneering models of social accounting for organizations with a social mission include the Social Impact Statement (Land, 1996), the Co-operative Social Balance (Vaccari, 1997), the Community Social Return on Investment (Richmond, 1999), the Expanded Value Added Statement (Mook, 2007; Richmond & Mook, 2001), the Socio-economic Impact Statement (Mook, 2007; Mook & Quarter, 2006), and the Socio-economic Resource Statement (Mook, 2007). In addition, models originally designed for for-profit organizations have also been applied to nonprofit organizations. Two examples of this are the Balanced Scorecard (Bull, 2007; Kaplan, 2001; Manville, 2007; Martello, Watson, & Fischer, 2008; Somers, 2004), and the Global Reporting Initiative NGO Sector Supplement (GRI, 2010). What all these models have in common is that they broaden the range of criteria incorporated in the accounting framework.

Originally, financial statements were designed for owners and shareholders of for-profit organizations to measure profits and losses. This model has been used by the nonprofit sector for many years, but the social objectives of the sector prompted the development of additional reporting approaches that go beyond profits and losses. Indeed, there are several significant differences between the operations of nonprofit organizations and for-profit ones that provide a rationale for considering alternate accounting frameworks (FASB, 1980; Riahi-Belkaoui, 2004). First, nonprofit organizations do not have owners and are prohibited from distributing their surpluses to individuals. This is called the nondistribution restraint (Hansmann, 1980). Second, nonprofit organizations involve significant amounts of volunteer labor and receive significant in-kind donations, items typically not included in the financial statements. Third, many nonprofits do not operate in the market. Fourth, those who contribute resources, (i.e., donations, labor), do not expect economic returns. Fifth, success can be hard to measure, as impacts are often intangible and many of them are only realized in the long term. Sixth, although nonprofits can make a profit (surplus), they are not primarily profit-oriented. These differences lead us to consider a different approach to nonprofit accounting using the lens of social accounting.

While existing social accounting models have made important contributions in terms of individual measures of nonprofit social performance, what is lacking is the integration of these measures into a performance measurement and management system. This article offers such a nonprofit integrated social accounting model (NISA). On the one hand, it addresses functions of resource control and accountability. On the other hand, it provides information for the organization and its stakeholders to gauge and improve the organization's economic and social performance.

This article continues as follows. First, it presents a conceptual framework to guide the development of the NISA model. Second, using the conceptual framework as a guide, it outlines possible components of such a system. Third, it discusses implementation issues. The last section provides a summary and conclusions.

CONCEPTUAL FRAMEWORK

This section presents a conceptual framework to guide the development of the NISA model (Fig. 1). First, it defines social accounting. Secondly, it sets out the boundaries of the reporting entity. Third, it identifies the objectives of nonprofit reporting. From these objectives, it considers the questions that have to be answered in order to know if the organization is achieving those goals. The questions also determine the type of analysis that is needed (Gair, 2009). The assumption underlying this (using the objectives of nonprofit reporting as a starting point) is that accounting drives behavior. As such, it plays an important role in shaping and communicating the "reality" of the organization. As pioneers in the critical accounting field have argued, including certain things and excluding others from the accounting statement

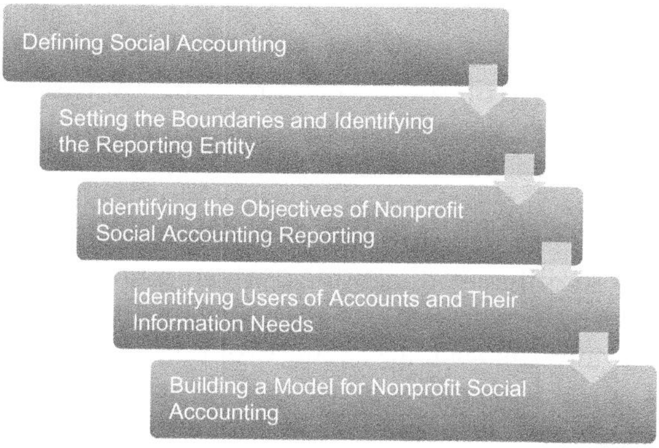

Fig. 1. A Conceptual Framework for a Nonprofit Integrated Social Accounting (NISA) Model.

affects how decisions and policies are made (Hines, 1988; Morgan, 1988). In this conceptual framework, the "things" that are considered important to include in the NISA model are those that help the organization move toward achieving its objectives. In the case of the NISA model proposed in this article, the "reality" that is being constructed is based on the economic and social factors deemed important to achieve mission and remain viable. In other words, in contrast to prior social accounting models, which primarily consist of individual measures of performance, the NISA model requires a balanced performance management system, where performance is measured across multiple domains from multiple perspectives. After setting out the objectives, the next step of the conceptual framework consists of identifying the users and their information needs, while recognizing that they may have competing interests. With all this information in mind, the final step is building the model.

Defining Social Accounting

As previously stated, social accounting can be defined as "a systematic analysis of the effects of an organization on its communities of interest or stakeholders, with stakeholder input as part of the data that are analyzed for the accounting statement" (Mook et al., 2007, p. 2). This definition expands the range of "what counts" – factors considered when measuring performance and looking at an organization in relation to its surrounding environment, both social and natural. Social accounting commonly addresses three factors: (a) financial (ensuring long term economic and financial performance); (b) social (creating value for society); and (c) environmental (through the responsible management and re-construction of natural resources) (Giovannoni & Fabietti, 2013, p. 29).

In taking an integrated social accounting approach, an organization would consider all three dimensions together. Inevitably there will be tensions between these different dimensions, which add to the complexity of nonprofit performance management. This needs to be kept in mind when designing and monitoring such a system. From a normative point of view, the purpose of social accounting is to "lead to action and change for the better" (Ball & Osborne, 2011, p. 1).

Setting Boundaries and Identifying the Reporting Entity

In order to help determine the boundaries of what we are accounting for, we need to define the unit of analysis. Defining the reporting entity, which typically is the same as the legal entity, allows us to measure and report on items for which the entity has control over and can influence. Following the IASB Framework (2010, p. 9), we identify three characteristics of a reporting entity:

1. Economic activities of an entity are being conducted, have been conducted, or will be conducted;
2. Those economic activities can be objectively distinguished from those of other entities and from the economic environment in which the entity exists; and
3. Financial information about the economic activities of that entity has the potential to be useful in making decisions about providing resources to the entity and in assessing whether the management and the governing board have made efficient and effective use of the resources provided.

In nonprofit organizations, economic activities include those of both paid staff and volunteers.

Identifying the Objectives of Nonprofit Social Accounting Reporting

Nonprofit organizations are guided by two main concerns: (1) achieving their mission and (2) remaining economically viable. However, early performance management systems dealt primarily only with financial measures based on traditional accounting systems (Manoochehri, 1999). This approach has two notable shortcomings for nonprofits. One is that traditional accounting frameworks were developed for for-profit organizations with different goals in mind. The other is that those systems do not recognize the importance of nonfinancial performance. Instead of mimicking business organizations, Mautz (1994, p. 56) argues that the focus of nonprofit accounting should instead be on addressing other types of questions:

1. What did the organization receive and from what sources?
2. What did the organization do with what it received?
3. How much does the organization have left?
4. What are its plans for the future?

More recently, the Irvine Foundation studied the best practices of other foundations in performance assessment. It came up with the following questions to evaluate its performance as it strives to achieve its mission "to expand opportunity for the people of California to participate in a vibrant, successful and inclusive society" (The James Irvine Foundation, 2014, p. 1):

1. What is the context in our program fields?
2. What progress are we making toward our program goals?
3. How do lessons from our program work improve our approach?
4. How is the foundation exercising leadership in the field?
5. How do key stakeholders perceive us and how do their perceptions inform our work?
6. How are we performing on measures of financial health and organizational effectiveness? (Canales & Rafter, 2012, pp. 3–4)

Whereas in traditional accounting the overriding objective is to measure profits for owners and shareholders, in the case of the NISA model, the overriding question is this: *is the organization moving toward achieving its mission in an effective and efficient manner, considering the interplay of economic, social, and environmental factors?* In answering this question, stakeholders are particularly interested in knowing that resources are used properly to achieve the mission of the organization in an ethical way. This leads to the consideration of the concepts of accountability and resource allocation.

Accountability

Implicit in the above question is the notion that the organization should be accountable for its actions. This begs two additional questions: accountable for what? and accountable to whom? For nonprofits, this is a complex matter as there are multiple stakeholders and thus multiple lines of accountability. As Keating and Frumkin (2001, p. 14) observe, "each of these groups has a different stake in the future of nonprofit organizations, and each is affected differently by charities that fail to achieve their goals or fulfill their mission." Indeed, accountability is a contested space (Kinder, 2011).

The decision to involve multiple stakeholders in the implementation of this model is guided by multiconstituency theory. This theory posits that performance goals such as effectiveness are socially constructed, and that this construction can differ amongst stakeholders and over time. Zammuto (1984, p. 614) defines organizational effectiveness as "human judgments about the desirability of the outcomes of organizational performance from the vantage point of the varied constituencies directly and indirectly affected by the organization." Thus, because there is variability in the way that concepts of organizational performance are constructed and judged, it is important to look at the perspectives of different stakeholder groups separately rather than their average (Herman & Renz, 1997).

Indeed, multiple studies confirm that there is significant variation in how effectiveness is viewed and evaluated by different stakeholders (Chan, Mook, & Kislenko, 2014; Fried & Worthington, 1995; Herman & Renz, 1997; Mistry, 2007). For those stakeholders with limited knowledge of the organization such as funders, or for outcomes that are difficult to measure, the degree to which correct procedures are followed typically becomes the proxy for effectiveness (Herman & Renz, 1997). For those internal to the organization, effectiveness takes on another meaning as there is more knowledge of how the organization operates.

In terms of organization strategy, it is important to understand these different perspectives as "an organization's life chances are improved when an organization conforms to the norms and expectations of its institutional environment" (Meyer & Scott, 1983, as cited in Hager, 1999, p. 26). By involving multiple stakeholders in monitoring organizational performance, risk is mitigated and organizations tend to be more successful (Kinder, 2011). Although recognizing multiple accountabilities and openly engaging with multiple stakeholders can bring out tensions and vulnerabilities, it also serves to create an atmosphere of trust, innovation, and reduced risk. For instance, in a study of social work middle managers in one county in Scotland, high involvement of multiple stakeholders (including clients) in formal and informal methods of designing and monitoring services led to better care, lower costs, reduced risk and community building (Kinder, 2011).

Resource Allocation

Regarding resource allocations, it is pertinent to consider the increased competition for resources – both financial and human – in the nonprofit sector

(Keating & Frumkin, 2001; Mautz, 1994). In this context, nonprofit organizations are seeking to become more efficient, looking to improve managerial practices in order to become more effective with fewer resources. Organizations also have to be very mindful of their liquidity and cash flow situations, and of the availability and recruitment of human resources, both paid and unpaid.

Taking into account the two concepts together (accountability and resource allocation), and following the work of Edwards and Hulme (1996), social accounting can provide information on functional accountability for resources, resource use and immediate impacts on the one, and on strategic accountability concerned with the impact of the organization's actions on others and the environment on the other hand. Our objective in the social accounting report, then, is to include information that will help with both short-term and long-term decision-making.

Identifying Users of Accounts and their Information Needs

The next step is to ascertain key stakeholders and their information needs. In examining nonprofits, Keating and Frumkin (2001) identified three key external stakeholders and two internal stakeholders, as well as their incentives and objectives. The first external stakeholder is donors, who are interested in knowing that their contributions are used for the purposes they made them for, and in a nonwasteful way. The second external stakeholder is clients, who may care about nonprofit performance so as to get the best quality and quantity of needed goods or services. The third external stakeholder is taxpayers, who want to see resources used in the best possible way in order to minimize their tax burden. The two internal stakeholders are board members and staff (both paid and unpaid). Board members have a legal responsibility for the organization, and thus are concerned with meeting their fiduciary duties. Staff members are responsible for ensuring that the programmatic and financial goals of the organization are met.

Another way to conceptualize key stakeholders in nonprofit organizations was proposed by Riahi-Belkaoui (2004, p. 184). This perspective includes four stakeholder groups:

1. The resource providers: lenders, suppliers, employees, taxpayers, members and contributors.
2. The constituents who use and benefit from the services rendered by the organization.

3. The governing and oversight bodies responsible for setting policies and overseeing and appraising the managers of nonbusiness organizations.
4. The managers of nonbusiness organizations.

Traditional approaches to stakeholder involvement tend to focus on gaining their support for the activities of the organization;

From this perspective, the corporation's continued existence requires the support of the stakeholders and their approval must be sought and the activities of the corporation adjusted to gain that approval. The more powerful the stakeholders, the more the company must adapt (Gray, Kouhy, & Lavers, 1995, p. 53).

A different perspective considers stakeholders as contributors to the impact of the organization in more creative ways. For instance, in a recent study of the impact of a social enterprise (Furniture Bank), stakeholders were asked for their ideas and opinions of the current and potential impact of the organization (Chan et al., 2014). The researchers adopted the idea of crowdsourcing, but instead of targeting the broader public (or the "crowd"), they targeted stakeholder groups, a process known as stakeholder-sourcing (Lim, Quercia, & Finkelstein, 2010). Participating in this research provided a creative outlet for stakeholders of the social enterprise. They managed to generate novel ideas that have great potential to increase the impact of the organization. This suggests that stakeholder contributions can go beyond time, money and in-kind items. Indeed, stakeholders' willingness to be part of the solutions to problems and their commitment to sharing ideas constitute important inputs to the organization that are not often included in stakeholder analysis. From a social accounting perspective, this is an important factor that should not be overlooked (Mook, 2013; Mook et al., 2007).

The research with Furniture Bank also highlighted the prevalence of multiple roles held by the same individual, adding another dimension to the understanding of stakeholder groups. For instance, those who have furniture picked up by the social purpose enterprise arm of the organization are both customers (concerned with the price of the pick-up service) and donors (wanting to make a social impact). Thus, the idea of stakeholder groups as distinct was challenged. In social accounting for nonprofits, it may be more appropriate to think in terms of stakeholder roles, while recognizing possible tensions between these roles.

Building a Nonprofit Integrated Social Accounting Model

Once we have identified the stakeholders and their information needs, the next step is to return to the nonprofit's twin objectives of achieving its mission while remaining viable. This leads us to consider three additional themes: (1) organizational failure; (2) integrating multiple dimensions; and (3) value creation or destruction.

Organizational Failure

One question that often arises regarding the viability of nonprofit organizations, is this: *why do some nonprofit organizations cease to exist?* In a study of nonprofit organizations that had closed down over a 15-year time period in one area of the United States, Hager (1999) identified eight factors that could explain nonprofit closure:

(1) The liabilities of newness and small size
(2) The inability to reproduce commitment
(3) Intraorganizational conflict
(4) Inability to mobilize human resources
(5) Lack of legitimacy
(6) Inability to compete for scarce or depleted financial resources
(7) Lack of connections to other organizations, and
(8) The completion of the organization's mission (Hager, 1999, p. iv).

After an extensive empirical analysis, Hager found that some factors were more prevalent in nonprofit closures than others. The most important ones relating to failure were newness and small size, inability to compete for scarce resources, and loss of key staff or volunteers. Some closures, however, were the result of success (e.g., completion of the mission of the organization). Some of these findings lend support to a focus on financial and human resources as integral components of a nonprofit accounting framework.

Integrating Multiple Dimensions

In the introduction, we made reference to the balanced scorecard. The balanced scorecard brings to the fore the need to consider multiple dimensions in the day-to-day operations and in the strategic planning of an organization (Kaplan & Norton, 1996). The balanced scorecard considers the organization's mission and strategy and translates them "into a comprehensive set of performance measures that provides the framework for a strategic measurement and management system" (Kaplan & Norton, 1996, p. 20). The balanced scorecard takes into account multiple dimensions of the organization and includes metrics that focus on finances, the customer, internal management processes, and learning and growth. In so doing, it recognizes a broader view of value creation, providing a more balanced view of the organization's performance.

Although the original focus and application of the balanced scorecard was with for-profit organizations, this approach has also been modified for nonprofit organizations (Kaplan, 2001). In this case, "the mission rather than the financial/shareholder objectives drives the organization's strategy," and the financial and customer perspectives are revised to focus on financial donors and recipients of services (Kaplan, 2001, p. 361). The perspectives of internal processes, and learning and growth remain the same. The idea of using a broader approach to measuring and monitoring the performance of a nonprofit organization falls directly in line with social accounting, which expands the items that are included in the accounting statement to encompass economic, social, and environmental factors (multi-bottom line). It also emphasizes the importance of acknowledging intangible assets such as skills and knowledge of employees and volunteers, relationships with other providers, reputation, and the like. These have also been termed "intellectual capital" and the value of such is rarely reflected on an organization's accounting statements.

Value Creation or Destruction

The focus on both tangible and intangible items can also be applied to the perspective of value creation. Value creating resources of an organization can be broken down into economic capital and intellectual capital. Tangible items such as financial and physical capital are already captured on traditional accounting statements. However, intellectual capital, often intangible, is another important source of value creation, and one we include in our social accounting model (Fig. 2).

Here we are concerned with the impacts of the nonprofit organization: *what economic, social, and environmental value added is created or destroyed by the organization through its activities?* Value added is an accounting concept that measures the wealth created by an organization as a result of transforming its externally purchased goods and services with labor and capital (Suojanen, 1954). As shown in Fig. 3, value added recognizes that the value created is greater than profit created for shareholders (as is the case in for-profit organizations). Instead, the value added statement reports the wealth created for a wider group of stakeholders, including employees, creditors, the public sector, and the organization itself (Mook et al., 2007).

For example, a small business creating a product such as gourmet pasta sauce, creates value added in the traditional sense by transforming externally purchased goods and services (such as tomatoes and jars) using labor (employees) and capital (such as a stove) into a finished product to be sold in the market. Value added is calculated by subtracting the cost of the

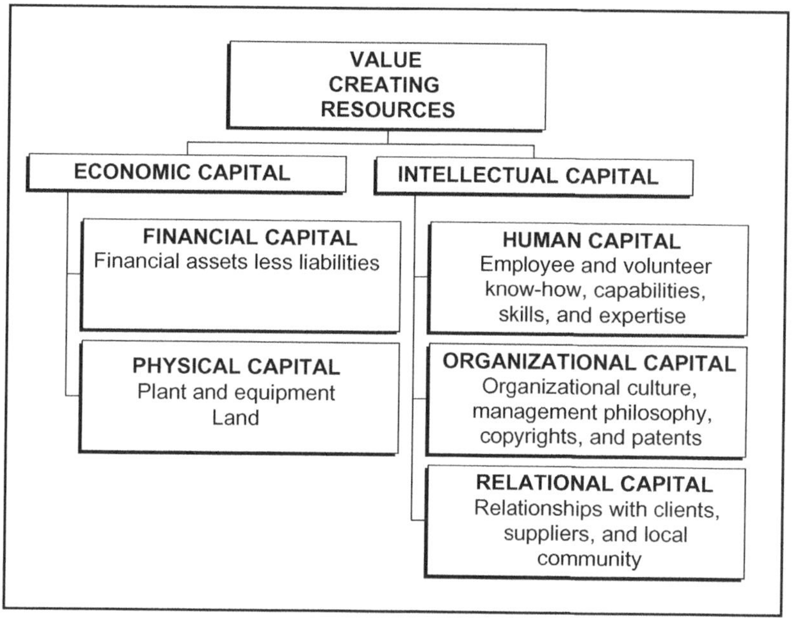

Fig. 2. Value Creating Resources of an Organization. Source: Mook et al. (2007, p. 100).

externally goods and services from the amount the pasta sauce was sold for. Value added is then distributed to different stakeholders such as employees (wages and benefits), creditors (interest), the public sector (income taxes), and the organization (depreciation and retained profits).

However, there are two shortcomings to the traditional calculation of value added, especially for nonprofit organizations. First, by relying only on financial data, an important component of nonprofit labor is missing – that of volunteers. Second, traditional value added does not take into consideration nonmonetized social and environmental impacts of the organization. To overcome these limitations, the Expanded Value Added Statement was developed (Mook, 2007). The Expanded Value Added Statement addresses three questions:

(1) *What economic value added is created in the transformation of goods and services using labor and capital?*
(2) *What social value added is created in the transformation of goods and services using labor and capital?*

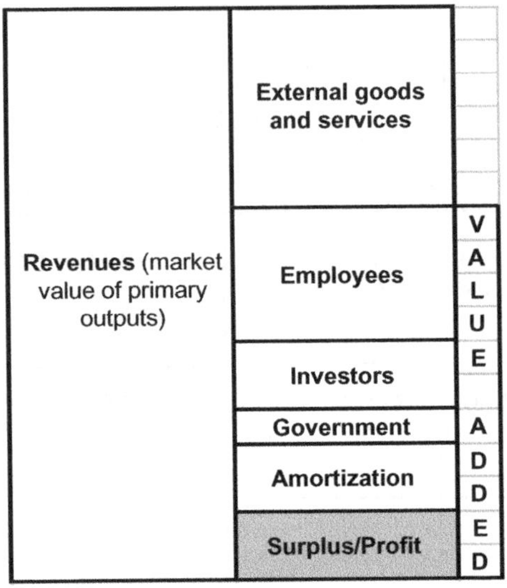

Fig. 3. Value Added. Source: Mook et al. (2007, p. 111).

(3) *What environmental value added is created in the transformation of goods and services using labor and capital?*

In our example of the gourmet pasta sauce, we can differentiate between a private business and an environmentally friendly social enterprise that employs individuals with disabilities who are often excluded from the formal labor market. In addition to the economic value added described previously, we can report the social value added created as a result of employing individuals who could not be employed elsewhere. We also could report the environmental value added as a result of using organic and local tomatoes, as well as using renewable energy to run its equipment. We now turn to operationalizing these issues.

ELEMENTS OF A NONPROFIT INTEGRATED SOCIAL ACCOUNTING MODEL

The main purpose of the NISA model is to determine whether or not the organization is moving toward achieving its mission in an effective and efficient manner. At the center of the NISA model are the objectives of the nonprofit organization: mission and resource sustainability. As with the Balanced Scorecard (Kaplan, 2001), multiple perspectives are considered, although modified. The four surrounding circles are the elements that need to be measured: (1) economic and human resources; (2) value creation (economic, social, and environmental); (3) internal systems and processes; and (4) learning, growth, and innovation (Fig. 4). The information gathered in these four elements will be used to improve the performance of the organizations through enhancing efficiency and effectiveness, strategic accountability, functional accountability, and feedback mechanisms (Fig. 5).

Economic and Human Resources

The first element is concerned with economic (financial and nonfinancial) and human resources. Close monitoring of these items is necessary to ensure the survival of the organization. This component addresses the question: *what level of economic and human resources does the nonprofit need to operate effectively and efficiently to achieve its mission?* Traditional accounting statements focus on financial resources and pay less attention to human resources. However, the role of human resources in achieving the mission of a nonprofit is crucial. Indeed, the largest expense in nonprofit organizations is wages and benefits (approximately between 50 and 80 percent of

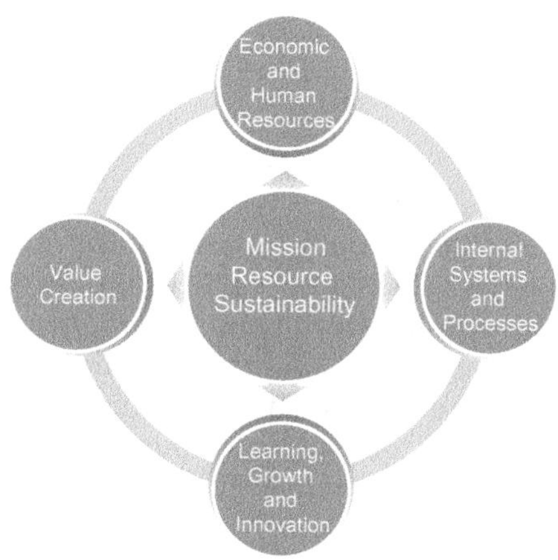

Fig. 4. Elements of a Nonprofit Integrated Social Accounting (NISA) Model. Adapted from Kaplan (2001); Mook et al. (2007).

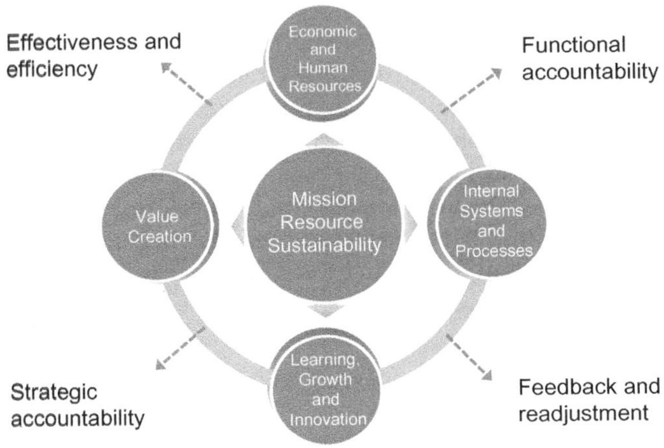

Fig. 5. Interaction of the Elements. Adapted from Kaplan (2001); Mook et al. (2007).

their budget) and more attention to this area is warranted (Pynes, 2013). Strong strategic human resource management practices are necessary to optimize effectiveness and efficiency of the organization. This applies to any organization, for-profit or nonprofit, however nonprofits also have a significant presence of volunteers. For instance, in the United States, volunteer contributions in 2011 amounted to almost 8 billion hours of service worth $171 billion (CNCS, 2012).

Value Creation

The second element, value creation, considers the integrated economic, social, and environmental value added created or destroyed by the organization. Here the question to be addressed is: *what difference is the organization making economically, socially, and environmentally?*

The Expanded Value Added framework discussed previously considers precisely the transformation of externally purchased goods and services into the organization's outputs, while noting the economic, social, and environmental value added or destroyed. It also takes a stakeholder approach and addresses this question from multiple vantage points.

Linking the first two elements (value creation and financial and human resources) are the notions of efficiency and effectiveness. Efficiency is measured in resource terms: "the amount of resources used to produce a unit of output" (Etzioni, 1964, p. 8), while effectiveness is a measure of goal attainment. Measures of effectiveness are rooted in available research, allowing the organization to focus on successful implementation (Fiennes, 2013). In other words, if the idea or mission of the organization is based on ideas that have been "proven" through prior research, the higher the quality of the idea and the higher the implementation, the greater the impact. This gets around issues of having to attribute and measure precisely outcomes and impact.

Internal Systems and Processes

The third element, internal systems and processes, focuses on the way an organization operates, and how it manages its human, organizational and relational capital. Here the question is: *what internal systems and processes does the organization need in place to successfully achieve its mission and remain viable?*

Managing Human Capital

Human capital can be thought of as consisting of employee and volunteer know-how, capabilities, skills, and expertise. A social accounting focus on the maximization of human capital has multiple benefits. First, it helps to make better decisions related to human resources, leading to higher engagement and lower turnover of volunteers and paid employees. Second, it allows for cost-benefit analyses of human resource development (e.g., training, volunteer management). Related to these, it can encourage management to consider human resources as assets to be maximized and not as costs to be minimized (Flamholtz, 1999; Mook et al., 2007).

Managing Organizational Capital

Organizational capital consists of organizational culture, management philosophy, copyrights, patents, and systems for undertaking the work the organization engages in. These are assets that differentiate one organization from another and could be recognized as having value in the social accounting statement through a variety of proxies (Mook et al., 2007).

Managing Relational Capital

Relational capital refers to relationships with clients, suppliers, supporters, and local community. Paying attention to relationship building and maintenance is the focus of this aspect of the model. Even though relational work is critical in much of nonprofit frontline work, accounts of it are noticeably absent (Benjamin, 2012).

Organizational Learning, Growth, and Innovation

The fourth element is organizational learning, growth, and innovation. Organizational learning is critical to move beyond short-term accountability to long-term performance (Ebrahim, 2005). This addresses the question, *what can the organization learn from itself and its stakeholders in order to improve its impact and sustainability?*

Incorporating the idea of "stakeholder-sourcing," mentioned previously, stakeholders contribute to advancing the work of the nonprofit by reflecting on the economic, social, and environmental impacts of the organization (Chan et al., 2014). The rationale for using stakeholder-sourcing is based on multiple constituency theory which posits that "different stakeholder groups evaluate a focal organization differently because stakeholders judge the focal organization against criteria unique to their interest" (Mackey, Brudney, Menoher, & Levy, 2008, p. 4). This is important because nonprofit organizations have multiple accountabilities and goals, and the different goals and interests of stakeholders lead to different constructions of effectiveness (Jun & Shiau, 2012).

Creating a space for creativity and innovation is also important. This includes learning from failure. For instance, the nonprofit Engineers Without Borders in Canada has created a culture of reflection and openness around failure and publishes an annual failure report that allows it to move forward (EWB, 2012). Reflection, learning, growth, and innovation are all important aspects of moving forward, yet are areas that are often neglected in resource – and time-strapped nonprofit organizations.

Interaction of the Elements

We already noted that the data collected for economic and human resources and value creation combine to allow measurement of effectiveness and efficiency. The value creation data and learning, growth, and innovation data connect to address strategic accountability, in other words, the impact of thc organization on others and the environment. Economic and human resource data connects with internal systems and processes data to address functional accountability, for instance, how resources are allocated and used up. Finally, learning, growth, and innovation data connected with internal systems and processes data move the organization forward in achieving its goals through feedback and readjustment (Fig. 5).

IMPLEMENTING THE NISA MODEL

There are two main challenges to address in moving the NISA model from conception to implementation for practitioners: (1) selecting the right metrics and (2) using imperfect information in decision-making. A key challenge in implementing any performance measurement system is selecting the right metrics. Not measuring the right things can lead to sub-optimal decision-making, counterproductive behavior, and delay in exposing real problems (Blackburn & Valerdi, 2009). It is common to over-measure items that are easier to measure such as costs, and under-measure items that are intangible and with uncertain or soft benefit. A related phenomenon is the halo effect which may bias the interpretation of nonfinancial results based on financial results. In other words, "when confronted with multiple measures of organizational performance, a person will form a general impression based on the financial results" (DeBusk, Killough, & Brown, 2005, p. 78).

To help avoid these pitfalls, and following Blackburn and Valerdi (2009, pp. 4–5) four main steps could be followed for selecting metrics:

1. Identify what you are trying to measure, the decision it is trying to support, and how it is part of a greater purpose.
2. Determine what you know and what you need to know.
3. Understand who is impacted by the metric and how it aligns vertically with different levels of the organization.
4. Have a systematic process and a measurement friendly culture; evaluate timeliness of information, quality, and whether or not the system has working feedback.

Once metrics have been selected and measured, their results are available for decision-making. Often, these data are imperfect and care must be taken in interpreting results (Kinder, 2011). Here it is better to rely on a small number of high quality metrics than be overwhelmed with too much data. Decision-makers must also be aware of different types of biases that can occur in evaluating data in order to reduce them and evaluate results in the most effective way (Blackburn & Valerdi, 2009). These biases include

(1) anchoring, wherein one relies on specific information or an arbitrary value and influences judgment;
(2) the "halo/horns" effect, wherein if people first see one attribute that predisposes them to favor or disfavor one alternative, they are more likely to interpret subsequent information in a way that supports their conclusion;
(3) bandwagon bias, wherein the presence of others and their interpretations affects one's judgment;
(4) hindsight bias, where people exaggerate what could have been anticipated in foresight, and consider the outcome having been relatively inevitable; and
(5) overconfidence or optimism bias, where people exaggerate the confidence and completeness of their own knowledge (Blackburn & Valerdi, 2009, pp. 10–11).

The implementation of a NISA model requires the cultivation of skills related to strategic thinking, the development and measurement of metrics, engagement of stakeholders, and the ability to bring together elements of performance across multiple dimensions. Here, professional education institutions have a role to play. In a previous work, we identified some of the skills that future social accountants and nonprofit organization leaders need to cultivate, including "collaboration, dialogue, creativity and innovation, systems-thinking, team work, active listening, stakeholder engagement, group decision-making, conflict management, qualitative and quantitative data gathering and analysis, story-telling, critical reflection, learning from failure, change management, strategic forecasting, and lifelong learning" (Mook & Pstross, 2013, p. 257). Hence, developing a mix of qualitative and quantitative skills is necessary.

SUMMARY AND CONCLUSIONS

Traditional accounting models were designed for for-profit organizations and are not always adequate to reflect the mission and the operational realities of nonprofit organizations. This article presented a conceptual framework to guide the development of a social accounting statement that addresses the particular reality of nonprofit organizations. Drawing on this framework, an a nonprofit integrated social accounting model was proposed. The NISA model includes four elements that direct data collection: (1) economic and human resources; (2) economic, social, and environmental value creation; (3) internal systems and processes; and (4) learning, growth, and innovation. These elements are guided by the main goal of nonprofits:

to achieve their mission and remain viable as an organization. In the social accounting statement proposed, these four elements connect around issues of effectiveness and efficiency, strategic accountability, functional accountability, and feedback and readjustment.

Those interested in applying the NISA model to a given nonprofit organization could focus on answering four main questions, each one related to an element:

1. Economic and Human Resources: *What level of economic and human resources does the nonprofit need to operate effectively and efficiently to achieve its mission?*
2. Value Creation: *What difference is the organization making economically, socially, and environmentally?*
3. Internal Systems and Processes: *What internal systems and processes does the organization need in place to successfully achieve its mission and remain viable?*
4. Organizational Learning, Growth, and Innovation: *What can the organization learn from itself and its stakeholders in order to improve its impact and sustainability?*

There is no one single set of metrics to answer these questions. The operationalization of the NISA model take into account the context of the particular nonprofit organization that is reporting, and its stakeholders. Thus, for nonprofits operating in different countries, and even regions, the answers to these questions may be significantly different based on the expectations of their stakeholders and regulatory systems. Having said that, it is important to consider that nonprofit organizations require an accounting and reporting model that recognizes and addresses their social and economic bottom lines and hence is different from for-profit sector models. For instance, the statement should recognize the fact that nonprofit organizations engage significant volunteer labor. For many nonprofits, this type of information is already being collected and it is a matter of assembling it in a different format and paying attention to the interconnections between the different elements.

In terms of research implications, this model adds to the literature on nonprofit performance management by using a social accounting lens. It also adds to the social accounting literature by considering how using this lens impacts performance management. Research could be conducted to test and further develop the NISA model, for instance using an in-depth case study approach. The model also raises questions to explore regarding stakeholder relationships that could add to stakeholder theory building.

Just as "'it takes a village' [of scholars] to develop, evaluate, elaborate, and exploit a fledging idea" in academia (Scott, 2005, p. 475) in academia, so does it take a village of stakeholders to evaluate an organization's performance. Future research involving case studies organizations applying the NISA model is planned, and will provide further insights.

REFERENCES

Ball, A., & Osborne, S. P. (2011). Introduction: Accounting – for the common good? In A. Ball & S. P. Osborne (Eds.), *Social accounting and public management: Accountability for the common good* (pp. 1–7). New York, NY: Routledge.

Benjamin, L. M. (2012). Nonprofit organizations and outcome measurement: From tracking program activities to focusing on frontline work. *American Journal of Evaluation, 33*(3), 431–447.

Blackburn, C., & Valerdi, R. (2009). *Navigating the metrics landscape: An introductory literature guide to metric selection, implementation & decision making.* 7th Annual Conference on Systems Engineering Research. Retrieved from http://dspace.mit.edu/handle/1721.1/84114. Accessed on May 1, 2014.

Bull, M. (2007). Balance: The development of a social enterprise business performance analysis tool. *Social Enterprise Journal, 3*(1), 49–66.

Canales, J. E., & Rafter, K. (2012). *Assessing one's own performance.* Stanford Social Innovation Review, Summer. Retrieved from http://www.ssireview.org/articles/entry/assessing_ones_own_performance. Accessed on May 1, 2014.

Chan, A., Mook, L., & Kislenko, S. (2014). Stakeholders' stories of impact: The case of Furniture Bank. In J. Quarter, S. Ryan, & A. Chan (Eds.), *Social purpose enterprises: Case studies for social change.* Toronto: University of Toronto Press.

Corporate Register. (2013). *CR perspectives 2013: Global CR reporting trends and stakeholder views.* Retrieved from http://www.corporateregister.com/a10723/58958-13th-15918660Y4561226712N-Gl.pdf. Accessed on May 14, 2014.

Corporation for National & Community Service (CNCS). (2012). *Volunteering and civic life in America 2012: Key findings on the volunteer participation and civic health of the nation.* Washington, DC: Author. Retrieved from http://www.volunteeringinamerica.gov/assets/resources/FactSheetFinal.pdf. Accessed on January 31, 2014.

DeBusk, G. K., Killough, L. N., & Brown, R. M. (2005). Financial measures bias in the use of performance measurement systems. *Advances in Management Accounting, 14*, 61–89.

Ebrahim, A. (2005). Accountability myopia: Losing sight of organizational learning. *Nonprofit and Voluntary Sector Quarterly, 34*(1), 56–87.

Edwards, M., & Hulme, D. (1996). Introduction: NGO performance and accountability. In M. Edwards & D. Hulme (Eds.), *Beyond the magic bullet: NGO performance and accountability in the post-cold war world* (pp. 3–16). West Hartford, CT: Kumarian Press.

Engineers Without Borders (EWB). (2012). *Failure report 2011.* Retrieved from http://legacy.ewb.ca/mainsite/pages/whoweare/accountable/FailureReport2012.pdf

Etzioni, A. (1964). *Modern organizations.* Englewood Cliffs, NJ: Prentice-Hall.

Fiennes, C. (2013). *Most charities shouldn't evaluate their work: Part two*. Stanford social innovation review blog. Retrieved from http://www.ssireview.org/blog/entry/most_charities_shouldnt_evaluate_their_work1

Financial Accounting Standards Board (FASB). (1980). *Concepts statement no. 4 objectives of financial reporting by nonbusiness organizations*. Norwalk, CT: FASB.

Flamholtz, E. (1999). *Human resource accounting: Advances in concepts, methods, and applications* (3d ed.). Boston, MA: Kluwer Academic Publishers.

Fried, B. J., & Worthington, C. (1995). The multiconstituency approach to organizational performance assessment: A Canadian mental health system application. *Community Mental Health Journal*, *31*(1), 11–24.

Gair, C. (2009). *SROI act II: A call to action for next generation SROI*. San Francisco, MA: REDF.

Giovannoni, E., & Fabietti, G. (2013). What is sustainability? A review of the concept and its applications. In C. Busco, M. L. Frigo, A. Riccagoni, & P. Quattrone (Eds.), *Integrated reporting* (pp. 21–40). Cham: Springer.

Global Reporting Initiative (GRI). (2010). *An introduction to the GRI NGO sector supplement*. Retrieved from http://www.globalreporting.org/NR/rdonlyres/19B9E00D-299D-4F3C-A5A7-6B9650EDC532/4207/AnIntroductiontotheGRINGOSectorSupplement.pdf

Gray, R., Dillard, J., & Spence, C. (2011). A brief re-examination of "The Social Accounting Project": Social accounting research as if the world matters. In A. Ball & S. P. Osborne (Eds.), *Social accounting and public management: Accountability for the common good* (pp. 11–22). New York, NY: Routledge.

Gray, R., Kouhy, R., & Lavers, S. (1995). Corporate social and environmental reporting: A review of the literature and a longitudinal study of UK disclosure. *Accounting, Auditing & Accountability Journal*, *8*(2), 47–77.

Hager, M. (1999). Explaining demise among nonprofit organizations. Unpublished doctoral dissertation, University of Minnesota.

Hansmann, H. B. (1980). The role of nonprofit organizations. *The Yale Law Journal* *89*(5), 835–901.

Herman, R. D., & Renz, D. O. (1997). Multiple constituencies and the social construction of nonprofit organization effectiveness. *Nonprofit and Voluntary Sector Quarterly*, *26*(2), 185–206.

Hines, R. D. (1988). Financial accounting: In communicating reality, we construct reality. *Accounting, Organizations and Society*, *13*(3), 251–261.

International Accounting Standards Board (IASB). (2010). *Conceptual framework for financial reporting: The reporting entity*. Exposure draft. Retrieved from http://www.ifrs.org/Current-Projects/IASB-Projects/Conceptual-Framework/EDMar10/Documents/EDConceptualFrameworkMar10.pdf

Jun, K., & Shiau, E. (2012). How are we doing? A multiple consitituency approach to civic association effectiveness. *Nonprofit and Voluntary Sector Quarterly*, *41*(4), 632–655.

Kaplan, R. S. (2001). Strategic performance measurement and management in nonprofit organizations. *Nonprofit Management & Leadership*, *11*(3), 353–370.

Kaplan, R. S., & Norton, D. P. (1996). *The balanced scorecard: Translating strategy into action*. Boston, MA: Harvard Business Press.

Keating, E. K., & Frumkin, P. (2001). How to assess nonprofit financial performance. Hauser Center for Nonprofit Organizations, Harvard University.

Kechiche, A., & Soparnot, R. (2012). CSR within SMEs: Literature review. *International Business Research*, *5*(7), 97–104.

Kinder, T. (2011). Evolving accountabilities: Experience and prospects from scottish public services. In A. Ball & S. P. Osborne (Eds.), *Social accounting and public management: Accountability for the common good* (pp. 147–162). New York, NY: Routledge.

KPMG. (2013). *The KPMG international survey of corporate sustainability reporting 2013*. Amsterdam: Author. Retrieved from http://www.kpmg.com/Global/en/IssuesAndInsights/ArticlesPublications/corporate-responsibility/Documents/corporate-responsibility-reporting-survey-2013.pdf. Accessed on May 16, 2014.

Land, K. (1996). Social indicators for assessing the impact of the independent, not-for-profit sector on society. Paper presented at a meeting of Independent Sector, Washington, DC.

Larrinaga-González, C. (2007). Sustainability reporting: Insights from neoinstitutinal theory. In J. Unerman, J. Bebbington, & B. O'Dwyer (Eds.), *Sustainability accounting and accountability* (pp. 150–167). Abingdon, UK: Routledge.

Lim, S. L., Quercia, D., & Finkelstein, A. (2010). StakeNet: Using social networks to analyse the stakeholders of large-scale software projects. *Proceedings of the 32nd International Conference on Software Engineering*, May 2–8, Cape Town, South Africa (pp. 295–304).

Mackey, C. K., Brudney, J. L., Menoher, B., & Levy, D. (2008). *Measuring the impact of hands on network: An evaluation of direct and secondary impact from the stakeholder perspective*. Washington, DC: Points of Light Network. Retrieved from http://successlinks.biz/wp-content/uploads/2010/08/ISR-Final.pdf. Accessed on May 1, 2014.

Manoochehri, G. (1999). Overcoming obstacles to developing effective performance measures. *Work Study*, *48*(6), 223–229.

Manville, G. (2007). Implementing a balanced scorecard in a not for profit SME. *International Journal of Productivity and Performance Management*, *56*(2), 162–169.

Martello, M., Watson, J. G., & Fischer, M. J. (2008). Implementing a balanced scorecard in a not-for-profit organization. *Journal of Business & Economics Research*, *6*(9), 67–80.

Mautz, R. K. (1994). *Financial reporting for nonprofit organizations: A fresh look*. New York, NY and London: Garland Publishing, Inc.

McLaughlin, T. A. (2009). *Streetsmart financial basics for nonprofit managers* (3rd ed.). Hoboken, NJ: Wiley & Sons.

Meyer, J. W., & Scott, R. (1983). *Organizational environments: Ritual and rationality*. Beverly Hills, CA: Sage.

Mistry, S. (2007). *How does one voluntary organisation engage with multiple stakeholder views of effectiveness?* Voluntary Sector Working Paper Number 7. Retrieved from http://eprints.lse.ac.uk/29245/1/VSWP7_Mistry.pdf. Accessed on May 1, 2014.

Mook, L. (2007). *Social and environmental accounting: The expanded value added statement*. Unpublished Ph.D. discussion, University of Toronto.

Mook, L. (2013). Social accounting for social economy organizations. In L. Mook (Ed.), *Accounting for social value*. Toronto: University of Toronto Press.

Mook, L., & Pstross, M. (2013). Social accounting: Lessons learned for the road ahead. In L. Mook (Ed.), *Accounting for social value* (pp. 249–259). Toronto: University of Toronto Press.

Mook, L., & Quarter, J. (2006). Accounting for the social economy: The socioeconomic impact statement. *Annals of Public and Cooperative Economics*, *77*(2), 247–269.

Mook, L., Quarter, J., & Richmond, B. J. (2007). *What counts: Social accounting for nonprofits and cooperatives* (2nd ed.). London: Sigel Press.

Morgan, G. (1988). Accounting as reality construction: Towards a new epistemology for accounting practice. *Accounting, Organizations and Society*, *13*(5), 477–485.

Pynes, J. E. (2013). *Human resources management for public and nonprofit organizations: A strategic approach* (4th ed.). San Francisco, MA: Jossey-Bass.

Quarter, J. (1992). *Canada's social economy: Co-operatives, non-profits, and other community enterprises*. Toronto: James Lorimer and Company.

Riahi-Belkaoui, A. (2004). *Accounting theory* (5th ed.). London: Thomson Learning.

Richmond, B. J. (1999). *Counting on each other: A social audit model to assess the impact of nonprofit organizations*. Ph.D. discussion, University of Toronto.

Richmond, B. J., & Mook, L. (2001). *Social audit for WCRI*. Toronto: Author.

Salamon, L. (1996). *Defining the nonprofit sector: The United States*. Baltimore: Johns Hopkins University. Retrieved from http://adm-cf.com/jhu/pdfs/CNP_Working_Papers/CNP_WP18.pdf

Scott, W. R. (2005). Institutional theory: Contributing to a theoretical research program. In K. G. Smith & M. A. Hitt (Eds.), *Great minds in management: The process of theory development* (pp. 460–484). New York, NY: Oxford University Press.

Somers, A. B. (2004). *Shaping the balanced scorecard for use in UK social enterprises*. London: Social Enterprises London.

Suojanen, W. W. (1954). Accounting theory and the large corporation. *Accounting Review*, *29*(3), 391–398.

The James Irvine Foundation. (2014). *Our mission*. Retrieved from http://irvine.org/about-us/mission. Accessed on May 1, 2014.

Vaccari, A. (1997). Constructing the social balance: Consumer cooperative Italy. In S. Zadek, P. Pruznan, & R. Evans (Eds.), *Building corporate accountability* (pp. 171–188). London: Earthscan.

Zammuto, R. F. (1984). A comparison of multiple constituency models of organizational effectiveness. *The Academy of Management Review*, *9*(4), 606–616.

VOLUNTARY DISCLOSURE IN A REGULATED CONTEXT: THE CASE OF ITALIAN SOCIAL ENTERPRISES

Ericka Costa

ABSTRACT

This article analyzes the interplay between regulation and social and environmental reporting in northern Italian social enterprises. Specifically, it investigates how "non-accredited" social enterprises discharge voluntary accountability before and after the introduction of regulation making social and environmental reporting compulsory for "accredited-social enterprises." By developing a content analysis on 170 stand-alone social and environmental reports, this article provides a longitudinal analysis of voluntary disclosures in a regulated context from 2006 (before regulation) to 2009 (after regulation). Based on the total number of disclosures and the average number of sentences per report, Italian "non-regulated" social enterprises showed increased voluntary disclosure on social and environmental matters from 2006 to 2009; however, when analyzing the average sentences per report, it emerges that the information contained in the stand-alone social and environmental reports decreased, especially disclosures related to "social-related issues." This article looks beyond crude noncompliance analysis with legislation and analyzes if the

Accountability and Social Accounting for Social and Non-profit Organizations
Advances in Public Interest Accounting, Volume 17, 223–249

ISSN: 1041-7060/doi:10.1108/S1041-706020140000017009

regulation influences organizations' voluntary disclosure. It analyzes all *of the social and environmental disclosures provided by northern Italian "non-accredited" social enterprises before and after the introduction of regulation. The novelty of this article rests in the fact that it does not analyze the social and environmental disclosure of "legal social enterprises"; rather, it considers the whole voluntary disclosure context for "non-accredited" social enterprises in a regulated environment.*

Keywords: Voluntary disclosure; social and environmental reporting; regulation; Italian social enterprises; compulsory standard

INTRODUCTION

Following broader conceptualization of social enterprises, the recent Italian law 118/2005 as well as the 2008 Implementation Decree has introduced the duty to conduct social and environmental reporting according to compulsory standards. These regulations target Italian "legal social enterprises," those that applied to the Italian Chamber of Commerce for legal accreditation. In 2009, the IRIS Network Reports (Zandonai & Borzaga, 2009) highlighted that "legal social enterprises" included only 623 out of more than 13,000 social enterprises, most of which have not registered to obtain legal accreditation. Why did so few Italian social enterprises seek legal accreditation? Many Italian authors (Andreaus, 2006, 2007; Costa, 2014; Rusconi & Signori, 2007) have pointed out that the model of social reporting proposed by the legislation focuses too much on the description of the governance mechanism and the activities of the social enterprises. Therefore, they described how the social enterprises are governed (with a multistakeholder approach) and highlight the carried-out activities. At the same time, Italian scholars claim that the current compulsory Italian standard for social enterprises is unable to measure the social enterprise's achievement of institutional purposes or mission. It also fails to consider the means by which the social enterprise pursues those objectives in accordance with the legitimate interests of all involved stakeholders under the constraint of long-term sustainability (efficiency). In this way, the social report[1] essentially is viewed as a further "cost"; it is inherently bureaucratic for the social enterprise. It does not represent an opportunity for self-evaluation or clear communication with relevant stakeholders.

The Italian regulation regarding social reporting for social enterprises recalls the academic debate regarding voluntary versus mandatory disclosure. Indeed, over the past decade, a growing number of studies on Corporate Social Reporting (CSRep) have investigated the role of mandatory and voluntary disclosure. These studies have been conducted for the following reasons: (i) to evaluate how companies discharge accountability (Adams, Coutts, & Harte, 1995; Day & Woodward, 2004) and (ii) to measure the degree of compliance of CSRep with legal standards or requirements (Criado-Jiménez, Fernàndez-Chuliàn, Husillos-Carqués, & Larrinaga-Gonzàlez, 2008; Larrinaga, Carrasco, Correa, Llena, & Moneva, 2002; Llena, Moneva, & Hernandez, 2007).

Scholars in this debate consider mandatory disclosure the most appropriate way to transparency and stakeholder disclosure, which consequently affects the organizations (Bebbington & Thy, 1999; Mobus, 2005). Many studies demonstrate that despite mandatory CSRep, a large number of companies still fail to make disclosures, or if they do make disclosures, the quality of the data is relatively low (Adams et al., 1995; Criado-Jiménez et al., 2008; Day & Woodward, 2004; Larrinaga et al., 2002; Llena et al., 2007).

This article looks beyond crude noncompliance analysis with legislation, aiming to analyze if regulation influences organizations' voluntary disclosure. The article provides a detailed analysis of *all* the social and environmental disclosures provided by northern Italian "non-accredited" social enterprises before and after the introduction of regulation. The novelty of this article rests in the fact that it does not analyze the social and environmental disclosure of "legal social enterprises." Instead, it considers the whole context of voluntary disclosure for "non-accredited" social enterprises in a regulated environment. The research question can be therefore summarized as follows: *Did the regulation influence the voluntary disclosure of social enterprises?* The research thus aims to learn if regulation has the power to influence voluntary practices of social and environmental reporting.

In order to accomplish this task, this article provides a content analysis of 170 stand-alone social and environmental reports from Italian "non-accredited social enterprises" from 2006 to 2009. The empirical evidence shows that the regulation has induced a large number of non-accredited social enterprises to voluntarily adopt a social and environmental reporting system. Indeed, the findings show that the number of social enterprises delivering a stand-alone social report has increased, thereby supporting the role of mandatory disclosures for social and environmental issues.

However, by analyzing the average sentences per report from 2006 to 2009, we discovered that the information related to social and environmental matters is actually less significant. The information contained in the stand-alone social and environmental reports have decreased, especially those involving "social-related issues." In fact, these disclosures suffer from regulatory limitations (i.e., Decree 1/24/2008); for instance, they focus too much on the governance structure and the description of social enterprise activities.

Following this brief introduction, the next section of this article presents the context of Italian social enterprises in light of the 2005 legal framework. Then, the section "The Debate Regarding Voluntary and Mandatory Social and Environmental Disclosure Within the Italian Context of Social Enterprises" describes the accountability duty of regulated social enterprises and discusses the academic debate regarding voluntary and mandatory social and environmental disclosure. The section "Research Design" presents the methodology of the research with reference to the sample description and methodology for the analysis. The section "Findings and Discussion" provides the research results, which are further discussed in the section "Conclusion" with specific attention to the international academic debate regarding voluntary disclosure. The article closes with concluding remarks.

THE CONTEXT: ITALIAN SOCIAL ENTERPRISES IN A NEW LEGAL FRAMEWORK

This section first provides worldwide definitions on this topic, with specific attention devoted to Europe and Italy. It also outlines the legal frameworks that social enterprises can adopt.

This article adopts the European concept of social enterprises developed by the EMES Research Network,[2] defining them as "not-for-profit private organizations providing goods or services directly related to their explicit aim to benefit the community. They rely on a collective dynamic involving various types of stakeholders in their governing bodies, they place a high value on their autonomy and they bear economic risks linked to their activity" (Defourny & Nyssens, 2008a, p. 5).

In Europe, the Italian experience represents the starting point for the concept of social enterprises. Indeed, even if some scholars previously used this concept (Dees, 1998; Dees & Economy, 2001), it became acknowledged in 1990 with the launch of a new Italian journal, entitled *Impresa Sociale* (Defourny & Nyssens, 2008b). Historical and cultural reasons may explain why innovative organizational models were needed to deal with the unmet social needs in Italy. Defourny and Nyssens (2008a) explain that the weak presence of the welfare state combined with the historical tradition of cooperation to give rise to new organizational forms, such as social enterprises. In this context where the government was unable to solve or ameliorate failures, social enterprises sprang up as mechanisms offering social services to citizens (Austin, Stevenson, & Skillern, 2006).

This section also considers the legal framework assumed by social enterprises. European social enterprises have assumed various legal forms, and the evolution of these regulations can be divided into two main phases. In the first phase, social enterprises were established as associations (similar to France and Belgium) and cooperatives (similar to Sweden, Finland, Spain, and Italy) (Borzaga & Defourny, 2001; Kerlin, 2006). In the second phase, some countries adopted specific legal forms for social enterprises (e.g., Italy). These adaptations occurred through cooperative legal frameworks or through the introduction of legal brands and categories that recognize the social commitment taken on by certain economic entities (e.g., the United Kingdom) (European Commission, 2013; Galera & Borzaga, 2009; see also Table 1).

In 1991, this process formally began when Law n. 381 on social cooperatives built the legislative framework for socially oriented organizations that spontaneously sprang up more than 20 years prior (Borzaga & Ianes, 2006). According to this law, social cooperatives can either provide caring or training activities (Thomas, 2004). Caring activities – so-called type A – refer to social health care and educational services, cultural activities, nurseries, and environmental protection initiatives. Training activities – so-called type B – introduce disadvantaged people to business activities and employment opportunities (work integration). These organizations are privately owned. Specifically, they are member-owned, operating in order to create social value for the community.

In the last few years, Italy has changed its legal framework for social enterprises, introducing new laws (Law 118/2005 and Legislative Decree Dlgs.n. 155/2006) in order to "cross the boundaries of all legal forms" (Defourny & Nyssens, 2010, p. 37). Indeed, it enables "various types of organizations (not only cooperatives and traditional nonprofit organizations (NPOs), but also investor-owned organization, for instance) to obtain the "legal brand" of social enterprise, provided they comply with the non-distribution constraint and organize the representation of certain categories

Table 1. Social Enterprise Qualifications for Various Legal Forms and Countries.

Country	Legal Forms Used	Definition of Social Aim
Belgium Law of April 13, 1995	Limited company; limited liability cooperative society; private limited liability society	Activities are aimed at pursuing a social goal. What constitutes a social goal results from constitutive elements foreseen by the legislation
Italy Law n. 118 of 13 June 2005	Associations; foundations; cooperatives; for-profit enterprises	Production or exchange of services in the sectors of social and health assistance, education and training, environmental protection, social tourism, cultural services, or work integration of disadvantaged persons independently from the field of activity of the enterprise
The United Kingdom Community interest company regulations 2005	Enterprises regulated by Companies Act of 1985	Wide range of activities that correspond to the needs of communities. Social definition assessed by the regulator
Slovenia Law on social entrepreneurship 2011	Legal persons without a profit goal (cooperative enterprises, share-holder companies, *zavods* (institutes), companies for disabled, associations, and foundations)	Provision of a wide set of services listed by the law
Finland Law n. 1351/2003	Social enterprise (all enterprises regardless of their legal form and ownership structure)	Work integration of people with disabilities and long-term unemployed individuals

Adapted from European Commission (2013).

of stakeholders, including workers and beneficiaries" (Defourny & Nyssens, 2008b, p. 26).

According to the current law, the social enterprise is not a new type of organization nor a new legal form; rather, it is only a "legal brand" in which all eligible organizations that respect the legal requirement may be included, regardless of their organizational structure (Fici, 2006; Galera & Borzaga, 2009). Social cooperatives, thus, fall *naturally* – but not *automatically* – under the banner of social enterprise. In order to obtain the legal status, they have to meet three additional requirements: (1) provide an annual stand-alone social report; (2) develop a participatory and open governance mechanism, including not only members but also other stakeholders; and (3) formally register at the Chamber of Commerce. The Italian law on social enterprises thus has introduced the duty to provide stand-alone social and environmental reports for "regulated" social enterprises. This law follows an established proforma containing 38 compulsory issues (with the Implementation Decree on January 24, 2008; see appendix).

THE DEBATE REGARDING VOLUNTARY AND MANDATORY SOCIAL AND ENVIRONMENTAL DISCLOSURE WITHIN THE ITALIAN CONTEXT OF SOCIAL ENTERPRISES

Four years after the law's passing, the IRIS Network Report noted that only 623 institutions had obtained their "legal brand" by registering at the Chamber of Commerce, a small number given the nearly 13,000 possible social enterprises (Zandonai & Borzaga, 2009). The data suggests that the recent legal framework partially has failed due to its inability to attract traditional social cooperatives into its new "legal brand" (Zandonai & Borzaga, 2009).

By analyzing the limits and potentials of the recent legislation, many Italian scholars of various disciplines have reflected on this "partial failure," including lawyers (Fici & Galletti, 2007; Iamiceli, 2009), economists (Ecchia & Viviani, 2006; Sacconi, 2006), and accountants (Andreaus, 2007; Costa, 2014; Marano, 2006; Rusconi & Signori, 2007; Travaglini, 2006, 2007). Their reflections stem from the debate regarding voluntary and mandatory disclosure in social and environmental accounting research. Simplifying a little, they blame the social reporting duty, particularly the compulsory guidelines established by the Implementation Decree on January 24th, 2008. By analyzing the 38 items required by the law (see appendix) and by attributing a "label" to each indicator by defining different areas of the disclosure, Costa (2014) showed that few indicators refer to social and environmental issues. Instead, the majority of the indicators refers to governance, activities, general information, and financial subjects. "Thus, it seems that the legislator put a list of items rather unrelated to social and environmental disclosure under the 'social accounting umbrella'" (Costa, 2014, p. 115). Italian scholars recognize two main limitations to this approach: first, they criticize the mandatory standard for social and environmental reporting; second, they suggest reinforcing the role of the mission statement in social enterprises' social and environmental reporting.

Several studies have indeed demonstrated that voluntary social and environmental disclosure faces two primary weaknesses. On one side, voluntary disclosure deals with a lack of neutrality and objectivity because it is subject to considerable managerial discretion (Adams, 2004; Deegan & Rankin, 1996). In addition, voluntary disclosure often is used as a "greenwashing" technique devoid of outcome-based results (Netwon & Harte, 1997), thus presenting misleading and self-laudatory communication (Mobus, 2005).

While the process of discharging voluntary disclosure may contribute to the creating and maintaining of stakeholder dialogue, the relative power relations between the company and stakeholders imply that the company inevitably comes to control the relationship with the stakeholder as well as the related disclosure (O'Dwyer, 2005; Owen, Swift, Humphrey, and Bowerman, 2000).

Therefore, a first step toward disclosure "systematization" is standardization. This standardization of voluntary disclosure should not be conceived of as a final solution to the above-mentioned problem. Suggesting the importance of standardization, some authors also have highlighted its associated problems (Lamberton, 2005). Indeed, the voluntary approach to social and environmental disclosure was rejected widely even though it was promoted by GRI, ISEA, and other organizations representing businesses (O'Dwyer, Unerman, & Bradley, 2005). To date, these standards have been built from private sector organizations, industry associations, or NPOs, and they have been made available for companies to freely choose their favored standard. This approach certainly creates flexibility for firms to find a system matching their needs, but it does not solve the problem of selective disclosure (Hess & Dunfee, 2007).

These disadvantages of voluntary disclosure have induced many scholars to affirm mandatory social and environmental disclosure as the most appropriate approach to improve corporate transparency (Bebbington & Thy, 1999; Deegan & Rankin, 1996; Gray, Owen, & Adams, 1996, p. 212; Hess & Dunfee, 2007; O'Dwyer et al., 2005; Owen, Gray, & Bebbington, 1997) while reducing manipulative intentions (Mobus, 2005). In particular, Larrinaga et al. (2002) argue that "legislation could improve environmental reporting by avoiding (a) the difference between companies that disclose and companies that do not; (b) opacity regarding bad news; (c) disclosure of non-audited information" (p. 724).

Several European countries are considering (or have considered) introducing mandatory social and environmental disclosure. Denmark, The Netherlands, Spain, Norway, and Sweden, for instance, have required companies to report on the social and environmental impacts of their activities since the late 1990s (Hess & Dunfee, 2007; Larrinaga et al., 2002). However, when corporate social disclosure is mandatory, research demonstrates that many companies do not comply with the legal requirements, and when they do, the quality of their social and environmental disclosure is fairly low (Adams et al., 1995; Criado-Jiménez et al., 2008; Day & Woodward, 2004; Larrinaga et al., 2002; Llena et al., 2007). Moreover, Adams et al. (1995), Larrinaga et al. (2002), and Criado-Jiménez et al. (2008) highlight how corporate social disclosure still is used to selectively manage public impression even in the presence of specific regulation. Therefore, the debate surrounding voluntary and mandatory disclosure continues because the introduction of corporate social regulation has failed to completely overcome the problems associated with voluntary disclosure.

This article seeks to contribute to this debate in a different way by looking beyond the distinction between voluntary and mandatory disclosure and by going further than investigating compliance with the standard. The current research seeks to investigate the interplay between the regulation and the overall voluntary disclosure of "non-regulated" social enterprises. Has the introduction of such legislation had an impact on the ongoing voluntary disclosure of non-regulated social enterprises?

RESEARCH DESIGN

Sample

The list of non-accredited social enterprises (which are social cooperatives) was collected using AIDA, a database that contains all of the data from the economic balance sheets of every company in Italy. AIDA is the Italian version of Amadeus and is available from Bureau van Dijk (http://www.bvdep.com/it/AIDA.html).

From the database analysis 5,337 social cooperatives existed in northern Italy in 2008 (Euricse, 2011). The decision to focus only on the northern social cooperatives was made for two reasons: first, social cooperatives historically have been developed mainly in northern Italy (Marocchi, 2002); second, future analysis will involve the development of a qualitative survey, and the travel costs associated with this research would be considerably less (Trento is centrally located in the northern region). After careful manual checking of the 5,337 northern Italian social cooperatives' financial statements, 395 were excluded from the analysis due to incompleteness of the balance sheet. Thus, for 2008, the final population is composed of 4,942 northern social cooperatives, as shown in Table 2.

The current research makes the assumption that bigger social enterprises more frequently provide a social report than smaller ones (Adams, Wan-Ying, & Roberts, 1998); thus, the sample of social enterprises has been selected according to population stratification.

A sample of 250 units has been built up with an error rate of 2% according to double stratification: (i) stratification by dimension (big social cooperatives with sales over €10,000,000 and medium-small social cooperatives with sales below €10,000,000) and (ii) stratification by region. Within every strata, the social cooperatives have been selected randomly. From the first strata, all the social enterprises (82) were selected, and the other 168 units were chosen by region, with a sample ratio of 0.036 (Table 1).

The researchers contacted each of the 250 social cooperatives by phone or e-mail in order to understand if they drew up social reports. Some social cooperatives no longer existed; thus, other samples were collected in order to replace the missing cooperatives. In the end, a total of 336 social cooperatives were contacted, and 231 were in operation. Out of 231 social cooperatives, 65 (28%) presented at least one social report during the period under investigation (2006–2009), 116 did not provide a social and/or environmental report, and the remaining 59 did not respond to our questions (pending cases) (see Table 3).

Out of the 65 responding social cooperatives, most did not deliver a social report for the entire period under investigation (2006–2009), or did not produce an annual social report. Table 4 shows the number of social reports collected by year and highlights those available on the Internet webpage of the social cooperatives. The table also indicates those reports that had to be collected manually by asking the social cooperatives to deliver a hardcopy. A total of 170 stand-alone social and environmental reports have been located, most (61%) of which have been collected manually by the researchers.

Table 2. The Population and Sample of Social Cooperatives in Northern Italy (2008).

Italian Regions	Total	Population			Sample	
		Big sales > €10,000,000	Medium-small sales ≤ €10,000,000	Others sales ≤ €0 or missing	Big	Medium-small
Bolzano	95	0	94	1	0	4
Emilia-Romagna	750	28	689	33	28	24
Friuli-Venezia Giulia	204	5	196	3	5	7
Liguria	366	5	345	16	5	12
Lombardia	1908	20	1798	90	20	65
Piemonte	724	16	665	43	16	24
Trento	91	1	86	4	1	4
Valle d'Aosta	42	0	42	0	0	2
Veneto	762	7	728	27	7	26
Total	*4942*	*82*	*4643*	*217*	*82*	*168*

Table 3. Number of Social Cooperatives with a Social Report.

Data	Description
336	Social cooperatives contacted
231	Existing social cooperatives
116	Do not have a social report (from 2006 to 2009)
59	Pending cases
65	*Have a social report (for at least one year from 2006 to 2009)*

Table 4. Number of Social Reports Analyzed over the Years.

Year	Hardcopy	PDF Online	Total
2006	20	9	29
2007	21	13	34
2008	32	17	49
2009	31	27	58
Total	*104*	*66*	*170*

Content Analysis

The article is based on a content analysis (Krippendorf, 1980) of 170 social and environmental reports from 2006 to 2009 (before and after the law was implemented) from social cooperatives located in northern Italy. Content analysis is a "technique for gathering data that consists of codifying qualitative information in anecdotal and literary form into categories for deriving quantitative scales of varying levels of complexity" (Abbott & Monsen, 1979, p. 504). It enables the researcher to collect large amounts of textual information and systematically identify its properties.

In the social and environmental accounting literature, the content analysis method usually has been classified into two main groups. The first group includes measures that quantify the amount of disclosure by defining the importance of each category (Unerman, 2000). This group consists of counting every word, sentence, page, or page proportion. The second measurement group uses a quality index to assess, compare, and explain differences in the quality of disclosed information (for a review, see Hooks & van Staden, 2011). The article adopts a sentences-count content analysis, as many scholars consider sentences the most appropriate unit of analysis (Hackston, David, & Milne, 1996; Milne & Adler, 1999). For the purpose of the analysis, this approach enables us to better understand the following: the amount of disclosure regarding the social and environmental impacts of social enterprises and the evolution of such information during the years under investigation (2006–2009). Through this information, the study seeks to comprehend the effects of the 2008 legislative decree on disclosure.

The content analysis method is based on the concept of reliability (Milne & Adler, 1999; Gray, Kouhy, & Lavers, 1995; Unerman, 2000), which has been assessed in several ways in this article. First, two researchers independently have carried out the analysis of 170 reports over three rounds to ensure stability and reproducibility. Discrepancies between the two researchers then were re-analyzed and differences resolved. Second, in order to guarantee accuracy, the two researchers established a priori rules in order to facilitate the distribution of the information into coding units; they then distributed these coding units into categories (Stemler, 2001) selected using the national guidelines for social enterprises, as provided by the Implementation Decree (January, 2008; see appendix for details). The Implementation Decree set out guidelines containing a list of indicators attributable to the following areas of disclosure: general (information regarding the formal structure of the social enterprise), governance, social workers, consolidation, context, social beneficiaries, financial, activities, and social environment. As a third reliability measure, the researchers performed a pilot test on a few corporate social reports.

The data have been collected manually. Although labor-intensive and time-consuming, manual collection has allowed the researchers to create a more detailed and sophisticated analysis (Unerman, 2000).

FINDINGS AND DISCUSSION

Table 5 considers all the disclosed information in the social and environmental reports of Italian social enterprises and presents it according to the categories provided by the Implementation Decree Some categories included "not-socially-related" issues: general, governance, consolidated, context, financial, and activities. Other categories involve more "socially related issues": workers, beneficiaries, and environment. This disclosure was completely voluntary as it had been addressed by social enterprises not accredited under the "legal brand." However, the analysis splits the overall disclosure in two main groups: (a) disclosure that could be encompassed under the guidelines set out by the Implementation Decree of January 2008

Table 5. The Volume of Disclosures by Area.

	Total 2006			Total 2007			Total 2008			Total 2009			Total 2006–2009		
	Impl. decree Jan 2008	Other	Total	Impl. decree Jan 2008	Other	Total	Impl. decree Jan 2008	Other	Total	Impl. decree Jan 2008	Other	Total	Impl. decree Jan 2008	Other	Total
Panel A: total volume of the disclosure															
General	562	2437	2999	771	2297	3068	1151	3149	4300	1197	2793	3990	3681	10676	14357
Governance	871	392	1263	1087	580	1667	1569	706	2275	1478	741	2219	5005	2419	7424
Consolidated	135	0	135	173	0	173	296	0	296	233	0	233	837	0	837
Context	255	446	701	333	777	1110	259	1115	1374	272	1097	1369	1119	3435	4554
Financial	321	712	1033	413	944	1357	614	836	1450	599	1142	1741	1947	3634	5581
Activities	2796	609	3405	2237	665	2902	3567	584	4151	5029	825	5854	13629	2683	16312
Total "not-social-related"	*4940*	*4596*	*9536*	*5014*	*5263*	*10277*	*7456*	*6390*	*13846*	*8808*	*6598*	*15406*	*26218*	*22847*	*49065*
Social workers	77	2439	2516	152	2362	2514	200	1884	2084	302	2343	2645	731	9028	9759
Social beneficiaries	729	467	1196	748	362	1110	1067	523	1590	1366	849	2215	3910	2201	6111
Social environment	0	3	3	0	34	34	0	79	79	0	72	72	0	188	188
Total "social-related"	*806*	*2909*	*3715*	*900*	*2758*	*3658*	*1267*	*2486*	*3753*	*1668*	*3264*	*4932*	*4641*	*11417*	*16058*
Total volume	*5746*	*7505*	*13251*	*5914*	*8021*	*13935*	*8723*	*8876*	*17599*	*10476*	*9862*	*20338*	*30859*	*34264*	*65123*
Panel B: Average by report															
General	19.4	84.0	1034	22.7	67.6	90.2	23.5	64.3	87.8	20.6	48.2	68.8	21.7	62.8	84.5
Governance	30.0	13.5	43.6	32.0	17.1	49.0	32.0	14.4	46.4	25.5	12.8	38.3	29.4	14.2	43.7
Consolidated	4.7	0.0	4.7	5.1	0.0	5.1	6.0	0.0	6.0	4.0	0.0	4.0	4.9	0.0	4.9

Context	8.8	15.4	24.2	9.8	22.9	32.6	5.3	22.8	28.0	4.7	18.9	23.6	6.6	20.2	26.8
Financial	11.1	24.6	35.6	12.1	27.8	39.9	12.5	17.1	29.6	10.3	19.7	30.0	11.5	21.4	32.8
Activities	96.4	21.0	117.4	65.8	19.6	85.4	72.8	11.9	84.7	86.7	14.2	100.9	80.2	15.8	96.0
Total "not-social-related"	*170.3*	*158.5*	*328.8*	*147.5*	*154.8*	*302.3*	*152.2*	*130.4*	*282.6*	*151.9*	*113.8*	*265.6*	*154.2*	*134.4*	*288.6*
Social workers	2.7	84.1	86.8	4.5	69.5	73.9	4.1	38.4	42.5	5.2	40.4	45.6	4.3	53.1	57.4
Social beneficiaries	25.1	16.1	41.2	22.0	10.6	32.6	21.8	10.7	32.4	23.6	14.6	38.2	23.0	12.9	35.9
Social environment	0.0	0.1	0.1	0.0	1.0	1.0	0.0	1.6	1.6	0.0	1.2	1.2	0.0	1.1	1.1
Total "social-related"	*27.8*	*100.3*	*128.1*	*26.5*	*81.1*	*107.6*	*25.9*	*50.7*	*76.6*	*28.8*	*56.3*	*85.0*	*27.3*	*67.2*	*94.5*
Total average	*198.1*	*258.8*	*456.9*	*173.9*	*235.9*	*409.9*	*178.0*	*181.1*	*359.2*	*180.6*	*170.0*	*350.7*	*181.5*	*201.6*	*383.1*

and (b) disclosure that has been added according to the previously mentioned categories. Both of these groups provided information voluntarily.

Panel A displays a total number of 65,123 reported sentences within social enterprises' sustainability reports. Within this panel, most (75%) reported information unrelated to social and environmental matters, mainly providing descriptions of the activities carried out by the social enterprises in order to achieve their mission (16,312 sentences from 2006 to 2009; 25% of the disclosure). The other major category included general information (14,357 sentences from 2006 to 2009; 22%).

Common features emerge when analyzing the data over the years: there is a great deal of description of activities as well as general information about the social enterprises and their governance structures. Issues related to activities cover 26% of total disclosures in 2006, 21% in 2007, 24% in 2008, and 29% in 2009. The same trend occurred with regard to general and governance issues. Overall, the "not-social-related" issues were preponderant from 2006–2009, accounting for more than 70% of the overall disclosures in Italian social enterprises' social and environmental reports.

In the 2008 reports, the Implementation Decree had been introduced. Paradoxically, beginning in 2008, the "not-social-related" information increased to the detriment of the "social-related" information. More precisely, the overall number of disclosures increased from 2006 to 2009 (from 13,251 sentences to 20,338; +53%); however, their composition substantially changed in favor of more social and environmental information. Indeed, in 2008, there was a significant increase with regard to general information and information specifically related to activities (+40% and +43%, respectively). At the same time, there was an inadequate increase of 3% in "social-related" issue reporting and a decrease (−17%) in information related to the workers. Regarding the social information of the beneficiaries, the analysis reveals that it represents approximately 9% of the total disclosure and, even if it noticeably increased from 2007 to 2008 (+43%), its weight within the total disclosure remained unchanged.

Panel A shows that from 2006 to 2009, and more specifically from 2007 to 2008 (the year of the change), there have been overall increases in the social and environmental reports of Italian social enterprises; however, disclosures related to the social and environmental impacts of these enterprises has not emerged as primary objectives. The social impact on the workers has been measured and explained less within the report: 19% in 2006, 18% in 2007, 12% in 2008, and 15% in 2009. At the same time, there has been increasing attention to "not-social-related" issues.

By analyzing the average number of sentences per report, Panel B displays that from 2006 to 2009, there were decreases in the average amounts of disclosed information. Again, by comparing the "not-social-oriented" issues with the more "social-oriented" ones, it emerges that the former decreased less than the latter. For instance, the "not-social-related issues" moved from 328.8 average sentences in 2006 to 256.6 average sentences in 2009 (−19%). Meanwhile, the "social-related issues" went from 128.1 average sentences per report in 2006 to 85 average sentences in 2009 (−34%).

By comparing the data from 2006 (before regulation) and 2009 (after regulation), it becomes clear that the social and environmental reports of Italian social enterprises became "less-social-oriented" after the introduction of the 2008 Implementation Decree. Indeed, in 2006, the 28% of global voluntary disclosures was employed to provide accounts to the workers (19%) and beneficiaries (9%). Seventy-two percent of the disclosures dealt with more general information, not focused on discharge accountability on the social and environmental impact of social enterprises' activities. In particular, the disclosures focused on general information (23%) and description of activities (26%). The impact on voluntary disclosure for non-accredited social enterprises was very low following the 2008 introduction of a mandatory standard for social reporting for "accredited social enterprises." In fact, there was decreased reporting regarding workers (13%) and beneficiaries (11%) in favor of increased reporting of "not-social-related" issues (76%).

Generally speaking, considering both the total disclosure (Panel A) and the average number of sentences per report (Panel B), there was increased voluntary disclosure from 2006 to 2009 on social and environmental matters in the Italian "non-regulated" social enterprises. This increase is connected to an increasing amount of social reporting (see Table 4). However, when analyzing the average sentences per report, it emerges that the information contained in the stand-alone social and environmental reports have decreased, especially those in the "social-related issues" category. Therefore, on one side, there is an increasing number of social enterprises – even if not accredited – which are dealing with the problem of accounting for their social and environmental impacts; on the other side, the information related to social and environmental matters has lessened from 2006 to 2009. These results have implications for the stream of academic debate relating to the role of accountability as well as voluntary versus mandatory disclosure in social enterprises. Generally, studies regarding the role of voluntary and mandatory disclosure on social and environmental matters agree that mandatory corporate social and environmental disclosure is the best solution to several problems (Bebbington & Thy, 1999; Deegan & Rankin, 1996; Gray et al., 1996, p. 212; Hess & Dunfee, 2007; Larrinaga et al., 2002; O'Dwyer et al., 2005, 1997). Hess and Dunfee (2007) propose a solution that is not only mandatory but also standardized; they advocate for a "single standardized format established by a government body, but including sufficient flexibility to be relevant to all firms" (p. 24). This solution parallels the one offered by the Italian government for the "accredited" social enterprises. The solution proposed Hess and Dunfee (2007) could be helpful in avoiding two kinds of problems: the ability of firms to selectively disclose and stakeholders' lack of knowledge with respect to what information a corporation has or could acquire. A mandatory and standardized disclosure obligates companies to follow the same information and sets out the information firms should be able to disclose.

Nevertheless, this solution does not consider the effects on voluntary disclosure in a regulated environment. What is the impact on an organization's overall disclosure when a law has taken force in a country? In the Italian case, there are social enterprises that have not taken the legal accreditation; therefore, they are not obliged to draw up stand-alone social and environmental reports. However, before and after the introduction of this law, they started and continue to provide social reporting to their stakeholders. This article has highlighted that, from 2006 to 2009, overall disclosure regarding social and environmental matters on "non-accredited" Italian social enterprises increased, as seen by the trend in increased reports. However, the average sentences per report decreased during the period under investigation. Though an increasing number of firms are motivated to disclose social information, it is not clear if this motivation results from a desire to make voluntary disclosure available to the stakeholder. Hess and Dunfee (2007) argue that there are two main drivers of voluntary disclosure: first, there must be a significant benefit in disclosure, which is not the case for "non-accredited" Italian social enterprises. Second, there must be a strong belief in the notion of accountability.

This second point regarding the concept of accountability could be the key for interpreting the rationales for voluntary disclosure, even in a regulated context, such as the case presented in this article. Recently, Costa (2014) has highlighted that before the introduction of a mandatory scheme for social reporting for the "regulated" Italian social enterprises, some social enterprises "felt the need to enlarge their accountability and accounting systems by providing additional information closer to their identity (Unerman & O'Dwyer, 2006) and their activity mission purposes" (p. 104).

Therefore, in the Italian case, voluntary disclosure could be seen as a way to be accountable to the stakeholders; perhaps for the same reason, most Italian social enterprises decided not to seek accreditation as a "legal social enterprise."

In this regard, Italian scholars reprimand the content of the Italian guidelines for straying from the acknowledged norms for social reporting; these guidelines have seemingly been unable to provide a new legal framework creating greater accountability. Two primary limitations have been addressed regarding the guidelines. First, Iamiceli (2009) highlights how the amount of detail required for the social report – which has to contain 38 issues – discourages social enterprises from participating in the challenging social accounting process. Second, Sacconi (2006) and Andreaus (2006) point out that the standards primarily are devoted to controlling the mission-oriented purpose. In other words, as structured by the legislature, the social report is not able to effectively "account" on the relationship with stakeholders. As Sacconi (2006) highlights, the social report required by law "is defined as an instrument to verify the correspondence with the social aim required to be a social enterprise. [...] Thus, the guidelines suggest mainly how to account for the quantity and quality of social value goods and services provided. In this way, the social report is likely to be understood as a social statement of the core business and its results (production of a good social utility)" (p. 58).

There are two missing points in this regulated environment: the centrality of the mission and the relationship with the stakeholders. The law, thus, is unable to highlight the central role of the mission, which is a distinctive feature of every NPO (Johnston, 2001; Kanter & Summers, 1987). Moreover, the guidelines proposed by the legislator fail to account on the stakeholder's legitimate needs in the social enterprise (Bouckaert & Vandenhove, 1998; Rusconi & Signori, 2007). In this sense, the social report seems to be more a cost and constraint than a strength and opportunity for an NPO willing to acquire the status of "regulated social enterprise." These issues could be a disincentive for social reporting.

CONCLUSION

This article aimed to investigate if regulation influences organizations' voluntary disclosure by analyzing the overall voluntary disclosure of Italian social enterprises in a regulated context from 2006 (before the introduction of specific regulation making social reporting compulsory) to 2009 (after regulation).

Social enterprises number approximately 13,000 in Italy with a turnover of more than 10 million Euros and 520,000 employees. In 2005 and later in 2008, the Italian government set forth laws introducing a formal accreditation process for social enterprises, including mandatory social and environmental reporting for these "legal" social enterprises. Most Italian social enterprises did not acquire this "legal accreditation" (Zandonai & Borzaga, 2009) and did not comply with the mandatory standard for social reporting.

The academic debate to date has supported the relevance of mandatory disclosure rather than the voluntary form (Adams et al., 1995; Gray et al., 1996, p. 212; Hess & Dunfee, 2007; Larrinaga et al., 2002; Llena et al., 2007; Owen et al., 1997). This article makes a contribution by investigating the interplay between voluntary disclosure and regulation. More specifically, it analyzes the evolution of voluntary disclosure for "non-regulated" social enterprises from 2006 to 2009 in a regulated context, following the introduction of a specific law making social reporting compulsory.

By evaluating the number of sentences devoted to singles areas of the disclosure, the article develops an in-depth content analysis of the overall disclosure while measuring the extent of the disclosures. The analysis not only evaluates the items encompassed under the Implementation Decree of 2008 but also considers all of the social and environmental disclosures provided by social enterprises.

The empirical evidence shows that Italian social enterprises increased their attention on social reporting practices. From 2006 to 2009, the number of social enterprises that drew up a social report increased, and the overall disclosure rate increased as well. Nevertheless, the average number of sentences per report decreased during the period under investigation, especially information related to social issues.

Therefore, on one side, we argue that mandatory disclosure is the preferred way for providing accountability, even if regulation is insufficient for the advancement of social and environmental accountability. Many studies have presented unacceptable results for voluntary reporting; therefore, we agree with Larrinaga et al. (2002) and question the "simplistic" view (p. 737) according to which the regulation of social and environmental reporting prevents all the shortcomings of voluntary disclosure. We do not believe that Hess and Dunfee's view (2007) on a standardized voluntary accountability represents the best solution to the aforementioned problems;

the only way to better perform both voluntary and mandatory disclosure is to enhance the accountability of every organization (Adams, 2004).

On the other side, by expressing skepticism toward Hess and Dunfee's (2007) proposal, we agree with Italian scholars claiming that the Italian mandatory standard for social enterprises is too focused on social enterprise governance structure and description of the activities (Andreaus, 2006, 2007; Marano, 2006; Rusconi & Signori, 2007; Sacconi, 2006; Travaglini, 2006, 2007). Two major concerns have been raised to date: first, the legislation paid too much attention to the details, thus building a strictly formal accountability system. This formal social and environmental reporting seems to discourage social enterprises from facing the challenging social accounting process. Second, the standard promoted by the new legal framework primarily is devoted to controlling the governance requirement. The main information relates to governance and activities, acting as a formal control of the requirements to become a regulated social enterprise.

These concerns also could contribute to the ongoing debate regarding policy implications. There is a current European debate on the need to adopt (or not adopt) a European standard for social impact measurement for social enterprises (GECES, 2014). This article could help Italian and European legislators in understanding that – in my opinion – a mandatory standardized approach to social and environmental reporting is improper. As the analysis clearly shows, the duty to provide an account positively affects the voluntary disclosure of social enterprises, but the content of these reports suffers due to the limitations imposed by the standards. It is a complex process to set out proper standards because of the myriad of different social enterprises.

The results coming from the current analysis also could be related to the role of social reporting for social enterprises, thereby representing a starting point for future examination. The analyzed social and environmental reporting indeed focuses primarily on governance and activities issues. Therefore, they described how the social enterprises are governed (with a multistakeholder approach) quite well. They also highlight the kinds of activities that are carried out. This analysis roughly confirms the existence of a managerial and accounting dilemma in the social enterprise (Bouckaert & Vandenhove, 1998; Cornelius, Todres, Janjuha-Jivraj, and Wallace, 2008; Rusconi & Signori, 2007). A social enterprise could be managed in a socially irresponsible way because from a socially oriented perspective, it does not follow ethical processes defined by managerial and accounting guidelines.

NOTES

1. Please note that, in this article, "social report," "social and environmental report," and "social reporting" are used interchangeably. As Gray (2002) highlights, social accounting appears under various labels: "social responsibility accounting, social audits, corporate social reporting, employee and employment reporting, stakeholder dialogue reporting as well as environmental accounting and reporting" (Gray, 2002, p. 687).

2. Begun in 1996, the EMES (The Emergence of Social Enterprise in Europe) Project conducts research on social enterprise in European Union countries with funds from the European Commission. It is the basis for the European EMES network that annually holds an international conference on social enterprise in Trento, Italy.

REFERENCES

Abbott, W. F., & Monsen, R. J. (1979). On the measurement of corporate social responsibility: Self-reported disclosures as a method of measuring corporate social involvement. *Academy of Management Journal*, *22*(3), 501–515.

Adams, C. A. (2004). The ethical, social and environmental reporting performance portrayal gap. *Accounting, Auditing & Accountability Journal*, *17*(5), 731–757.

Adams, C. A., Coutts, A., & Harte, G. (1995). Corporate equal opportunities (non-)disclosure. *British Accounting Review*, *27*, 87–108.

Adams, C. A., Wan-Ying, H., & Roberts, C. B. (1998). Corporate social reporting practices in Western Europe: Legitimating corporate behaviour? *British Accounting Review*, *30*, 1–21.

Andreaus, M. (2006). La legge delega sull'impresa sociale: Quali implicazioni dal punto di vista aziendale. *Impresa Sociale*, *75*(3), 100–113.

Andreaus, M. (2007). Quale modello di rendicontazione per l'impresa sociale? *Impresa Sociale*, *76*(1), 59–78.

Austin, J., Stevenson, H., & Skillern, J. W. (2006). Social and commercial entrepreneurship: Same, different, or both? *Entrepreneurship Theory and Practice*, *January*, 1–22.

Bebbington, J., & Thy, C. (1999). Compulsory environmental reporting in Denmark: An evaluation. *Social and Environmental Accounting*, *19*(2), 2–4.

Borzaga, C., & Defourny, J. (2001). *The emergence of social enterprise*. London: Routledge.

Borzaga, C., & Ianes, A. (2006). *L'economia della solidarietà. Storia e prospettive della cooperazione sociale*. Roma: Donzelli Editore.

Bouckaert, L., & Vandenhove, J. (1998). Business ethics and the management of non-profit institutions. *Journal of Business Ethics*, *17*, 1073–1081.

Cornelius, N., Todres, M., Janjuha-Jivraj, S., & Wallace, J. (2008). Corporate social responsibility and the social enterprise. *Journal of Business Ethics*, *81*(2), 355–371.

Costa, E. (2014). Social reporting for Italian social enterprises. Did the Italian legislator miss an opportunity? In Z. Hoque & L. Parker (Eds.), *Performance management in nonprofit organizations: Global perspectives* (pp. 93–131). New York, NY: Routledge.

Criado-Jiménez, I., Fernàndez-Chuliàn, M., Husillos-Carqués, F. J., & Larrinaga-Gonzàlez, C. (2008). Compliance with mandatory environmental reporting in financial statements: The case of Spain (2001–2003). *Journal of Business Ethics*, *79*, 245–262.

Day, R., & Woodward, T. (2004). Disclosure of information about employees in the directors' report of UK published financial statements: Substantive or symbolic? *Accounting Forum*, *28*, 43–59.

Deegan, C., & Rankin, M. (1996). Do Australian companies report environmental news objectively? An analysis of environmental disclosures by firms prosecuted successfully by the environmental protection authority. *Accounting, Auditing & Accountability Journal*, *9*(2), 50–67.

Dees, J. G. (1998). *The meaning of social entrepreneurship*. Retrieved from http://www.fuqua.duke.edu/centers/case/documents/dees_SE.pdf. Accessed on July 12, 2011.

Dees, J. G., & Economy, P. (2001). Social entrepreneurship. In J. G. Dees, J. Emerson, & P. Economy (Eds.), *Enterprising nonprofits: A toolkit for social entrepreneurship* (pp. 1–18). Canada: Wiley.

Defourny, J., & Nyssens, M. (2008a). *Conceptions of social enterprises in Europe and the United States: Convergences and divergences*. Paper presented at the Second EMES International Conference on Social Enterprise, University of Trento, Italy. Retrieved from http://www.emes.net/fileadmin/emes/PDF_files/Conferences/JD_MN_EU-US_final_Trento _2009.pdf. Accessed on July 1–4, 2009.

Defourny, J., & Nyssens, M. (Eds.). (2008b). *Social enterprise in Europe: Recent trends and developments*. EMES Working Paper No. 08/01.

Defourny, J., & Nyssens, M. (2010). Conceptions of social enterprise and social entrepreneurship in Europe and the United States: Convergences and divergences. *Journal of Social Entrepreneurship*, *1*(1), 32–53.

Ecchia, G., & Viviani, M. (2006). *Responsabilità sociale e impresa sociale*. Working paper AICCON No. 34. Retrieved from http://www.aiccon.it/working_paper.cfm

Euricse. (2011). La cooperazione in Italia – 1° Rapporto. Trento: Euricse.

European Commission. (2013). *Social economy and social entrepreneurship – Social Europe guide*, volume 4, Retrived from http://ec.europa.eu/social/main.jsp?catId=738&langId = it&pubId=7523

Fici, A. (2006). La nozione di impresa sociale e le finalità della disciplina. *Impresa Sociale*, *75*(3), 23–41.

Fici, A., & Galletti, D. (2007). Commentario al decreto sull'impresa sociale (D.lgs. 24 marzo 2006, n. 155). Torino: Giappichelli.

Galera, G., & Borzaga, C. (2009). Social enterprise: An international overview of its conceptual evolution and legal implementation. *Social Enterprise Journal*, *5*(3), 210–228.

GECES. (2014). *Proposed approaches to social impact measurement in European commission legislation and in practice relating to: EuSEFs and the EaSI, GECES sub-group on impact measurement* (following initial publication on 28th November 2013). Retrived from http://ec.europa.eu/internal_market/social_business/docs/expert-group/social_impact/140605-sub-group-report_en.pdf. Accessed on February 16, 2014.

Gray, R. H. (2002). The social accounting project and accounting organizations and society privileging engagement, imaginings, new accountings and pragmatism over critique? *Accounting, Organizations and Society*, *27*, 687–708.

Gray, R. H., Kouhy, R., & Lavers, S. (1995). Corporate social and environmental reporting: A review of the literature and a longitudinal study of UK disclosure. *Accounting, Auditing & Accountability Journal*, *8*(2), 47–77.

Gray, R. H., Owen, D. L., & Adams, C. (1996). *Accounting and accountability: Changes and challenges in corporate social and environmental reporting*. London: Prentice Hall.

Hackston, D., & Milne, M. J. (1996). Some determinants of social and environmental disclosures in New Zealand companies. *Accounting, Auditing & Accountability Journal*, *9*(1), 77–108.

Hess, D., & Dunfee, T. W. (2007). The kasky-nike threat to corporate social reporting. Implementing a standard of optimal truthful disclosure as a solution. *Business Ethics Quarterly*, *17*(1), 5–32.

Hooks, J., & Van Staden, C. J. (2011). Evaluating environmental disclosures: The relationship between quality and extent measures. *The British Accounting Review*, *43*(3), 200–213.

Iamiceli, P. (2009). La disciplina dell'impresa sociale: Potenzialita`, limiti e prospettive. In C. Borzaga, & F. Zandonai (Eds.), *L'impresa sociale in Italia* (pp. 87–102). Rome: Donzelli editore.

Johnston, R. (2001). Defining your mission. In J. G. Dees, J. Emerson, & P. Economy (Eds.), *Enterprising nonprofits: A toolkit for social entrepreneurship* (pp. 19–42). Canada: Wiley.

Kanter, R. M., & Summers, D. V. (1987). Doing well while doing good: Dilemmas of performance measurement in nonprofit organizations and the need for a multiple-constituency approach. In W. W. Powell (Ed.) *The non profit sector – A research handbook* (pp. 154–164). New Haven, CT:Yale University Press.

Kerlin, J. A. (2006). Social enterprise in the United States and Europe: Understanding and learning from the differences. *Voluntas: International Journal of Voluntary and Nonprofit Organizations*, *17*, 247–263.

Krippendorf, K. (1980). *Content analysis: An introduction to its methodology*. Beverly Hills, CA: Sage Publications.

Lamberton, G. (2005). Sustainability accounting-a brief history and conceptual framework. *Accounting Forum*, *29*, 7–26.

Larrinaga, C., Carrasco, F., Correa, C., Llena, F., & Moneva, J. M. (2002). Accountability and accounting regulation: The case of the Spanish environmental disclosure standard. *The European Accounting Review*, *11*(4), 723–740.

Llena, F., Moneva, J. M., & Hernandez, B. (2007). Environmental disclosures and compulsory accounting standards: The case of spanish annual reports. *Business Strategy and the Environment*, *16*(1), 50–63.

Marano, M. (2006). *L'accountability e i processi informativi dell'impresa sociale alla luce del d. lgs.* 155/2006. Working Paper AICCON No 38, Retrieved from http://www.aiccon.it/file/convdoc/n.38.pdf

Marocchi, G. (2002). I dati ministeriali: Una fotografia della cooperazione sociale. In C. G. M. Centro Studi (Ed.), *Comunità cooperative. Terzo rapporto sulla cooperazione sociale in Italia*. Torino: Fondazione Giovanni Agnelli.

Milne, M. J., & Adler, R. W. (1999). Exploring the reliability of social and environmental disclosures content analysis. *Accounting, Auditing & Accountability Journal*, *12*(2), 237–256.

Mobus, J. L. (2005). Mandatory environmental disclosures in a legitimacy theory context. *Accounting, Auditing and Accountability Journal*, *18*(4), 492–517.

Netwon, T., & Harte, G. (1997). Green business: Technicist kitsch? *Journal of Management Studies*, *34*(1), 75–98.

O'Dwyer, B. G. D. (2005). The construction of a social account: A case study in an overseas aid agency. Accounting, organizations and society. *Accounting, Organizations and Society*, *30*(3), 279–296.

O'Dwyer, B. G. D., Unerman, J., & Bradley, J. (2005). Perceptions on the emergence and future development of corporate social disclosure in Ireland: Engaging the voices of non-governmental organisations. *Accounting Auditing & Accountability Journal, 18*(1), 14–43.

Owen, D., Gray, R. H., & Bebbington, J. (1997). Green accounting: Cosmetic irrelevance or radical agenda for change? *Asia-Pacific Journal of Accounting, 4*(2), 175–198.

Owen, D. L., Swift, T., Humphrey, C., & Bowerman, M. (2000). The new social audits: Accountability, managerial capture or the agenda of social champions? *European Accounting Review, 9*(1), 81–98.

Rusconi, G., & Signori, S. (2007). Responsabilità sociale e aziende nonprofit: Quale declinazione? *Impresa Sociale, 76*(1), 39–58.

Sacconi, L. (2006). La legge sull'impresa sociale come selettore di organizzazioni con motivazioni necessarie all'efficienza: Quasi un'occasione mancata. *Impresa Sociale, 75*(3), 42–65.

Stemler, S. (2001). *An overview of content analysis.* Practical Assessment, Research & Evaluation, 7(17). ISSN 1531-7714. Retrieved from http://pareonline.net/getvn.asp?v=7&n=17

Thomas, A. (2004). The rise of social cooperatives in Italy. *Voluntas: International Journal of Voluntary and Nonprofit Organizations, 15*(3), 243–263.

Travaglini, C. (2006). L'informazione contabile nell'impresa sociale. *Impresa Sociale, 75*(3), 88–99.

Travaglini, C. (2007). Dal gruppo nonprofit al gruppo dell'impresa sociale: Dieci anni di sviluppo delle attività e di accountability nonprofit. *Impresa Sociale, 76*(1), 79–90.

Unerman, J. (2000). Methodological issues, reflection on quantification in corporate social reporting content analysis. *Accounting Auditing & Accountability Journal, 13*(5), 667–680.

Unerman, J., & O'Dwyer, B. (2006). Theorising accountability for NGO advocacy'. *Accounting, Auditing & Accountability Journal, 19*(3), 349–376.

Zandonai & Borzaga. (Eds.). (2009). L'impresa sociale in Italia. *Economia e Istituzione dei beni Comuni*. Rome: Donzelli Editore.

APPENDIX: THE LIST OF THE COMPULSORY ISSUES REQUESTED BY THE ITALIAN LAW ON SOCIAL ENTERPRISES

		Area of the Disclosure
1	**Introduction. Description of the Methodology Used for the Social Report**	General
	A. General Information about the Institution/Organization and the Administrator(s)	
2	Name of the organization	General
3	Registered office	General
4	Secondary office	General
5	Name of the administrator(s)	General
6	Names of people in charge as institutional office	General
7	Sector of activity	General
	B. Structure and Corporate Governance	
8	Mission	General
9	Information about the social/legal form adopted	General
10	Corporate governance information required from statute	Governance
11	Appointment of directors criteria	Governance
12	Appointing directors with delegated powers	Governance
13	Number of members	Governance
14	Summary of associative life	Governance
15	Map of stakeholders	Governance
16	Payments to directors	Governance
17	Payments to financial controller	Governance
18	Min. and max. value of compensation for worker	Social workers
19	Compensation for temporary workers	Social workers
20	Total number of women workers	Social workers
21	Analysis of the subsidiaries	Consolidated
22	Major networks and collaborations with third parties	Context
23	Total number of active volunteers in the organization	Social workers
24	Number and types of beneficiaries	Social beneficiaries
25	Evaluation of the economic and financial risk provided by the directors	Financial
	C. Aims and Activity	
26	Main purposes of the institution	Activities
27	Summary of main activities	Activities
28	Analysis of the relevant factors to achieve the objectives	Activities
29	Evaluation of achieved results and in particular analysis of the impact on the social fabric of reference	Social beneficiaries
30	Forms of involvement of employees and beneficiaries	Social workers and beneficiaries

Appendix. *(Continued)*

		Area of the Disclosure
31	Description of fund-raising activities	Financial
32	Indication of long-term strategies and outline future plans	Activities
	D. Economic and Financial Information	
33	Analysis of revenue and income	Financial
34	Analysis of costs and expenses	Financial
35	Analysis of how the costs have supported the key objectives of the institution	Financial
36	Analysis of the availability of funds – budget and constrains	Financial
37	Costs related to fund-raising activities, income obtained through fund-raising activities and the percentage of this revenue used to defray the costs of fund-raising	Financial
38	Analysis of the investment carried out and analysis of their funding	Financial

INTELLECTUAL CAPITAL REPORTING IN THE ITALIAN NONPROFIT SECTOR. AN IMAGE-BUILDING OR AN ACCOUNTABILITY TOOL?[☆]

Stefania Veltri and Giovanni Bronzetti

ABSTRACT

The purpose of this article is to analyze intellectual capital (IC) measurement, management, and reporting practices at organizational level, with the aim to address a relevant research question: are IC reports used as accountability or as image-building tools? The article presents a single in-depth case study of an Italian nonprofit organization (NPO) which has been measuring and reporting its IC for several years. The research

[☆]Though the chapter is the fruit of joint reflection and collaboration, for academic reasons the sections *Introductory remarks, Literatures review and hypotheses development, Research methodology, Research template, Analyzing the IC reporting practices of ANPAS Piemonte* are to be attributed to Stefania Veltri and the sections *Description of the case study and of its nonprofit setting* and *Conclusions* are to be attributed to Giovanni Bronzetti.

Accountability and Social Accounting for Social and Non-profit Organizations
Advances in Public Interest Accounting, Volume 17, 251–278

ISSN: 1041-7060/doi:10.1108/S1041-706020140000017010

project was conducted using an interpretative approach, by analyzing organizational IC reports in the light of a framework, derived from corporate social responsibility (CSR) and IC literature, able to provide researchers with useful insights to interpret the role played by IC report in the investigated organization. The lenses provided by the designed framework give researchers the opportunity to offer a skillful interpretation of the information provided by the IC report. From the analysis, it results that the investigated NPO use IC report more as a managerial rather than an accountability tool. Even though the use of a single case study provides in-depth and rich data, it also limits the generalizability of the observations to other companies. Moreover, the results obtained can be influenced by the model built and adopted to address the research question. The findings can support companies to enable IC reporting practices and readers to understand the orientation of the companies towards a reputation or an accountability approach by reading the IC report using the research model. The article fills a gap in the research of voluntary disclosure of NPOs from a different approach (i.e., to analyze IC reports to make evident the approach followed in disclosing IC information). So doing, the article contributes to narrowing the gap between IC theory and practice and offers new insights on the reasons why NPOs disclose IC.

Keywords: Intellectual capital; IC report; case study; Italy; nonprofit sector; model

INTRODUCTORY REMARKS

The advent of the knowledge economy has increased the importance of knowledge-based resources as key driver of firm performance, putting high in the agenda of managers and academics the need to measure, manage, and report intangible resources (Marr, 2005).

Anyway, the majority of intangible resources are not accounted for in traditional financial statements (Guthrie, Steane, & Farneti, 2009), instead information on Intellectual Capital (IC), the dynamic and firm-specific system of knowledge resources, could be included in the narrative part of the annual report (AR) or in a more elaborate autonomous supplementary report, the so-called IC report (ICR).[1]

IC management, measurement, and reporting, originally a private sector oriented metaphor, is increasingly viewed as a new conceptual framework for nonprofit (NP) setting (Kong, 2007; Veltri, 2011). On a macro (contextual level), NP organizations (NPOs) are today operating in a highly competitive environment, characterized by increasing demand of services from the community, growing competition for contracts with the public and for-profit sector, declining volunteer support and a generally tighter government funding source (Kong, 2010). On a micro (firm) level, intangible resources play a really relevant role in NPOs as their outputs (services) are intangible in nature and their production processes are based heavily on inputs such as skilled personnel and other intangible factors (Sillanpää et al., 2010).

The article adopts a reporting perspective (Mouritsen, Bukh, & Marr, 2005), focusing on the analysis of external IC reporting practices of a NPO operating within the Italian NP sector. The main research question is whether intellectual capital reports (ICRs) are used as an image-building or an accountability tool by NPOs.

To develop the research questions we refer to two main literature streams. The first theoretical stream considered collect all theoretical positions based on stakeholder/accountability theory, according to which NPOs have to be financially sustainable and social responsible to all of their multiple stakeholders, in order to create social value and achieve their organizational goals (Andreaus, 2007; Costa, Ramus, & Andreaus, 2011). The second stream collect all theories according to which at best NPOs voluntary self-report on their trustworthiness as part of a reputation-building process (Owen, Swift, & Hunt, 2001). In other words, we can say that the first is a form of "strong" accountability, whilst the second, coherently with Owen et al. (2001), can be considered a "soft" form of accountability.

To address the research questions we employ the qualitative methodology of the case study, appropriate when a researcher needs to conduct a holistic analysis of a complex phenomenon in its real-life context (Parker, 2012; Yin, 2003). As such, this method is particularly suitable for exploring IC, which is complex and context-dependent by nature (Mouritsen, 2006). In detail, the article analyzes the single longitudinal case study of ANPAS Piemonte, an NPO providing public interest services within the territory of Italy, considered an attractive NP sector as it has profoundly changed its role in recent years, moving from being a marginal to becoming a key player in supplying social services (Borzaga & Fazzi, 2011). From an IC perspective, the choice is interesting because of the organization's early adoption, since 2003, of an IC measurement, management, and reporting (ICMMR) system.

Through a document analysis applied to the ICRs disclosed on the organizational web site, we analyze whether ANPAS Piemonte's ICRs are used as an effective tool to account for organizational stakeholders or just as an image-building tool not able to highlight how the organization uses its IC. In order to answer to this research question, we build a theoretical framework against which we test our research hypothesis, under an interpretative approach (Demartini & Paoloni, 2013).

Several are the contribution of the research. Firstly, the research aims to fill a gap in IC theoretical and empirical literature. Theoretically speaking, there is a paucity of papers aimed to disclose a theoretical framework for voluntary IC disclosure; most studies on voluntary IC disclosure fail to provide theoretical basis for interpreting their findings, while other studies provide only a partial vision on a single theory (An, Davey, & Eggleton, 2011). Empirically speaking, to the best of our knowledge this is the first article that test two competing research hypotheses filtering information provided by ICRs, understood following an interpretative approach, against a theoretical framework implemented to answer to the research question. In addition, as very few papers examine IC reporting practices (Lonnqvist et al., 2009), and even less in the NP sector (Guthrie et al., 2009; Sillanpää et al., 2010), the research contributes to narrow the gap between theory and practice, enhancing the understanding of IC dynamics at organizational level (Chiucchi, 2013).

LITERATURES REVIEW AND HYPOTHESES DEVELOPMENT

Before to analyze the main studies belonging to different literature streams from which we drawn the two competing hypotheses at the basis of the article, we need to posit a relevant methodological note. The relevant studies quoted in this section mainly belong to the social and corporate social responsibility (CSR) area. This is because of two main reasons. The first reason is related to the circumstance that IC literature is a relatively young discipline, with a less pronounced doctrinal corpus. IC studies published in management, accounting or specialist IC journals rarely make any significant analysis of the theoretical literature which affects the choices to disclose IC information in ad hoc reports, except for the study of An et al. (2011). The second reason is that IC research can be legitimately included in the social research area (Gray, 2002). Of course, the reference to theories grounded in the CSR literature will be analyzed, if possible, through the IC lens.

Accountability Perspective

Within the accountability paradigm, in the same vein of ARs and financial statements, IC reports should be seen as essential to provide an account to stakeholder groups and for management to discharge its accountability (Palmer, 2011).

Numerous definition of accountability has been proposed by scholars and researchers (Costa et al., 2011). In the article we accept the Christensen and Ebrahims' (2006) conceptualization of accountability as "being answerable to stakeholders for the action of the organization" (p. 196), where stakeholders are identifiable "with any group of individual who can affect or is affected by the achievement of the organization's objectives" (Freeman, 1984, p. 46).

NPOs are mission-oriented and multi-stakeholders organizations (Christensen & Ebrahim, 2006; Costa et al., 2011), therefore the need to address different accountability expectations of multiple stakeholders without compromising the NPO mission make really complex and challenging the NP accountability (Balser & McClusky, 2005; LeRoux, 2009).

In conceptual papers (Freeman, 2010) a holistic view of the stakeholders' needs has been called for, and several models (Andreaus, 2007) show that NPOs should be accountable to their stakeholders contemporaneously under an economic, institutional, and social profile. Some of these models (Bagnoli & Megali, 2011) underline that the dimension of social accountability should be interpreted as being accountable not only for the impact on the collectivity of the services provided, but also for the effective use of their resources. This approach allows us to read IC concept under an accountability perspective. In fact IC can be defined as the system of knowledge-related intangibles resources and intangible resources are definitely strategic resources for NPOs (Kong, 2010). The rationale of this claim lies not only in the consideration that NPOs are organizations that, like all others, operate in a knowledge economy, in which competitive advantage relies in knowledge-related resources (Lev, 2001), but above all considering the relevance of intangible resources for NPOs. NPOs are value-driven instead of profit-driven organizations, their inputs and outputs are mainly intangibles, their production process is based on knowledge of their managers, employees, and volunteers (Sillanpää et al., 2010).

Moreover, the NP sector went through radical changes that made the management of NPOs much more complex than before (Helmig, Jegers, & Lapsley, 2004) The introduction of New Public Management (NPM), a reform agenda firstly aimed at restructuring the public sector according to private sector principles (Hood, 1995), dramatically altered the values, activities, and methods that traditionally characterized the NP sector (Alexander, 2000; Ramia & Carney, 2003). As consequence, NPOs ended up operating in a highly competitive environment, characterized by increasing demand of services from the community, growing competition for delivering services with the public and for-profit sectors, a decline in volunteer support and a decreasing amount of government funding (Kong, 2010). These changes are pushing towards the adoption of measurement, management and reporting systems able to allow NPOs to manage their strategic resources and to disclose to their stakeholders the efficient use of these resources. To gain strategic advantage in this competitive NP environment, NPOs have to demonstrate to their stakeholders not only their efficiency and effectiveness in using their existing resources (Moxham, 2009) but, above all, their capability to generate and manage effectively new resources which have knowledge as their basic constituent (Kong, 2010).

In the accountability perspective, therefore, NPOs are ethical organizations, meaning that they accept social responsibility as an ethical obligation (e.g., Donaldson & Preston, 1995), integrating in their social accountability a responsibility towards an efficient and effective use of their intangible resources (Surroca, Tribó, & Waddock, 2010). Ethical, political, and integrative theories of CSR suggest that firms/managers have an incentive to be honest, trustworthy, and ethical in their business processes, and thus tend to adhere to a high standard of behavior (Garriga & Melé, 2004).

On the basis of the above literature, we propose the following hypothesis:

H1. NPOs disclose IC in the ICRs to be accountable towards their stakeholders

Reputational Perspective

Another stream of literature, that we call reputational theory, can explain the willingness of a firm to disclose social and IC information to its stakeholder. Under a reputational perspective, communicating CSR an organization can provide a positive signal regarding the reputation of the firm (e.g., Simaens & Koster, 2013) and CSR activities can be seen as a form of reputation-building or maintenance (Linthicum, Reitenga, & Sanchez, 2010).[2]

Reputation can be defined as the public's perception regarding the NPO's consistency, trustworthiness and reliability (Bennett & Rentschler,

2003). Within the accounting literature, Goddard and Assad (2006) and Gray, Bebbington, and Collison (2006) contend that accountability systems and mechanisms are used by NPOs as part of the processes for establishing and maintaining trust, primarily in relation to their donors.

Also studies focused on legitimacy theory (which suggests that there is a "social contract" between the organization and the society in which it operates) support the view according to which it is necessary for organizations to disclose their CSR on a voluntary basis to indicate that they are complying with the expectations and norms of society, or to deflect the attention of the community (or media) from the prevailing negative influence of the organization's activities (Deegan, 2006). Prior empirical research, such as Abeysekera and Guthrie (2005), Guthrie, Petty, and Ricceri (2006), Petty and Cuganesan (2005) and Whiting and Miller (2008), has attempted to apply legitimacy theory to explain voluntary IC disclosure practices by firms.

We can comprehend in this approach as well studies suggesting that CSR can potentially be linked to the pursuit of managers' self-interest and/or that firms could adopt CSR to cover up the impact of some corporate misconduct (Brown & Fraser, 2006; Hemingway & Maclagan, 2004). Thus, firms may engage in CSR as a form of reputation insurance, which then gives them a "license to operate" committing irresponsible CSR activities. This motivation indicates that decisions to participate in CSR activities may be made to give stakeholders the impression that the firm is transparent, when, in fact, the firm "hides" behind the appearance of transparency while engaging in irresponsible CSR activities.

The reputational view, therefore, focuses on risk-management implications of CSR activities. According to the risk-management argument, a firm could serve the interests of its shareholders by managing its positive CSR reputation, which can potentially mitigate the risk associated with negative corporate events (Bebbington, Larrinaga, & Moneva, 2008). Godfrey, Merrill, and Hansen (2009) and Minor and Morgan (2011) find evidence in support of the risk-management argument. Their results suggest that (1) reducing irresponsible CSR activities and/or increasing responsible CSR activities can enhance a firm's positive CSR reputation, and (2) a positive CSR reputation provides some degree of insurance protection against the risk of market, political, regulatory, and social sanctions when negative corporate events occur.

On the basis of the above literature, we propose the following hypothesis:

H2. *NPOs disclose IC in the ICRs to build their reputation towards their stakeholders*

RESEARCH METHODOLOGY

The purpose of the study has been pursued using a case study approach, appropriate when a researcher conducts an analysis of one particular phenomenon or topic (Parker, 2012; Yin, 2003), especially if the phenomenon is under-researched (Birkinshaw, Brannen, & Tung, 2011). Yin (2003) postulates five rationales for single case design: (a) when it represents the critical case in testing a well-formulated theory; (b) when the case represents an extreme case or a unique case; (c) when it is the representative or typical case; (d) when it is a revelatory case; and (e) when it is a longitudinal case.

The article provides a critical analysis of the IC reports of an Italian NPO, namely ANPAS Piemonte, a branch of the biggest NP voluntary organization providing public interest services within the territory of Italy. The case selected represents a typical NPO case, as it refers to a voluntary organization. This case can represent a unique case as well, as it is, to the best of our knowledge, the only longstanding and certified experience of a NPO in reporting its IC in Italy. Moreover, this case is a longitudinal case, using data from 2003 to 2012. A long-lasting case of implementation of an IC measurement and reporting system is seldom used as an empirical starting point. As such, the company under consideration is an extremely interesting case under an IC reporting perspective. Using a longitudinal case study to address the aim of the article is considered appropriate since IC is a social object and, in order to be understood, it has to be "contextualized," that is, put into the specific time, space, and minds in which it develops (Jørgensen, 2006).

These rationales serve as the main reasons for conducting this single case study.

Moreover, the choice to focus on a single case enhances the in-depth nature of the analysis because it allows the researchers to get a richer understanding of the phenomenon and the context in which it takes place, in terms of quality and quantity of information on the phenomenon under analysis and therefore of opportunities to generate theoretical reflections on the phenomenon under investigation (Montemari & Chiucchi, 2013).

The study aims to address the strong call for critically investigating IC practices that has been raised by several leading authors in the area (Dumay & Garanina, 2013; Guthrie et al., 2012), and that has been gathered by several researchers, mainly in the profit sector (Chiucchi, 2013; Demartini & Paoloni, 2013). The article contributes to this research area by proposing the analysis of IC measuring, managing and reporting practices in an NPO, in order to shed light on how and why IC is measured and reported in a real organization, thus filling the gap between theory and practice.

The research has been carried out under a qualitative approach (Moll et al., 2006; Parker, 2012) and employed the qualitative tool of document analysis under the theoretical paradigm of the interpretivist model. In the light of interpretivism, sociological phenomena cannot simply be observed but must also be interpreted by the researcher. This means that there is not one absolute reality, but rather different possibilities are generated by the perspective adopted to interpret the facts (Demartini & Paoloni, 2013; Ryan, Scapens, & Theobald, 2002). Coherently with Mouritsen and Larsen (2005), we believe that ICRs can be read analytically to give information on a research question. The two authors, trying to make sense of the readership of ICRs' of Coloplast in relation to the management control of knowledge resources, build a template according to which they interpret the content of the ICR as follows along four dimensions: knowledge narrative, management challenges, initiatives, and indicators (DMSTI, 2003a).[3] In turn, the IC indicators investigate the knowledge *resources*, the *activities* carried out to improve them, the *effect* of the activities on the knowledge company resources (DMSTI, 2003b).

In a similar vein, we build a theoretical template able to help us to interpret the ANPAS Piemonte's ICRs in the light of research question of the article (*the ICR are used as an image building or an accountability tool?*).

RESEARCH TEMPLATE

The research question has been pursued through a thought analysis of ICRs of ANPAS Piemonte. In other words IC information provided by ICRs, following an interpretative approach, has been read and understood within a research template created *ad hoc* to address the research question. In detail the four dimensions that will be examined to answer the research question are: the IC measurement, management, and reporting (ICMMR) model followed by the selected NPO, the informative power of its IC indicators, the attitude of the organization towards its stakeholders, the main aim of assuring its ICRs.

The IC Measurement, Management, and Reporting Models

Methods for IC measurement and reporting, originally conceived for for-profit organizations, can be classified in four basic categories (Sveiby, 2010): market capitalization; return on asset; direct IC; and scorecard methods. The first three models focus on the financial side of measurement and the monetary value of intangible assets, whereas scorecard approaches look for indicators able to measure intangible resources and activities.

Scorecard methods, that do not measure intangible assets in financial terms are usefully applied with this aim by NPOs, government-sector agencies and organizations with environmental and social objectives. Historically speaking, scorecard methods conceptually evolved from a first to a second stage (Chiucchi, 2004) even if in the real world, early ICMMR models co-exist with the advanced ones (Veltri, 2011).

In the first stage, ICMMR models focused their attention on the definition of the IC subcategories content. The dominant vision is a typical accounting vision, according to which IC is an aggregate of intangible resources, conceptually similar to balance sheet assets. The mainstay of these models is IC value measurement and their main aim is to explain the causes of the differential between accounting and market value, mainly attributed to IC, a key resource that cannot be reported in the organization's annual account because of the construction rules of these documents. The Navigator proposed by Edvinsson and Malone (1997) and the Intangible Asset Monitor (IAM) proposed by Sveiby (1997) are typical examples of first stage models. The second stage ICMMR models adopt the evolved notion of IC as a dynamic system of intangible resources based on knowledge. In these kinds of models, attention is focused on the interactions between the IC items, at the basis of the organization's creation of value and on intangible activities essential for the production, maintenance and development of intangible resources. The assumption behind these models is knowledge management, and their main aim is to identify the paths of the organization's creation of value based on knowledge. The ICMMR models proposed by the Danish guidelines (DATI, 2000; DMSTI, 2003a) and by the EU-sponsored MERITUM project (Meritum Project, 2002) are typical examples of the second stage models (Veltri, 2007). The vision of IC behind the first stage models is a static vision, according to which IC is a set of intangible resources; conversely the vision of IC at the basis of second stage models is a dynamic vision, according to which IC is a dynamic system of intangible resources and activities (Veltri, 2011).

On the basis of the above analysis, we hypothesize that organizations that consider their IC report as an accountability tool are willing to disclose the efficient and effective use of their resources, therefore the second stage ICMMR models are the ideal candidates, as they are more likely able to highlight the contribution of intangibles to the process of organizational value creation, the synergies between IC subcategories and to disclose to the organizational stakeholders the efficient and effective use of knowledge resources.

The Informative Power of IC Indicators

If we refer to the first stage ICMMR models, we can say that the primary objective of these models is to analyze the causes of the differential between market and book value (Chiucchi, 2004). According to this vision, IC represents the sizeable part of the differential, its priority explicatory factor and can be abstractly expressed in three categories which essentially break down as human, organizational and relational capital (RC). Briefly, human capital (HC) is composed of tacit knowledge, capabilities, and competences possessed by the employees. Organizational capital (OC) is made up of structured knowledge in the form of patents, databases, procedures, etc. It also comprises "softer" elements such as organizational and managerial processes, the organizational structure, the company philosophy, etc. Lastly, RC encompasses the relations which a company develops with the stakeholders (customers, suppliers, institutions, etc.).

Regarding the measurement of IC, the categories become the preferential, object of analysis and measurement, and IC indicators are focused on IC subcategories even if, theoretically at least, the scholars of this first stage ICMMR models (i.e., Edvinsson & Malone, 1997; Sveiby, 1997) recognize that the value of IC is generated by interaction among the categories. In addition, particular stress is placed on the importance of utilizing not only monetary, but also nonmonetary indicators in that these express more efficiently the characteristics, the level, and the quality of intangible resources, even though the monetary ones conserve a relevant weight.

If we turn our attention to the IAM proposed by Sveiby (1997), we can say that IAM is a diagram model which illustrates how IC can be usefully broken down into three large typical categories: external structure, internal structure, and staff skills under three profiles: innovation and growth, efficiency, and stability, under which the tangible assets also are monitored. In detail, the growth/renewal indicators point out the meaningful increment of defined organizational phenomena; the efficiency indicators point out the achievement of a process by minimizing the cost, whereas the stability indicators allow the state of organization, or process or competences to be pointed out for a determined period (Sveiby, 1997). The method at its base is the same for all companies, but different indicators can be included from time to time according to the characteristics of a given company and the industry it operates in, its critical and competitive variables, the company history, and its organizational and managerial culture.

As regards the second stage ICMMR models, while there may be some differences in terminology, especially between the Danish model and the MERITUM project (i.e., while Meritum project validates the three-way division of IC into human, structural and RC, the Danish Guidelines do not give a classification of IC, instead they give a classification of knowledge resources: employees, customers, processes, and technologies), there is in fact a substantial similarity. First of all, the knowledge strategy must be defined, then it must be translated into objectives, which reflect critical success factors (management challenges or critical intangibles) followed by an outline of those actions which are necessary to implement it. The focus of the measurement consequently shifts from the categories to the actions which then become the main object of the monitoring process. The indicators are therefore centered on the intangible resources, on the actions and on their effects. Furthermore, the pinpointed systems are never of the input-output sort, but are manifested as networks of intangibles and, as such, the relationships which can develop among the indicators are never univocal but rather are of "concomitant cause and multiple effect." The measurement systems, then, evolve to facilitate the management of knowledge which is the key to creating value. Each model presents its own specific features of visualization, but the concepts of a network of intangibles, of connectivity, of managing knowledge are central.

If we turn our attention to the Danish Guidelines (DMSTI, 2003a), we can say that IC report is constituted of four elements: knowledge narrative, management challenges, actions, and indicators, following an iterative process: each phase influences and is influenced as well by the other phases.

The *knowledge narrative* expresses the company's ambition to increase the value a user receives from a company's goods or services (use value). It shows which types of knowledge resources are required to create the use value the company wants to supply and how company create use value. The second element is a set of (knowledge) *management challenges* which highlight the knowledge resources that need to be strengthened to reach knowledge aims. The third element is a set of *initiatives* that can be started to do something about the management challenges. The initiatives are concerned with how to compose, develop, and procure knowledge resources and how to monitor their extent and effects. The fourth element is a set of IC *indicators* which makes it possible to follow up whether the initiatives have been launched or whether the management challenges are being met. These four elements are interrelated and work together.

In 2003, the Danish Ministry of Technology and Innovation published a document, *Analysing intellectual capital statements*, in which it introduced a matrix analysis model with the aim to evaluate and compare the firm's IC reports (DMSTI, 2003b). The analysis model is not a narrow input-output one, but an accounting system; just as in an accounting system, the model only shows the effects and does not attempt to explain where they come from. In the analysis model IC statement indicators are positioned with respect to two dimensions: the four types of knowledge resources (employees, customers, processes, and technologies) and the three evaluation criteria (effects, activities, and resources).

On the basis of the above analysis, we believe that IC indicators of second stage ICMMR models have a greater informative power for organizational stakeholders, as they are included in a system that improve the readability of IC information provided by ICRs.

The Attitude of the Organization Towards its Stakeholders

Stakeholder theory, which expands the traditional shareholder theories (e.g., agency theory), is concerned with the relationships of an organization with a variety of stakeholders in society. Stakeholder theory naturally relates to the term accountability, and accounting information disclosure is considered to be an important means for organizations to discharge their accountability (An et al., 2011). In this context, IC information has being increasingly demanded by various stakeholders in recent years (Yi & Davey, 2010).

Nonetheless there exist two branch as for how to discharge accountability to various stakeholders: an ethical (moral) branch, and a positive (managerial) branch.

In accordance with Deegan and Samkin (2009), within the ethical branch of stakeholder theory, the organization should provide all stakeholders information regarding how its activities affect them, even though they may choose not to use the information or even though they may not be able to impact directly the organization. The positive branch of stakeholder theory, instead, requires the organization to identify and then manage those stakeholders considered significant for the long-term success of the organization (O'Dwyer, 2003).

These two different approach are indicative of two different concept of accountability: a "soft" accountability, typical of the reputational perspective, "whereby organisations engage in stakeholder dialogue for the purpose of voluntary self-reporting on their trustworthiness as part of a reputation building process" (Owen et al., 2001, p. 275) and a "strong" accountability, typical of the accountability perspective, whose proponents share the idea that organizations are accountable for the use of the vast financial, human, and community resources entrusted to them and that affected parties need safeguards against potential abuses of corporate power. In this process, IC information can be viewed as providing an important monitoring role. Translating these two kind of accountability into organizational attitude towards their stakeholders, we can identify two different attitude: stakeholder management, that is the management of stakeholders' expectations and stakeholders' engagement, meaning that organizations involve their stakeholders in decision-making processes and making them participants in the business management by sharing information, dialoguing and creating a model of mutual responsibility (Manetti, 2011).

On the basis of the above consideration, we believe that organizations following a stakeholder engagement approach achieve a strong accountability towards their stakeholders, while the propensity for stakeholder management matches an opportunistic and strategic approach to the stakeholder theory (Freeman, 1984). We evaluate the attitude of ANPAS Piemonte towards the organizational stakeholders by reading throughout its ICRs, analyzing a series of elements indicative of the quality of stakeholder engagement, that is if stakeholders are included in collaboratively designing IC performance metrics with organizations, and if they are regularly approached to receive or provide feedback on subsequent ICRs.

The Main Aim of Assuring IC Reports

There is much debate whether social, environmental, and ethical reports should be audited and on the quality and usefulness of audit or assurance statements (Mori, Best, & Cotter, 2014; Zorio, García-Benau, & Sierra, 2013), nonetheless there is relatively little research on the voluntary purchase of assurance for sustainability reports (Simnett, Vanstraelen, & Fong Chua, 2009) and even less for ICRs.

Briefly, we can say that modalities of auditing a social report are different under the two approaches. Under the reputational approach, the claim is that companies seeking to enhance the credibility of their reports and build their corporate reputation are more likely to have their sustainability reports assured, although it does not matter whether the assurance provider comes from the auditing profession (Simnett et al., 2009). Under the accountability approach, instead, the main aim of the social audit is to account for to stakeholders, and accountability to stakeholders, rather than stakeholder management, should be one of the core principle of the social audit (Adams & Evans, 2004; Owen et al., 2001).

On the basis of the above consideration, we believe that exists a relationship between the organizational attitude towards its stakeholders and the aim for which an organization assure its ICRs: "accountable" organizations will have as main aim of the social audit to account for to stakeholders, whilst "reputational" organizations will consider the external audit as an additional tool to build/maintain their image.

DESCRIPTION OF THE CASE STUDY AND OF ITS NONPROFIT SETTING

ANPAS Piemonte is a regional division (*comitato regionale*) of ANPAS (*Associazione Nazionale Pubbliche Assistenze*), the largest Italian volunteer federation of public assistance groups, comprehending more than 860 "Pubbliche Assistenze" (free, secular, and democratic associations of volunteers providing public services) deployed across 19 Italian Regions.[4]

ANPAS Piemonte has the aim to coordinate all the 81 public assistance groups in the Piemonte Region, acting as trait de union between these associations and the regional health system (ANPAS Piemonte Intellectual Capital reports, 2004–2012).

ANPAS Piemonte started to communicate to its stakeholders its intangible resources in 2003, in a changed NP scenario, characterized by the shortage of financial resources, the subsequent increased demand for the control and rationalization of the services supplied or financed by the public authorities, the growing competition with the public and for-profit sectors (Kong, 2010; Salamon, 2010).

Due to the relevant weigh of public funding on the NPOs, in Italy financial public management reforms have had a dramatic effect on these organizations (Borzaga & Fazzi, 2011). This effect has been even greater for NPOs, such as ANPAS Piemonte, which provide essential public health services (more than 40% of the annual budget comes from running public health services) and which are largely funded from the public purse.

Italy represents an interesting NP context in which to investigate IC management and reporting practices. Over the past 20 years, the third sector has substantially grown in all the Western countries, and in Italy the role of the third sector has profoundly changed from a marginal one to that of a key factor in the supply of social services (Borzaga & Fazzi, 2011). The recent national census (ISTAT, 2013) shows an ever-growing sector, both in terms of number of NPOs (+28% respect to the 2001 datum) and in terms of volunteers (+43.5%) and employees (+39.5%). Currently, more than three hundred thousand NPOs employ almost 1 million people and involve almost five million volunteers (ISTAT, 2013). The sector is characterized by the presence of many small-sized NPOs, struggling to survive because of limited human and financial resources: the average NPO has 16 volunteers, 2 employees and 1 external worker and 54.9% of Italian NPOs have a budget that does not exceed 15,000 euros per year (CNEL-ISTAT, 2008).

As regards the positioning of ANPAS Piemonte within the Italian NP context, we can say that the organization show features different from those of the average Italian NPO. ANPAS Piemonte is a legally recognized association located in northern Italy, operating in multiple areas of social services, mainly in health services, while the majority of Italian NPOs assume the form of nonlegally recognized association (63.3%) and focuses on a single social service, mainly in the area of culture and sport (63.4%) (CNEL-ISTAT, 2008). Moreover, ANPAS Piemonte is one of the oldest Italian NPOs, having been founded in 1974 and characterizes itself as a big, strong and wealthy NPO: it has 350 employees and 9,150 volunteers and its budget exceeds 1400.00 Euros (ANPAS Piemonte Intellectual Capital reports (2004–2012)).

As regards IC measurement, management, and reporting, this aspect is almost unknown among Italian NPOs. A recent research study provides evidence that the Italian NP sector organizational culture is not knowledge oriented. This context does not favor the development of HC, as the sampled NPOS neither use structured procedures to select the best candidates, nor consider training as a tool for strategic management of human resources (Benevene & Cortini, 2010).

In this context ANPAS Piemonte is different in its (communication) attitude towards IC, having issued 10 audited IC reports, but it remains to investigate whether IC reports are seen as accountability or as image-building tools.

ANALYZING THE IC REPORTING PRACTICES OF ANPAS PIEMONTE

The information on IC of ANPAS Piemonte is not incorporated in the AR, but in an autonomous document that can be read independently, although the aim of the ICR is to integrate the economic and financial information provided by the AR (ANPAS Piemonte Intellectual Capital reports, 2004–2012). ICR is not aimed to a more specific audience than AR: both documents are addressed to account for the regional public assistance groups, public (mainly Piemonte region) and private institutions and citizens, as results from the organizational web site. It operates essentially as an externally focused "brochure" that summarizes the year's IC objectives and indicators to its stakeholders.

The IC Measurement, Management, and Reporting Model

In its ICR, ANPAS Piemonte declares to follow both IAM and Danish Guidelines to report its intangible resources. Nonetheless, after having analyzed its ICRs, we can conclude that ANPAS Piemonte is not following Danish guidelines: its IC indicators are not systematized in a logic path which has its starting point in the organization's (knowledge) strategy and the actions to carry out to reach strategic aims are not made explicit in the ICRs (DMSTI, 2003a). Instead, ANPAS Piemonte properly follows the Sveiby's IAM's model (Sveiby, 1997). The vision of IC of ANPAS Piemonte is typical of the first stage ICMMR model, as in its ICR, it explicitly defines IC as "a set of intangible resources" (ANPAS Piemonte Intellectual Capital reports, 2004–2012). ANPAS Piemonte's ICRs concentrate on classifying the different categories of IC, validating the robust heuristics of IC as tripartite in human, organizational and RC, and the focus is definitely on measuring IC categories.

The Informative Power of IC Indicators

The section aims to answer key questions: Are the readers of the ICRs able to systemically interpret the organizational IC indicators? In other words, the IC indicators tell them the story of the firm under an IC perspective?

To make readable IC reports, IC indicators should answer to questions related to the firm's *portfolio* of resources, to the *activities* carried out to improve them and to the *effects* of the activities. DMSTI prepared a framework to make readable IC statements (DMSTI, 2003b; Mouritsen & Larsen, 2005), and ANPAS Piemonte says to follow Danish guidelines, so it is supposed also to follow the framework implemented by DMSTI to interpret the IC indicators (DMSTI, 2003b), but it does not. Instead, ANPAS Piemonte appears to follow IAM model (Sveiby, 1997), as the IC indicators are calculated for each IC subcategory on the basis of the IAM model classification (innovation and growth, efficiency, and stability indicators), applied to the tripartition of IC into human, organizational and RC and are mainly indicators focused on intangible resources (Table 1).

If we turn our attention to the HC indicators, we can say that they express HC in terms of number of employees and volunteers (certified and not certified), number of training hours, ages and working climate. It should be underlined that, in the ANPAS Piemonte's ICR the benefits of the training hours are not revealed, the correlation among the training hours and greater numbers of certified personnel and volunteers in subsequent years are not provided, neither are other eventual benefits gained from the higher training hours. Moreover, the HC indicators do not include a measure for either employee (or volunteer) turnover, measure that would be helpful to managers, funders and other stakeholders. The satisfaction percentages for directors, workers, and trainers are all very high, but the data do not provide any useful guidance for making improvements, as it do not report why they are satisfied/unsatisfied.

If we turn our attention to the OC indicators, we can say that they focus on the structure of ANPAS Piemonte (in terms of number of manuals distributed and projects managed) and its associates (in terms of number of volunteers, number of training course attended and of their satisfaction). As we can notice, the section of growth/renewal indicators focuses on ANPAS Piemonte, the efficiency section on its associates. If we focus on the efficiency section, which comprehends the most of OC indicators, we can say that many of these are not truly efficiency indicators, they are simply raw numbers. The indicators could be far more revealing and useful if they were expressed in terms such as number of services per employee, or number of kilometers per vehicle. Moreover, in the organizational section it is difficult to discern what are the most important outcomes for ANPAS Piemonte. If, as we believe, the number of services offered by associations is one of the most important outcomes, then the types of services should be broken down further, so that trends for each service type can be tracked.

If we turn our attention to the RC indicators, we can say that the RC indicators identify the relationships that ANPAS Piemonte entertain with its associates and the other organizations and the investments made to improve its image. In this section it is particularly difficult to determine what are the key indicators for measuring success. If, as we believe, it is the number of first aid courses offered to firms, then ICR should provide data to understand why that indicator declined 2010 and which activities allow

Table 1. The ANPAS Piemonte IC Framework.

Indicators	Human Capital	Organizational Capital	Relational Capital
Growth/renewal	Certified and not certified volunteers (S.A.R.A.)	No. of "aid scenarios" manuals distributed	Degree of satisfaction of associates (from 1 to 10)
	No. of training hours for employees	No. of units of ANPAS Piemonte employees	Associative quotes cashed
	Average years of the members of the board of directors and employees	No. of hours of external consultancy to associations	First aid courses in firms
		No. web site contacts	Trained students in first aid courses
		No. telephone contacts	Number of associations
		No. email contacts	Investments in communication
		Documental project published	
		International project managed	
		Internal coordination meetings	
		External coordination meetings	
Efficiency	Certified and not certified volunteers (118)	No. of associations' employees	Degree of satisfaction of public and private organizations dealing with ANPAS (1–10)
	Certified and not certified volunteers (118; years 1997–2002)	No. of associations' ambulances	No. of articles/advertisements on media
		No. associations' other vehicles	No. of families participating in meetings on international adoptions
		No. of services offered by associations	No. of associates' volunteers

Table 1. *(Continued)*

Indicators	Human Capital	Organizational Capital	Relational Capital
		No. of km covered by associations	No. of external associates' members
		No. of canine-unit associations	No. of volunteers in civil service
		% of associations with audited report	
		No. of associations certified on administrative and fiscal transparency	
		No. of 118 positions managed by certified associates	
		Refund conventions for health emergency 118 to associates	
		% of increment of 118 annual costs	
		Medium refund for 118 position	
		Social value of 118 voluntary work	
Stability	Internal customer satisfaction	Turnover of service suppliers	Customer satisfaction on courses offered
		% of associates on the total number of institutions authorized to transport disabled peoples	

Source: ANPAS Piemonte Intellectual Capital Reports 2003–2012.
S.A.R.A. = nonemergency transportation with ambulances; 118 = emergency transportation with ambulances.

the indicator to go back to grow in 2012. Again, the efficiency indicators do not truly measure efficiency; they should attempt to capture outcomes (or output) per unit of input, for instance how is ANPAS Piemonte capturing the value of its increased investments in communication and advertising. A further breakdown of the satisfaction indicators would also be helpful, together with the explanation of why the satisfaction ratings are missing for certain groups in some years and what this indicate to stakeholders.

Summarizing, the ANPAS Piemonte's IC indicators does not appear to be organized systematically to improve the readability of IC report; they are not articulated into resources, activities, and effect indicators, and even the articulation into growth/renewal, efficiency, and stability indicators does not appear to reflect the original meaning of IAM classification.

The relationships of indicators with the narrative is lacking. Nonetheless the two reading should be related, in ANPAS' Piemonte ICRs the problem does not arise, and this open gaps for interpretation, making difficult an analytical reading of IC statements.

The Attitude of the Organization Towards its Stakeholders

The ANPAS Piemonte ICRs lack almost completely to refer to its organizational stakeholders. There is just a general reference in the mission (included in ICRs) to the expectations and needs of associates, public institutions, and citizens, but the ICR does not either explains the impact of stakeholders' needs on IC indicators, or the role played by stakeholders in participating to the choice of the IC indicators to include in IC report or if.

Probably a prioritization exist or stakeholders could have impacted on the first choice of IC indicators, but it is not possible derive it reading IC reports.

Primary and secondary stakeholders are not identified (at least, not in the IC report) and the IC report appears to be oriented towards a stakeholder management instead of stakeholders engagement: the involvement of stakeholders in defining contents of IC reports appear low; there are no reference to dialogues with the organizational stakeholders or interviews with them to understand their perception of IC report, and the IC report does not appears to effectively follow in preparing IC reports guidelines able to facilitate the readability of ANPAS Piemonte from an IC perspective.

The Main Aim of the Assurance of IC Reports

The ANPAS Piemonte audited its IC reports since 2004, and it is, at the best of our knowledge, the only NPO assuring its IC statement. Assurance is needed to ensure credibility to external reports (Adams & Evans, 2004), even if assurance in itself is not enough to avoid criticism regarding the credibility of ICRs. It is true that auditors of social/IC reports have not guidelines specifying what type of audit opinion should be issued, but it also true that social/IC reports are prepared for a broad range of stakeholders, whose different and competing interests should make determination of the audit scope and decisions as what constitutes appropriate audit methods. As regards the auditor provider, he must act on the behalf of current stakeholders to ensure that they receive all the information they are entitled, and his primary concern should be the interests of stakeholders and not those of organization's managers. An obvious difficulty is that assurance provider is appointed by manager. In ANPAS Piemonte it is the case and it is also to be pointed out that the auditor provider is the same that helped ANPAS Piemonte to develop internally the framework used to report its IC, with obvious reflections on the independence of the audit provider. As regards the content of IC report, the IC audit should not be reduced to a review of company's systems of performance measurement, it should focus on the way in which an organization's performance is reported; it should report all outcomes that may affect stakeholders and stakeholders should rely on information in audited reports in making their decision. The ANPAS Piemonte IC report's audit be certification, available on the organization web site, analyses each indicator in relation to eight survey factors (relevance, verifiability, clarity, completeness, substance, evidence, neutrality, comparability), indicating a judgment which ranges from insufficient to good.

CONCLUSIONS

IC became the key driver of value creation for all kind of organizations, and IC measurement, management, and reporting systems, originally conceived for for-profit organizations are increasingly employed in public and NPOs (Kong, 2010). Under a reporting perspective, the main research question was if IC reports are used as accountability or image-building tools. In the first meaning, organizations could use IC reports as accountability tools, that is, account to their stakeholders for the effective use of its key, tangible and intangible, resources (Bagnoli & Megali, 2011); in the second meaning organizations adopt instead a managerial perspective (O'Dwyer, 2003), trying to handle stakeholders' expectations for their managerial purposes, instead of involving their stakeholders in decision-making process.

To address this research issue we investigated an Italian NPO with an outstanding experience in reporting its IC, from 2003 until now. To answer the research question, starting from the CSR and IC literature, we build a theoretical framework; thus, we read the IC reports of the investigated NPO through these theoretical lens. Briefly, we highlighted four different dimensions to investigate to address the research question, namely the ICMMR model used, the informative power of IC indicators for the stakeholders, the attitude of the organization towards its stakeholders, and the aim of the assurance of IC reports.

From the analysis of the ICRs, it emerges that ANPAS Piemonte seems to have a managerial rather than accountability aim. In fact, neither ANPAS Piemonte IC report seems to provide stakeholders with information useful to highlight the organization's value creation, nor its IC indicators help stakeholders to read the organization under an IC perspective. As regards ANPAS Piemonte's attitude towards stakeholders, its ICRs show that it is likely to have a stakeholder management instead of a stakeholder engagement attitude, and the IC report's audit does not meet the requirement of a stakeholders'-oriented report, instead it is likely used by managers to enhance the credibility of IC reports and build the corporate reputation.

Coherently with O'Dwyer (2003), we believe that managers, left free to determine their own conception of IC, perpetrated a form of managerial capture of its meaning. Nonetheless, a more thorough understanding could perhaps be achieved conducting interviews to ANPAS Piemonte managers to identify why and how they report IC. Further research could therefore investigate how IC measurement, management, and reporting are actually embedded in the organization using an "inside-out" perspective to effectively capture the role played by IC in the process value creation (Guthrie et al., 2009). Future research should also focus a broader exploration of the value IC brings to the organization, investigating how ANPAS Piemonte IC indicators relate with organizational performance, how the reporting on certain IC resources could be facilitated (e.g., employee competence), how knowledge activities impact on IC indicators, and if exists a process of negotiation and sharing on IC indicators among internal and external stakeholders (Ospina, Diaz, & O'Sullivan, 2002).

The use of an *ad hoc* research template constitutes both the main strength of the article, as it gives an original contribution to the IC literature, and also its main limit, as the observations and conclusions reached in the article are based on the authors' analysis of what the ICRs says as regards the role that the investigated NPO appoint to its ICRs.

Summarizing, we believe that this is a valuable research issue to investigate, as how organizations use IC tools in NP setting remains a scarcely investigated question, moreover in NPOs (Guthrie et al., 2009; Lönnqvist, Sillanpää, & Carlucci, 2009) and the model used in this research, opportunely improved, could be used for analyze organizations operating in other national and international context and sectors.

NOTES

1. In the article we use the term IC as a synonym for intangible or knowledge resources (Lev, 2001).
2. Signaling theory suggests that companies with a high quality should signal their advantages to the market. There are a number of means for companies to signal information about themselves. Among those, voluntary disclosure of positive accounting information (e.g., CSR and IC) is considered to be one of the most effective (An et al., 2011).
3. Coloplast is a Danish company, worldwide provider of healthcare products and services. Coloplast took part to the second stage of the project on IC reporting launched between 1997 and 2000 by the Danish Agency for Trade and Industry (DATI). The first stage of the project ended with the publication of guidelines for IC statements (DATI, 2000). Following implementation by around a hundred of companies and public organizations, in 2003 the Danish Ministry of Science, Technology and Innovation (DMSTI) produced a revised document entitled Intellectual Capital Statements – The New Guideline (DMSTI, 2003a).
4. The services provided by the 90,000 volunteers and 400,000 members of ANPAS ranging from emergency medical care and transportation (which are its prevailing activities), to blood donations, fire prevention, international adoptions, training, civil service, civil defense, solidarity's promotion, and animal rights defense.

REFERENCES

Abeysekera, I., & Guthrie, J. (2005). An empirical investigation of annual reporting trends of intellectual capital in Sri Lanka. *Critical Perspectives on Accounting*, *16*(3), 151–163.

Adams, C. A., & Evans, R. (2004). Accountability, completeness, credibility and the audit expectations gap. *Journal of Corporate Citizenship*, *14*, 97–115.

Alexander, J. (2000). Adaptive strategies of nonprofit human service organizations in an era of devolution and new public management. *Nonprofit Management and Leadership*, *10*(3), 287–303.

An, Y., Davey, H., & Eggleton, I. R. C. (2011). Towards a comprehensive theoretical framework for voluntary IC disclosure. *Journal of Intellectual Capital*, *14*(3), 395–413.

Andreaus, M. (2007). Quale modello di rendicontazione per l'impresa sociale? *Impresa Sociale*, *76*, 59–68.

ANPAS Piemonte Intellectual Capital reports. (2004–2012). Retrieved from http://www.anpas.piemonte.it/bilanci/bilanci.htm. Accessed on August, 2013.

Bagnoli, L., & Megali, C. (2011). Measuring performance in social enterprises. *Nonprofit and Voluntary Sector Quarterly*, *40*(1), 149–165.

Balser, D., & McClusky, J. (2005). Managing stakeholder relationships and non-profit organisation effectiveness. *Non-Profit Management and Leadership*, *15*, 295–315.

Bebbington, J., Larrinaga, C., & Moneva, J. N. (2008). Corporate social reporting and reputation risk management. *Accounting, Auditing & Accountability Journal*, *21*(3), 337–361.

Benevene, P., & Cortini, M. (2010). Interaction between structural capital and human capital in Italian NPOs. *Journal of Intellectual Capital*, *11*(2), 123–139.

Bennett, R., & Rentschler, R. (2003). Foreword. *Corporate Reputation Review*, *6*(3), 207–210.

Birkinshaw, J., Brannen, M. Y., & Tung, R. L. (2011). From a distance and generalizable to up close and grounded: Reclaiming a place for qualitative methods in international business research. *Journal of International Business Studies*, *42*, 573–581.

Borzaga, C., & Fazzi, L. (2011). Process of institutionalization and differentiation in the Italian third sector. *Voluntas*, *22*, 409–427.

Brown, J., & Fraser, M. (2006). Approaches and perspectives in social and environmental accounting: An overview of the conceptual landscape. *Business Strategy and the Environment*, *15*, 103–117.

Chiucchi, M. S. (2004). *Sistemi di misurazione e reporting del capital intellettuale: Criticità e prospettive*. Turin: Giappichelli.

Chiucchi, M. S. (2013). Measuring and reporting intellectual capital: Lessons learnt from some interventionist research projects. *Journal of Intellectual Capital*, *14*(3), 395–413.

Christensen, R. A., & Ebrahim, A. (2006). How does accountability affect mission? The case of a nonprofit serving immigrants and refugees. *Nonprofit Management & Leadership*, *17*(2), 195–209.

Consiglio Nazionale Economia Lavoro (CNEL)-Istituto Nazionale di Statistica (ISTAT). (2008). Primo Rapporto CNEL/ISTAT sull'economia sociale. Dimensioni e caratteristiche strutturali delle istituzioni non-profit in Italia. Consiglio Nazionale Economia Lavoro, Roma.

Costa, E., Ramus, T., & Andreaus, M. (2011). Accountability as managerial tool in non-profit organizations: Evidence from Italian CSVs. *Voluntas*, *22*, 470–492.

DATI – Danish Agency For Trade And Industry. (2000). *A guideline for intellectual capital statements*. Retrieved from http://www.vtu.dk. Accessed on January 3, 2010.

Deegan, C. (2006). Legitimacy theory. In Z. Hoque (Ed.), *Methodological issues in accounting research: Theories, methods and issues* (pp. 161–181). London: Spiramus Press.

Deegan, C., & Samkin, G. (2009). *New Zealand financial accounting*. Sydney: McGraw-Hill.

Demartini, P., & Paoloni, P. (2013). Implementing an intellectual capital framework in practice. *Journal of Intellectual Capital*, *14*(1), 69–83.

DMSTI – Danish Ministry of Technology And Innovation. (2003a). *Intellectual capital statements. The new guidelines*. Retrieved from http://www.vtu.dk. Accessed on January 3, 2010.

DMSTI – Danish Ministry of Technology And Innovation. (2003b). *Analyzing intellectual capital statements*. Retrieved from http://www.vtu.dk. Accessed on January 3, 2010.

Donaldson, T., & Preston, L. (1995). The stakeholder theory of the corporation: Concepts, evidence, and implications. *The Academy of Management Review*, *20*(1), 65–91.

Dumay, J., & Garanina, T. (2013). Intellectual capital research: A critical examination of the third stage. *Journal of Intellectual Capital*, *14*(1), 10–25.

Edvinsson, L., & Malone, M. S. (1997). *Intellectual capital – Realizing your company's true value by finding its hidden brainpower*. New York, NY: Harper Business Publisher.

Freeman, R. E. (1984). *Strategic management: A stakeholder approach*. Boston, MA: Pitman.

Freeman, R. E. (2010). Managing for stakeholders: Trade-offs or value creation. *Journal of Business Ethics*, *96*, 7–9.

Garriga, E., & Melé, D. (2004). Corporate social responsibility theories: Mapping the territory. *Journal of Business Ethics*, *53*(1–2), 51–71.

Goddard, A., & Assad, M. J. (2006). Accounting and navigating legitimacy in Tanzanian NGOs. *Accounting, Auditing & Accountability Journal*, *19*(3), 377–404.

Godfrey, P. C., Merrill, C. B., & Hansen, J. M. (2009). The relationship between corporate social responsibility and shareholder value: An empirical test of the risk management hypothesis. *Strategic Management Journal*, *30*(4), 425–445.

Gray, R. (2002). The social accounting project and accounting organizations and society privileging engagement, imaginings, new accountings and pragmatism over critique? *Accounting, Organizations and Society*, *27*(7), 687–708.

Gray, R., Bebbington, J., & Collison, D. (2006). NGOs civil society & accountability: Making the people accountable to capital. *Accounting, Auditing & Accountability Journal*, *19*(3), 319–348.

Guthrie, J., Petty, R., & Ricceri, F. (2006). The voluntary reporting of intellectual capital: Comparing evidence from Hong Kong and Australia. *Journal of Intellectual Capital*, *7*(2), 254–271.

Guthrie, J., Ricceri, F., & Dumay, J. (2012). Reflections and projections: A decade of intellectual capital accounting research. *The British Accounting Review*, *44*(2), 68–82.

Guthrie, J., Steane, P., & Farneti, F. (2009). IC Reporting in the Australian red cross blood service. *Journal of Intellectual Capital*, *10*(4), 504–519.

Helmig, B., Jegers, M., & Lapsley, I. (2004). Challenges in managing nonprofit organizations: A research overview. *Voluntas*, *15*(2), 101–116.

Hemingway, C., & Maclagan, P. (2004). Managers' personal values as drivers of corporate social responsibility. *Journal of Business Ethics*, *50*(1), 33–44.

Hood, C. (1995). New public management in the 1980s: Variations on a theme. *Accounting, Organizations and Society*, *20*(2–3), 93–109.

ISTAT. (2013). 9 censimento generale dell'industria, dei servizi e del non profit. Retrieved from http://www.istat.it/it/files/2013/07/Fascicolo_CIS_PrimiRisultati_completo.pdf

Jørgensen, K. M. (2006). Conceptualising intellectual capital as language game and power. *Journal of Intellectual Capital*, *7*(1), 78–92.

Kong, E. (2007). The strategic importance of intellectual capital in the nonprofit sector. *Journal of Intellectual Capital*, *8*(4), 721–731.

Kong, E. (2010). Intellectual capital and non-profit organizations in the knowledge economy: Editorial and introduction to special issue. *Journal of Intellectual Capital*, *11*(2), 97–106.

LeRoux, K. (2009). Managing stakeholder demands: Balancing responsiveness to clients and funding agents in nonprofit social service organizations. *Administration & Society*, *41*(2), 158–184.

Lev, B. (2001). *Intangibles: Management, measurement, and reporting*. Washington, DC: Brookings.

Linthicum, C., Reitenga, A., & Sanchez, J. (2010). Social responsibility and corporate reputation: The case of the Arthur Andersen Enron audit failure. *Journal of Accounting and Public Policy*, *29*(2), 160–176.

Lönnqvist, A., Sillanpää, V., & Carlucci, D. (2009). Intellectual capital management in practice: Assessment of implementation and outcome. *Knowledge Management Research and Practice*, *7*, 308–316.

Manetti, G. (2011). The quality of stakeholder engagement in sustainability reporting: Empirical evidence and critical points. *Corporate Social Responsibility and Environmental Management*, *18*, 110–122.

Marr, B. (2005). Introduction. In B. Marr (Ed.), *Perspectives on intellectual capital* (pp. 13–18). Amsterdam: Elsevier.

Meritum Project. (2002). *Guidelines for managing and reporting on intangibles*. Fundaciòn Aritel Mòvil.

Minor, D., & Morgan, J. (2011). CSR as reputation insurance: Primum non nocere. *California Management Review*, *53*(3), 40–59.

Moll, J., Major, M., & Hoque, Z. (2006). The qualitative research tradition. In Z. Hoque (Ed.), *Methodological Issues in accounting research: Theories and methods* (pp. 375–398). London: Spiramus.

Montemari, M., & Chiucchi, M. S. (2013). The problematization of IC indicators in action. Paper presented at the 9th EIASM Interdisciplinary Workshop on "Intangibles, Intellectual Capital and Extra-Financial Information", Copenhagen, 26–27 September 2013.

Mori, R., Best, P. J., & Cotter, J. (2014). Sustainability reporting and assurance: A historical analysis of a world-wide phenomenon. *Journal of Business Ethics*, *120*, 1–11.

Mouritsen, J. (2006). Problematising intellectual capital research: Ostensive versus performative IC. *Journal of Intellectual Capital*, *19*(6), 820–841.

Mouritsen, J., Bukh, P. N., & Marr, B. (2005). A reporting perspective on intellectual capital. In B. Marr (Ed.), *Perspectives on intellectual capital* (pp. 69–81). Amsterdam: Elsevier.

Mouritsen, J., & Larsen, H. T. (2005). The 2nd wave of knowledge management: The management control of knowledge resources intellectual capital information. *Management Accounting Research*, *16*, 371–394.

Moxham, C. (2009). Performance measurement: Examining the applicability of the existing body of knowledge to non-profit organisations. *International Journal of Operations & Production Management*, *29*(7), 740–763.

O'Dwyer, B. (2003). Conceptions of corporate social responsibility: The nature of managerial capture. *Accounting, Auditing and Accountability Journal*, *16*(4), 523–557.

Ospina, S., Diaz, W., & O'Sullivan, J. F. (2002). Negotiating accountability: Managerial lessons from identity-based non-profit organizations. *Non-profit and Voluntary Sector Quarterly*, *31*(1), 5–31.

Owen, D., Swift, T., & Hunt, K. (2001). Questioning the role of stakeholder engagement in social and ethical accounting, auditing and reporting. *Accounting Forum*, *25*, 264–282.

Palmer, P. D. (2011). Exploring attitudes to financial reporting in the Australian not-for-profit sector. *Accounting & Finance*, *53*(1), 217–241.

Parker, L. D. (2012). Qualitative management accounting research: Assessing deliverables and relevance. *Critical Perspectives on Accounting*, *23*, 54–70.

Petty, R., & Cuganesan, S. (2005). Voluntary disclosure of intellectual capital by Hong Kong companies: Examining size, industry and growth effects over time. *Australian Accounting Review*, *15*(2), 40–50.

Ramia, G., & Carney, T. (2003). New public management, the job network and non-profit strategy. *Australian Journal of Labour Economics*, *6*, 249–271.

Ryan, B., Scapens, R., & Theobald, M. (2002). *Research method and methodology in finance and accounting*. London: Thomson.

Salamon, L. M. (2010). Putting the civil society sector on the economic map of the world. *Annals of Public and Cooperative Economics*, *81*(2), 167–210.

Sillanpää, V., Lönnqvist, A., Koskela, N., Koivula, U., Koivuaho, M., & Laihonen, H. (2010). The role of intellectual capital in non-profit elderly care organizations. *Journal of Intellectual Capital*, *11*(2), 107–122.

Simaens, A., & Koster, M. (2013). Reporting on sustainable operations by third sector organizations. *Public Management Review*, *15*(7), 1040–1062.

Simnett, R., Vanstraelen, A., & Fong Chua, W. (2009). Assurance on sustainability reports: An international comparison. *The Accounting Review*, *84*, 937–967.

Surroca, J., Tribó, J. A., & Waddock, S. (2010). Corporate responsibility and financial performance: The role of intangible resources. *Strategic Management Journal*, *31*, 463–490.

Sveiby, K. E. (1997). *The new organizational wealth: Managing and measuring knowledge-based assets*. San Francisco, CA: Berrett-Koehler Publishers.

Sveiby, K. E. (2010). *Methods for measuring intangible assets*. Retrieved from http//www.sveiby.com/articles/IntangibleMethods.htm. Accessed on February 20, 2012.

Veltri, S. (2007). *Sistemi di misurazione del capitale intellettuale d'azien*. Milan: Franco Angeli.

Veltri, S. (2011). Main features of intellectual capital reporting models in the non-profit sector. In G. Bronzetti, R. Mazzotta, P. Puntillo, A. Silvestri, & S. Veltri (Eds.), *Intellectual capital reporting practices in the non-profit sector* (pp. 23–42). Sumy, Ukraine: Virtus Interpress.

Whiting, R. H., & Miller, J. C. (2008). Voluntary disclosure of intellectual capital in New Zealand annual reports and the 'hidden value'. *Journal of Human Resource Costing & Accounting*, *12*(1), 26–50.

Yi, A., & Davey, H. (2010). Intellectual capital disclosure in Chinese (mainland) companies. *Journal of Intellectual Capital*, *11*(3), 326–347.

Yin, R. K. (2003). *Case study research: Design and methods* (3rd ed.). Thousand Oaks, CA: Sage.

Zorio, A., García-Benau, M. A., & Sierra, L. (2013). Sustainability development and the quality of assurance reports: Empirical evidence. *Business Strategy and the Environment*, *22*, 484–500.

ABOUT THE AUTHORS

Louis Beaubien, PhD, CMA, CGA, is an Associate Professor of Accounting at the Rowe School of Business, Dalhousie University. His primary research areas are governance and reporting and he focuses much of his work on health systems research and research in the co-operative sector.

Carlo Borzaga is Professor of Economic Policy at the Department of Economics of the University of Trento (Italy) and President of the European Research Institute on Co-operative and Social Enterprises (Euricse). Trained in both Sociology and Economics, his research interests include cooperatives, social enterprise, the economic role of non-profit organizations and their interactions with the welfare policies. From 1997 to 2008 he was chairman of the Institute for the Development of Nonprofit Organizations (ISSAN), based at Trento University. Currently he is President of the European Research Institute on Cooperative and Social Enterprises (EURICSE). He is also member of the EMES European Research Network and chairman of the IRIS network, an Italian network of over 25 research centres on social enterprises. He sits on the editorial board of several Italian and European journals and is co-editor of the newly launched international Journal of Entrepreneurial and Organizational Diversity. He has written and co-edited numerous books and papers on labour economics, labour and welfare policies, social and co-operative enterprises. He has participated and coordinated numerous research projects funded by the EU, the Italian government and local authorities. He has also consulted widely for international organizations, including the OECD, ILO and European Commission.

Giovanni Bronzetti is associate professor of Business Economics within the Faculty of Political Sciences of the University of Calabria. His main research interests are management control and the third sector. On these research themes he has published books, book chapters, journal articles and presented papers to national and international congresses.

Massimo Contrafatto is a lecturer and Assistant Professor in the Department of Management, Economics and Quantitative Methods at the University of Bergamo, where he teaches social accounting and management accounting. His research interests are primarily in: (i) social and environmental accounting and reporting; (ii) accountability and stewardship; (iii) institutional theory; and (iv) organizational change. Massimo has conducted several pieces of research on these topics, including fieldwork with several organizations (e.g. multinationals, social economy, co-operative, foundations). Massimo is also a member of the Executive Council of CSEAR (Centre for Social and Environmental Accounting Research) based at St Andrews University.

Jacques Defourny is full professor of economics at HEC Management School, University of Liege (Belgium), where he also acts as a director of the Centre for Social Economy. He was a founding coordinator (1996–2001) and then the first president (2002–2010) of the 'EMES European Research Network', which now gathers 15 university research centres and individual scholars working on social enterprise and the third sector across Europe. His work focuses on the emergence of social enterprise in various parts of the world and on conceptual and quantitative analyses of the third sector in developed and developing countries. Besides numerous articles in academic journals, he has authored or (co-)edited 14 books, among which Tackling Social Exclusion in Europe. The Role of the Social Economy (Ashgate, 2001), The Emergence of Social Enterprise (Routledge, 2001 and 2004), The Worldwide Making of the Social Economy (Acco, 2009) and Social Enterprise and the Third Sector (Routledge, 2014).

Giulia Galera holds a multidisciplinary PhD in International Studies obtained from the University of Trento (Italy) and is currently senior researcher at the European Research Institute on Cooperative and Social Enterprises (Euricse). She has collaborated with several international institutions, including the European Commission, ILO, UNDP and OECD. Her main fields of research interest include the role of social enterprises in the welfare systems; social and cooperative enterprises in post-transition contexts; social enterprises and economic development; the legal evolution of social enterprises.

Laurie Mook is Assistant Professor in the Nonprofit Leadership and Management program, School of Community Resources and Development at Arizona State University. She is also research associate at the ASU Lodestar Center for Nonprofit Innovation and Philanthropy. She is co-author of What Counts: Social Accounting for Nonprofits and Cooperatives, now in its second edition (Sigel Press, 2007), and of Understanding the Social Economy: A Canadian Perspective (University of Toronto Press, 2009). Her other recent edited books include Accounting for Social Value (University of Toronto Press, 2013), and with Jack Quarter and

Sherida Ryan, Businesses with a Difference: Balancing the Economic and Social (University of Toronto Press, 2010) and Researching the Social Economy (University of Toronto Press, 2009). Her areas of interest are non-profit management, social accounting, social economy and volunteerism.

Victor Pestoff earned his PhD in political science at Stockholm University, later became Professor at Mid-Sweden University in Östersund and now is Professor Emeritus at the Institute for Civil Society Studies, Ersta Sköndal University College in Stockholm. He is also a Guest Professor at the Graduate School of Human Sciences, Osaka University. He published many articles and books on consumer organizations, cooperative movements, co-production, the third sector and welfare state. His three most recent books are A Democratic Architecture for the Welfare State (Routledge, 2009), New Public Governance, the Third Sector and Co-Production (Routledge, 2012) and Social Enterprise & the Third Sector: Changing European Landscapes in a Comparative Perspective (Routledge, 2014). For more information contact: www.esh.se or www.emes.net.

Fernando Polo-Garrido, PhD, is accredited Associate Professor at the Universidad Politécnica de Valencia, Secretary-General of CEGEA (Centre for Research in Business Management), Director of the International Research Network on Accounting for Cooperatives and Mutual Entities (ACCOOP), coordinator of the Co-operative Accounting Committee of the Spanish Association on Accounting and Business Administration (AECA). He has been member of the Working Group in Co-operatives of ICAC (the Spanish Standard Setter) and the principal researcher in two international research projects. He has published in Accounting Horizons, Journal of International Financial Management and Accounting Revista Española de Financiación y Contabilidad and others, as well several books, book chapters and papers for congresses.

Daphne Rixon, PhD, FCMA, is Associate Professor of Accounting at the Sobey School of Business, Saint Mary's University and is also the Executive Director of the Centre of Excellence in Accounting and Reporting for Co-operatives (CEARC). Her research interests include performance reporting for co-operatives and accounting in the NFP sector.

Stefania Veltri is Assistant Professor in Business Economics within the Faculty of Economics of the University of Calabria. Her main research interests are related to strategic and management control, the performances of university systems, and intellectual capital measurement systems. On these research themes she has published books, book chapters, journal articles and presented papers to national and international congresses.

LIST OF REFEREES

Louis Beaubien
Enrico Bracci
Giovanni Bronzetti
Valeria Cavotta
Laura Corazza
Jacques Defourny
Hannele Makela
Giovanna Michelon
Sara Moggi
Caterina Pesci
Silvia Pilonato
Fernando Polo-Garrido
Tommaso Ramus
Daphne Rixon
Silvana Signori
Rosanna Spanò
Antonino Vaccaro
Petros Vourvachis

ABOUT THE EDITORS

Ericka Costa (PhD in Business Economics, University of Udine, Italy) is Assistant Professor of Accounting, University of Trento. He also spent several visiting periods in other Universities: in 2011 in the Centre for Social and Environmental Accounting Research at the University of St Andrews (Scotland); in 2011 and 2013 at the University of Burgos (Spain) and in 2012 she was at the CEARC – Centre of Excellence in Accounting & Reporting for Co-operatives, St Mary University, Sobey Business School (Halifax, Canada). She is International Associate for Italy in the Centre for Social and Environmental Accounting Research (CSEAR) networks. She also participated in several researches project on accounting and social accounting for non-profit organizations at large and she has attended national and international conferences to present papers on the results of these research projects. Recently she is involved with the OECD and the European Commission in delivering a 'policy brief' on social impact measurement on social enterprises.

Her research interests are aimed at investigating Sustainability Accounting and Corporate Social Responsibility both for profit and non-profit organisations. She has written a number of chapters in books and articles and papers that have been accepted for national and international journals and conferences. Her research has appeared in international publications, including: *Social and Environmental Accountability Journal*, *Journal of Business Ethics*, *Voluntas* and *Service Business*. Together with these research interests, she has matured her professional experience as a consultant and executive educator on accounting and performance measurement both for profit and non-profit organisations.

Lee D. Parker (B.Ec. (Adel), M.Phil. (Dundee), Ph.D. (Monash) FCA FCPA FAIM CPMgr) Professor in Accounting in the School of Accounting at RMIT University, Melbourne, Australia and Professor of Accounting in the School of Management at Royal Holloway College, the University of London. His previous academic posts include the Universities of Glasgow, Dundee, Monash, Griffith, Flinders and Adelaide. He has also held visiting professorships at Case Western Reserve University, Cleveland,

Ohio; London School of Economics; University of California, Berkeley; University of Otago, New Zealand; Kuwait University; University of Mississippi; Nanyang Technological University, Singapore; University of Dundee, Scotland, University of Alabama; The University of Trisakti, Jakarta, Indonesia; University of Manchester; Royal Holloway College, the University of London; Glasgow University; Singapore Management University; University of Aberdeen.

He has published over 200 articles and books on management and accounting internationally and is a regular presenter and plenary speaker at international conferences and seminars. Professor Parker is joint founding editor of the internationally prominent and ISI listed interdisciplinary research journal *Accounting Auditing & Accountability Journal* (published by Emerald publishing) and serves on 30 journal editorial boards internationally. He is a founding Fellow of the Centre for Social and Environmental Accounting Research at the University of St Andrews, a panel member of the Hong Kong Research Grants Council, and has been a reviewer for government research granting authorities in Canada, the UK, Italy and Australia and international advisor to past Accountancy Panels of the British universities Research Assessment Exercises.

Professor Parker has been a president of the Academy of Accounting Historians (USA), the American Accounting Association Public Interest section and Vice-President International of the American Accounting Association. He is also a past president of CPA Australia (SA Division), past deputy president of the Australian Institute of Management (SA Division) and has also served on CPA Australia's national Education Advisory Committee. He is currently Chair of the American Accounting Association's Centennial Celebrations Committee and a board member of the Adelaide College of Divinity.

Michele Andreaus (PhD in Business Economics, University of Venice, Italy) is Full Professor of Business Administration, Accounting and Social Accounting, and since September 2008 has been Head of the Department of Computer and Management Sciences (DISA). He is also a member of the steering committee and of the scientific board of the European Research Institute on Cooperative and Social Enterprises (Euricse). Since 2006, he has been a member of the European Business Ethics Network (EBEN), and since 2008, he has been a member of the Board of EBEN, Italy. His current research interests include Social Accounting, Accounting in non-profit organisations, and Corporate Social Responsibility both in large companies and SMEs. In 2007, he concluded a two-year research project funded by the Italian Ministry of Education (PRIN 2005) on 'Value Communication and Protection of Institutional Interests in Corporate Groups'. Together with these research interests, he has matured his professional experience both as a consultant and executive educator. As a consultant he has worked in helping start-up and turnaround initiatives, while as executive educator he has been responsible for seminars addressed to banks, SMEs and chartered accountants. He has also written a number of chapters in books and articles and papers that have been accepted for national and international journals and conferences.

Printed and bound by CPI Group (UK) Ltd, Croydon, CR0 4YY

17/09/2026

14964145-0002